Praise for *The Pagan Man*

"Characteristically exciting, original, perceptive, and challenging."
—Ronald Hutton, author, *Triumph of the Moon*

"I like Isaac's work because it is direct and incisive but often laced with his distinctive brand of humour. The questions he tackles are deeply serious, but he believes we can have fun while exploring them. An excellent book!"   —Philip Carr-Gomm, Chosen Chief, OBOD, and author, *The Rebirth of Druidry*

"A timely and necessary book, a vitally important book in the emerging Post-Feminist Pagan literature, general in scope so as to be informative and widely relevant, personal in voice so as to be genuine, communicative, and just plain useful. Hopefully, it will inspire imitators, but will retain permanent value."
—Harold Moss, founder, Church of the Eternal Source

"What a glorious testament and vindication to all the dedicated men in our Pagan community whose devotion to the Goddess and Her avatars—the women in our lives—is our all-consuming passion."
—Oberon Zell-Ravenheart, founder, Church of All Worlds, and author, *Grimoire for the Apprentice Wizard*

"Once again, Isaac dares to go where few others have gone before, namely into the hearts and minds of Pagan men. An excellent survey of the issues and themes facing Pagan men of all traditions. Great for men starting on the path who want to know what they are getting into and experienced practitioners who are looking for a fresh perspective on Paganism."
—Christopher Penczak, author, *Sons of the Goddess*

"A *must-read* for Pagan men and women everywhere, *The Pagan Man* is a valued and useful resource for Pagan men and women to use in achieving a better understanding of themselves as Pagans and as a guide in improving their religious, social, sexual, personal, and family lives." —Searles O'Dubhain, founder, www.summerlands.com

"A well-researched book offering fresh insights on what it means to be a Pagan man. Isaac offers a captivating glimpse of the world of male spirituality.   —Kerr Cuhulain, author, *The Wiccan Warrior*

"Bonewits, possibly the best-known and most widely acquainted of living Pagan writers, provides introductions to Celtic, Druidic, Norse, Egyptian, Hellenic, and other forms of modern Pagan practice, and how the differing polytheologies impact the individual male in communities growing out of those practices.

"As always, his fluent style is punctuated with a reverent irreverence, by which the highly approachable author refuses to take himself too seriously. He presents his important material with a smile rather than a stern grimace, and the reading is much the better for it."
—Ramfis S. Firethorn, author, *Blindfold on a Tightrope*

BOOKS BY ISAAC BONEWITS

Real Magic
Authentic Thaumaturgy
Witchcraft: A Concise Guide
Rites of Worship

Forthcoming:
Bonewits's Essential Guide to Witchcraft and Wicca
Bonewits's Essential Guide to Druidism

The Pagan Man

Priests, Warriors, Hunters, and Drummers

ISAAC BONEWITS

Never thirst!

Isaac

CITADEL PRESS
Kensington Publishing Corp.
www.kensingtonbooks.com

CITADEL PRESS BOOKS are published by

Kensington Publishing Corp.
850 Third Avenue
New York, NY 10022

Copyright © 2005 Isaac Bonewits

All Kensington titles, imprints, and distributed lines are available at special quantity discounts for bulk purchases for sales promotions, premiums, fund-raising, educational, or institutional use. Special book excerpts or customized printings can also be created to fit specific needs. For details, write or phone the office of the Kensington special sales manager: Kensington Publishing Corp., 850 Third Avenue, New York, NY 10022, attn: Special Sales Department; phone 1-800-221-2647.

CITADEL PRESS and the Citadel logo are Reg. U.S. Pat. & TM Off.

First printing: December 2005

10   9   8   7   6   5   4   3   2   1

Printed in the United States of America

Library of Congress Control Number: 2005928266

ISBN 0-8065-2697-1

To my great-great-grandfathers
and my great-great-grandsons,
physical and spiritual,
from another link in the chain.

And to Fred, Kirk, and Steve:
Patrons of the Art

Contents

	Acknowledgments: Who to Blame	ix
	Introduction	xi
1	What Is Paganism?	1
2	Varieties of Modern Paganism	14
3	Where Do They Get Those Ideas?	39
4	Founding Fathers	50
5	Pagan Men as Priests and Wizards	67
6	Pagan Men as Artists and Musicians	87
7	Pagan Men as Warriors and Hunters	113
8	Pagan Men as Fathers	127
9	Pagan Men as Brothers	137
10	Pagan Men as "Queers"	152
11	Pagan Men, Pagan Women, and Sex	163
12	Pagan Men and Ritual	182
13	To Be a Pagan Man	208
	Bibliography	235
	Online Resources	239
	Index	243
	About the Author	251

Who to Blame
~~Acknowledgments~~

Three thousand years' worth of sages, wizards, priests, druids, bards, warriors, blacksmiths, farmers, troublemakers, and curmudgeons.

James Edwin Bonewits, James Emmons Bonewits, Peter Bonewits, Jacob Bonewitz, Joseph Bonewitz, Jacob Bonewitz, Johann Adam Bonnawitz, and his unknown fathers.

The Pagan men and boys who answered all my silly sounding questions seriously and my serious questions amusingly.

Bob Shuman, the toughest editor I've ever worked with, who improved this book immensely.

The makers of Manhattan Special brand Espresso Coffee Soda and Captain Morgan brand Original Spiced Rum—perfect together.

Introduction

In New Jersey, a Pagan priest gives a friendly greeting to a Unitarian Universalist (UU) woman at his local UU society, telling her that he is looking forward to her presentation on "Cakes for the Queen of Heaven," a series of programs for UU women on goddess worship. Her jaw drops, then she tells him that "Goddess worship is just for women."

He says, "That's odd. I've been leading Druid rituals to the Earth Mother for twenty-five years."

She responds, "That's impossible," and walks away.

In North Carolina, the members of the Royal Order of the Knights of Herne, a Pagan men's group, are discussing what their charitable activities for the next three months will be. Eventually, they settle on a toy drive for hospitalized children and some weekends in a local soup kitchen.

In California, the two men in an extended Pagan polyamorous marriage are sorting out the complexities of the upcoming Feast of Lupercalia (Valentine's Day to the rest of the world). With three women to keep happy, each with her unique preferences, it takes some fancy scheduling.

In Oklahoma, a group of Pagan men and a couple of women are clearing land for a new Pagan sanctuary. The women are running the rented bulldozer and one of the chainsaws, while the men are using axes and weed-wackers to clean up after them.

In Miami, a Santeria worshipper invokes his patron deity, Chango, the West African god of thunder, to come down and possess him.

Suddenly, he is seemingly transformed from a slightly built, unathletic man into a swaggering, powerful warrior reaching for his symbolic axe and a bottle of 150-proof rum. After the ritual is done, the worshipper will return to his normal state of consciousness, but stronger, more assertive, and braver than before.

In New York, the members of the Council of Hermes, a Pagan men's discussion group, are listening as one member holding a ritual caduceus speaks about his problems at work with a biased supervisor. After he puts the snake wand down, the others brainstorm on suggestions, both magical and mundane, to improve his situation. Then they turn to planning a coming-of-age ritual for the son of one of their members.

In Texas, a group of Asatruar men are doing a private rite in honor of Thor, the Norse god of thunder. The godi (priest) raises a symbolic hammer and calls on Thor to accept the offered sacrifice of mead and to bless his worshippers.

These are Pagan men: straight, gay, bisexual, monogamous, polyamorous, plumbers, programmers, shopkeepers, writers, musicians, dancers, and drummers. They and their traditions come from all over the world.

Why This Book?

This book is about what it means to be a boy or a man in a faith community that worships both gods and goddesses and that honors strong women. As fathers, sons, brothers, lovers, hunters, healers, warriors, breadwinners, and cheerleaders for the women and girls in their lives, Pagan men are blazing new trails into unknown social, cultural, and political territories. This book will tell some of their stories as individuals and as members of ancient and modern Pagan men's groups. I will be quoting throughout from interviews I've conducted with Pagan men, both famous and obscure, as well as from correspondence, answers to a questionnaire I circulated[1] while writing this book, and thoughts from my own attempts to figure out just what Pagan manhood consists of and how one manifests it.

If I don't explain who the man giving me a particular quote is, it's because I know little beyond his name. You will also notice that many Pagan men use unusual-sounding names. They do this for the same reason that Catholic monks and nuns often take special names: as a spiritual exercise in the magical Law of Names. By changing his name to a new one that is inspirational to him, a Pagan man has a frequent if not constant reminder of who he wants to be.

Some of what I quote from Pagan men will be inspiring, some amusing, and some of it really annoying, especially to many of our Pagan sisters reading them. But if they, and you, really want to know what Pagan men are thinking and feeling, we are going to have to accept their sentiments as genuine, however much we agree or disagree with what they say. There is a great deal of irony here, especially in terms of the impact of feminism on the Pagan movement, which I will comment on near the end of the book.

Many people may have heard the slogan, "Witchcraft is wimmin's religion!" I've often heard references to Wiccan priests as "glorified altar boys," and for many years initiatory lineages in Wicca were traced (in most groups) only through the female lines—one was initiated in a sacred circle cast by a priestess who was initiated in a circle cast by an earlier priestess, and so on. When people in the Neopagan movement think of "famous Pagans," or when the mass media is looking for "Pagan representatives" to interview, women such as Starhawk, Z Budapest, Selena Fox, Silver Ravenwolf, and so on are usually the ones that come to mind. Much of this, of course, has to do with the femaleness of the witch archetype in Euro-American culture.

Obviously, if a man thinks that the only things Pagan men get to do is hand ceremonial tools to their priestesses (who get to do all the fun stuff), that he will be relegated to staying in the kitchen minding the baby while his wife is interviewed for a magazine story about Paganism, or that honoring a goddess means that he always has to do what his wife or some other female tells him to, he probably won't find this a very attractive prospect.

Unfortunately, these are the clichés that Wicca has attracted to itself, and since Wicca is the only kind of modern Paganism most people know about, many assume that men are either excluded from or can only play supportive or backstage roles in modern Pagan religions. Indeed, in the first few decades of the Neopagan movement, some women[*] actively promoted the view that it was "their turn" to be the top dogs (though they never phrased it quite that way) and that the guys could "see how they liked" being second-class citizens of a religion. It is a tribute to the attractive power of the Old Gods and Goddesses that enough men put up with this attitude long enough for these ladies to mature and discover that the goddesses love their sons as much as their daughters. Some twinges of wariness still remain among men who were Wiccans during this time and they are often hypersensitive and defensive about real or alleged gender insults.

Ironically, most of the modern Pagan movements such as Asatru (Norse Paganism), Druidism (and other forms of Celtic Paganism), Kemetism (Egyptian Paganism), the Church of All Worlds (science-fiction and Gaian Paganism), as well as the earliest versions of Wicca, were started by men, including Sveinbjörn Beinteinsson, Ross Nichols, Harold Moss, Oberon Zell-Ravenheart, and Gerald Gardner (all of whom you'll meet later in this book). Today, almost all Neopagan and most Mesopagan groups (with the obvious exception of those that are gender exclusive) are run by both men and women working as equals. There are many roles that men can and do play that can manifest their masculinity while still honoring their Pagan sisters, without having to be ashamed of their Y chromosomes.

[*]And no, I'm not going to mention names here—I like all my body parts where they are!

In a movement seemingly dominated by strong and visible women such as those famous ones mentioned, I am one of the few well-known male writers and teachers. I've watched the Neo-pagan community grow and evolve for nearly forty years and have in my earlier writings articulated many of the core concepts now accepted by hundreds of thousands of Neopagans. I've also made a lot of mistakes over the years as I tried to define my own Pagan manhood, and I want to share what I have learned from these mistakes.

I hope this book will be enjoyed by men (and the women who love them) who want to know how to be male in a Pagan path, without slipping back into the sexist and homophobic patterns of the mainstream cultures in which they were raised or having to suppress their own personal powers as men. I hope my sisters will accept this book as my contribution to improving their relations with our brothers, and vice versa, leading, one hopes, to greater sibling revelry.

Stumbling Down Memory Lane

In 1989, I was unfortunate enough to be among those who consumed contaminated L-tryptophan tablets, which gave me a condition the Centers for Disease Control and Prevention decided to call Eosinophilia-Myalgia Syndrome. This had, among its many other debilitating effects, the result of wiping out large clusters of neurons involved in memory storage, especially those portions recording my personal memories before the age of forty (when I got ill). Fortunately, the two dozen or so personal stories that I was in the habit of using in my lectures and workshops* were stored in other locations in my brain—the ones where my frequently

---

*Such as the one about my leaving the Catholic seminary, which I'll relate in chapter 5.

repeated intellectual information was kept. Those sectors were left 80 percent intact and I have been able to restore most of the academic and magical knowledge I had memorized, although I still have trouble footnoting references I used to know by heart.

All this is to explain that I can only clearly remember a tiny fraction of my first forty years, usually highly emotionally charged events such as near-death experiences and incidents of being abused. The rest of my personal memories before 1992 or so are almost all blurry or absent (as are a lot of the ones since then, alas). Nonetheless, I can still reconstruct some of them based on old letters, school records, photos, published interviews, and so on. I have called on those resources to help me remember most of the personal stories I will use in this book, because I realized that as a Pagan man I should be able to relate this book's topics to my own life if I'm going to help others relate them to their own.

What We'll Be Looking At

In the pages that follow, I'll explain just what Paganism has been and is today, some of the different kinds of Pagan religions that now exist, and a little bit of literary and philosophical history behind the modern movements. Then we'll look at several of the founding fathers of modern Paganism, followed by chapters about Pagan men as priests, wizards, artists, musicians, warriors, and hunters. We'll take a look at the joys of being a Pagan father, as well as at different kinds of Pagan men's groups.

I've included a chapter on gay and bisexual men because modern Pagan faiths are some of the only religions that don't exclude, either theologically or socially, men who belong to sexual minorities. Perhaps the most controversial chapter will be the one where Pagan men talk about Pagan women!

Since the potential for a lively sex life and the opportunity to use magic actively are two of the things that attract men to Paganism, yet they are both fraught with pitfalls for the unwary, I felt it useful to include some information and tips about these topics specifically directed to the needs and concerns of Pagan males. Naturally, I added some ritual materials here, too, just for Pagan men to enjoy and use.

At the end of several chapters I've included exercises for you to do, based on that chapter's discussion. Most of them involve thinking and meditating about particular ideas, then writing or drawing your answers to questions or the results of your experiments. So, I recommend getting a small blank book that you can keep by your side as you read these pages.

Throughout this book I hope to show that modern Pagan men, like their distant forefathers, can be strong, creative, smart, loving, and magical—and that their sisters, mothers, and daughters (not to mention most of the goddesses) like them that way!

The Pagan Man

CHAPTER 1

What Is Paganism?

"Paganism" is one of those words that almost everyone has an opinion about. The dictionaries aren't much help, as they all give multiple meanings. Today, for hundreds of thousands (if not millions) of people, "paganism" means religions that honor nature and whose members worship many different gods and goddesses. As a modern Westerner, you probably know some of the names of these deities from your childhood: Zeus and Hera, Venus and Mars, Thor and Freya. There are hundreds of old gods and goddesses being worshiped today, even in the heart of the most sophisticated modern cities, in countries all around the world and as they were throughout history.

There are Druids saying prayers in stone circles, Norse Pagans offering mead to Odin, Santeros dancing for and being possessed by the Orisha, and, yes, people offering cakes to the Queen of Heaven, just as the Bible says they're not supposed to.

Perhaps the best-known modern Pagans are the Witches or "Wiccans," as many of them prefer to be called:

> Though you thought you had destroyed
> The memory of the Ancient Way,
> Still the people light the bale fires

Every year on solstice day.
And on Beltane Eve and Samhain
You can find us on the hill,
Invoking once again
The Triple Will.[1]

Thanks to the broadcasting of such television shows as *Buffy the Vampire Slayer, Angel, Charmed,* and *Sabrina the Teenaged Witch,* as well as the release of popular movies such as *Practical Magic, The Witches of Eastwick,* and a thousand lurid horror flicks, the general public now has a lot of (mostly exaggerated and wrong) information about Witchcraft. Many, many books have been published about Witchcraft over the last few centuries, with hundreds appearing in the last few decades alone. Whether for or against whatever their authors thought Witchcraft was or is, many of these books are filled with stereotypes, unverified assumptions, obsolete research, or just plain nonsense. Even those works written by Wiccans for Wiccans often contain errors based on scholarly and pseudo-scholarly works written from the nineteenth through the mid-twentieth century, include feminist dogmas from the 1980s, or repeat naively the unverifiable claims made by founders of modern Wiccan groups (before anyone began paying attention). Fundamentalist Christian authors have written extensive critiques of Wicca, based on their belief that any form of religious or magical practice that isn't their own is automatically "a demonic deception"—of course, most of those books are filled with enough accidental or deliberate mistakes to sink a battleship.[2]

Fortunately, over the sixty-plus years of its history, Wicca has attracted enough sincere, intelligent, playful, and deeply spiritual people that there are now hundreds of thousands of Wiccans and tens of thousands of Wiccan covens around the world, many of whom actually know what they are talking about.

And while it might not be obvious from *Buffy,* nearly half of those Wiccans, indeed half of all Pagans worldwide, are guys!

How Many Kinds of Pagans Are There?

You can count them several ways. Pagans can be counted by historical categories, ethnic or pantheon (collections of deities) categories, and the "Wicca versus everybody else" category.

The historical categories, which will be defined, include the Paleopagans, Mesopagans, Recon-Pagans, Buddheo-Pagans, and Neopagans.[3] Most of them today just call themselves and each other Pagans (if that) but the differences are important.

Paleo means "old" and the Paleopagans were the original polytheists (worshipers of many deities) all around the world. This category includes the ancient peoples of Africa, Asia, Europe, North and South America, Australia, and everywhere else. Even the Cro-Magnons and Neanderthals seem to have had religious practices. In fact, every human being who had ever lived before the invention of monotheism (one-godism) 2,500 years ago, was a Paleopagan, as were most of those who came afterward. Today, Paleopaganism has pretty much vanished from the earth (though there are a few Mesopagans and Buddheo-Pagans who will *claim* to be Paleopagan). Only a handful of tribes hiding deep in the jungles of Africa, New Guinea, or the Amazon might still be practicing a form of Paleopaganism in the twenty-first century. But what about Hinduism, Taoism, or Shinto? Those three faiths all started out Paleopagan but became Mesopagan and/or Buddheo-Pagan over time. Hinduism was heavily influenced first by Buddhism, then by Zoroastrian dualism, Islam, and Christianity, while Taoism and Shinto have both incorporated concepts from Buddhism into their beliefs and practices.

Meso means "middle" and Mesopaganism occurs (both historically and philosophically) after Paleopaganism and before Neopaganism. Mesopagan religions are ones that are a mix of one or more kinds of Paganism and one or more kinds of monotheism or dualism. Some Mesopagan religions, such as Sikhism, are a blend of polytheistic faiths—in this case, Hinduism—with monotheistic Islam. Most, however, such as Theosophy, Rosicrucianism, Freemasonry, Voodoo, or the fraternal Druid orders of the nineteenth century, are a mix of Pagan ideas (often from several faiths) with ones from Christianity.[4] Usually, the founders thought (or at least said) they were reviving or continuing what their Paleopagan ancestors (or people they admired) had done. Mesopagans will often believe (or at least say publicly) that they are good Christians or Muslims, while holding to beliefs and practices from Pagan sources. The various African Diasporic or Voodoo religions discussed in the next chapter, for example, often use the names and images of Christian saints to refer to West African or Native American deities. The fraternal Druid organizations of the eighteenth and nineteenth centuries frequently claimed that the Paleopagan druids had been monotheists like them, despite the lack of historical evidence to back up these claims (and the huge amount against them). Wicca itself started as a Mesopagan religion, influenced by the childhood Christianity of its founders, and only gradually became Neopagan as the Christian influences (such as dualism, exclusive truth claims, the transcendental nature of deities, the apostolic succession, and so on) were dropped by its more liberal members after coming in contact with Neopaganism.

Neo means "new" and the Neopagan religions are ones that have tried to revive old Paleopaganisms, modify current Mesopaganisms, or simply invent brand new polytheistic faiths (such as the Church of All Worlds, based on a science-fiction novel, or Discordianism, based on the humorous worship of a goddess of chaos) out of thin air—without accepting Jewish, Christian, or Islamic influences or assumptions. Most of them go back to the 1960s or 1970s, but like Mesopaganisms, new Neopaganisms are being constantly created.

Recon is short for "Reconstructionist" and Recon-Pagans are people who may be either Meso- or Neopagans. What makes them distinctive is a strong emphasis on scholarship in their work, a wide streak of conservatism in their practices ("if the ancients didn't do it, we won't either"), and a dislike of organizational structures and leaders. Celtic Recon-Paganism, for example, has been described as "Druidism without the druids," by which they mean that no one takes (or is given) religious authority as a priest or priestess, either because individuals focus on solitary worship and/or because the members of a group take turns leading rituals or providing other services usually associated with clergy. In this, they may be seen as "Protestant" Pagans, following Martin Luther's principle of "every man his own minister." Some Recon-Pagan groups that are liberal about dropping ancient customs (such as celebrating holy days on specific dates) and adopting modern ones (such as celebrating them on the nearest weekend) may choose to use the term "Revivalist" Paganism.

Buddheo is another way to say "Buddhist," and Buddheo-Pagans are Buddhists who worship various Paleopagan deities as Buddhas and Boddhisatvas (Enlightened Ones). Oddly enough, while the term is a modern one, it has a useful historical application. Buddhism was originally a nontheistic religion, in that the Paleopagan deities of ancient India were recognized as existing, but were considered beings who were trapped in the wheel of reincarnation as much as mortals were. Worshipping them would only bind them to the wheel tighter and provide no benefit to the worshippers. Even the Buddha himself was not worshiped in the beginning of Buddhism, and it is likely that the early Buddhists would have described their beliefs and practices as a philosophy rather than as a religion. These nontheistic Buddhists still exist today and are called Theravada (Doctrine of the Elders) Buddhists by themselves and Hinayana (Lesser Vehicle) Buddhists by their offshoot, Mahayana Buddhism.

This later form of Buddhism began around 100 BCE when Buddhist missionaries brought their beliefs to the Paleopagans living in Tibet, China, and Japan. They found it easier to convert these Paleopagans by incorporating their local deities into a Buddhist pantheon as Boddhisatvas (much as the early Christian Church transformed European deities into saints), rather than by denying them completely. This coincided with a doctrinal shift to emphasizing the principle of compassion and the Boddhisatvas' superior spiritual merits as beings who had renounced their personal entrance into nirvana in favor of helping to enlighten others. The result was a new variety of Buddhism that its members called Mahayana (Greater Vehicle) Buddhism and that some today might call Buddheo-Pagan. The term was coined in the 1970s by Neopagans who fell in love with some of the Buddhist goddesses, especially the White and Green Taras.

All these historical terms for different types of Paganism refer to overlapping trends and groups of people. After all, one of the advantages of being a polytheist is the ability to belong to more than one religion at a time! So polytheistic religions, by their pluralist nature, tend to have looser philosophical or polytheological boundaries than monotheists might find comfortable.

Many people find it handier to refer to Pagans by the name of their favorite pantheon or ethnic/cultural preferences. So people will talk about Celtic Pagans, Norse Pagans, Egyptian Pagans, African American Pagans, and so on. You have to be careful about jumping to conclusions about the ethnic heritages of people based on these labels, however, as you will find members of almost every race and color in all of those groups just mentioned!

What about "Wicca versus Everybody Else"? Well, for the first few decades of the Pagan revival, that distinction made sense. Well into the late 1980s, the overwhelming majority of Neopagans appeared to those of us in the movement to be Wiccans, with an occasional Celtic, Norse, or Egyptian Pagan here and there. There certainly seem to be more non-Wiccans around in the modern Pagan movements these days, but it's hard to be sure.

To begin with, it's nearly impossible to figure out how many Pagans there are in the world today, as a whole or by various subcategories, for a wide variety of definitional and methodological reasons. The lack of agreed on criteria for defining/describing modern Pagans, the social and economic repercussions of being revealed as a Witch or Pagan in bigoted communities, and secular/academic biases against treating "magical religions" as serious faiths will continue to make it nearly impossible to arrive at any firm numbers for the foreseeable future.[5]

Take the figures from the 2001 City University of New York's *American Religious Identification Study*[6] for people who were willing to call themselves Wiccans (134,000), Druids (33,000), or Pagans (140,000) to a stranger on the phone, for example, then add the 19 percent of Unitarian Universalists (total 629,000) who said in a 1999 survey that they consider themselves "earth religionists" (119,500), and you get 426,500 semipublic Neopagans just in the United States. Factor in the many people in the United States who fear persecution or discrimination if their minority religious beliefs become public knowledge—11 million people refused to answer the question in the CUNY study—and the real number could be much larger. The Neopagan movement *may* be larger in the United States than in other nations, but even if you decide to just multiply it by two or three times to cover the rest of the globe, we are looking at 1 or 2 million Neopagans in the world.

The number of Mesopagans, however, dwarfs those figures, even if we only count the West African–based Mesopagans (followers of Voodoo, Santeria, Candomble, Macumba, etc.). There are nearly a billion of those in North, Central, and South America, the Caribbean, and Africa. Considering how many of them in the Western Hemisphere are usually counted as Catholics by observers, it makes me wonder how many of Islam's supposed billion-plus members are actually African or Asian Mesopagans in hiding. Add in all the Mahayana Buddhists, Hindus, and surviving followers of aboriginal religions in other parts of Africa, the Americas,

China, and Australia, and we're looking at some pretty big numbers—nearly half of the world's population! Most of these polytheists are *not* Wiccans or witches of any flavor.

Back home in the American and Canadian Neopagan community, I can make some guesstimates, based on forty years of obser-
vation. I would say that around three-quarters of these Neopagans
are Wiccans or otherwise identified with the term "witch," about 7
to 10 percent are Druids, about 5 to 8 percent Asatruar, and the
rest are members of other Neopagan paths to be discussed later in
this book. Of course, we have to remember that many will belong
to two, three, or more categories at the same time.

What Do Pagans Believe?

This is a far more difficult question than it may seem. I can tell
you what most Neopagans seem to generally believe, most of the
time. Describing Mesopagan beliefs, however, is a great deal
harder, since there are so many varieties of Mesopaganism. So,
let's start with what most Neopagans seem to agree on, and use
that as a base from which to discuss differences between and
within Meso- and Neopaganism as they come up in this book. [7]

- Divinity is both immanent (internal) and transcendent (external). Deities can show up at any point in space or time
  they might choose, including within people.

- Children are born holy, since they have nothing between
  them and their indwelling deities. So we can believe in "Original Blessing" rather than "Original Sin" and we thus see no
  need for salvation.

- Divinity is immanent in both women and men, so the word
  "goddess" makes just as much sense as the word "god."
  Therefore, women and men are spiritually equal and masculine and feminine attitudes, values, and roles are of equal

importance, regardless of the physical gender of those exercising them.

- There are many gods and goddesses, as well as lesser beings such as ancestors, nature spirits, spirit guides, totems, elementals, and so on, many of whom are worthy of respect, love, and worship.

- There is no divine or semidivine figure of ultimate Evil. The Devil is a figure in Christian, Islamic, and related theologies—not modern Pagan ones! More importantly, Neopagan religions are not dualistic—we do not believe that the multiverse is split between warring armies of spiritual beings, or that black and white thinking works very well (see the discussion later on about dualism).

- No one religion, philosophy, scripture, or other approach to understanding can explain the infinite complexities of the multiverse. This particular belief specifically rejects absolute truth claims by other religions and philosophies, as well as the religious intolerance that inevitably comes with them.

- Because of divine immanence, personal experience can be just as important a source of truth as logic or reason might be, depending on how many and which levels of reality (areas of discussion, argument, experience, or application) are involved in a given situation. This belief is particularly upsetting to theologians, who often confuse their intellectual maps with living spiritual territories.

- It is necessary to respect and love Mother Nature as divine in her own right, and to accept ourselves as part of nature and not her rulers. Many accept the Gaia theory, that the Earth's entire biosphere can be usefully seen as a single living "superbeing" on multiple levels of reality—rocks as her bones, the oceans and atmosphere as her circulatory system, plants and fungi as her skin, and so forth, all tied into an infinitely complex network of feedback systems. Such metaphors are useful in geology, biology, atmospheric and oceanic sciences, and ecology. We humans are her children, but so are all other living beings, and any special privileges we might have are balanced by equal responsibilities. As the one superbeing that every human lives within, and without whom we would all die, Mother Nature is worthy of that respect called "worship," for we recognize her worth.

- Ethics and morality should be based on joy, love, self-esteem, mutual respect, and the avoidance of actual harm to others and ourselves. Most Neopagans believe in some variant of the principle of karma and affirm that the results of their actions will always return to them, sooner or later—not as rewards or punishments, but as consequences.

- People were meant to lead lives filled with joy, love, pleasure, beauty, and humor. Neopagans may be carnivores, vegetarians, or omnivores, depending on their individual religious beliefs, but most are sensualists.

- Sexual ecstasy is a divine blessing and it can be a major source of spiritual growth and enlightenment, though we vary widely in how, with whom, and under what circumstances we seek such ecstasy. Most Neopagans have very strong ethical opinions in this department, many of them hard won after observing their own and others' blunders.

- With proper training, art, discipline, and intent, human minds and hearts are capable of performing most of the magic and miracles they are ever likely to need. The use of (real) magic* is a central practice in Wicca and is common in most forms of Neopaganism, as is divination (fortune-telling). Not every person can do every kind of magic or

---

*As a matter of fact, there's a well-known book with that title.

psychic work, just as not everyone can paint pictures or play a musical instrument, but most people can do some sort. Therefore, the ability to perform magic or miracles has little to do with the accuracy of one's theological opinions, no matter what religious founders or followers might believe.

- It is important to celebrate the solar, lunar, and other cycles of our lives. Most of us consciously observe the winter and summer solstices, the fall and spring equinoxes, and the points in between, as well as the phases of the moon, and the major passages of our lives (birth, puberty, marriage, death, etc.).

- Some sort of afterlife exists, as well as does reincarnation, often involving rest and recovery in "the Summerland" before reincarnating. Neopagan beliefs in this area have not been deeply developed, since we tend to pay much more attention to our current lives then to theoretical future ones

- We must practice what we preach, if we are to achieve any of our goals. Neopaganism, like any other religion, should be a way of life, not a hobby or a pose to impress others. Many Neopagans, for example, as worshipers of Gaia, believe they have a religious obligation to recycle their trash and to be active in environmental movements.

- Healthy religions should have a minimum amount of rigidity and a maximum amount of flexibility. Neopaganism is an assortment of organic religions, which are growing, changing, merging, splitting, and producing offshoots. Anyone who wants to is free to start his or her own denomination, special interest group, charity, and so on.

- Freedom of worship and belief is a right that all religious groups and individuals (who are willing to grant us our freedoms in return) should have. We see religious tolerance as a sign of spiritual strength and confidence, not weakness or uncertainty, and we are quick to defend our freedoms.

We will see over the course of this book that a few of these principles directly affect the experiences of Neopagan men as members of their faith traditions. Obviously, religions that believe in gender equality and that encourage worship of and role modeling from both goddesses and gods, are not going to put up with the same old sexism and limited gender roles that the mainstream religions have created and are going to offer men many different divine images to pattern themselves after. A Neopagan man (and most Mesopagan ones) can choose to be at any moment a warrior, a lover, an artist, a lawmaker, a magician, a priest, a seer, a farmer, a hunter, a child nurturer, a cook, or an inventor—and always have a god (or goddess) to imitate or be inspired by.

Some principles of Neopaganism do seem to clash directly with the mainstream culture's ideas that "real men" only behave in certain ways. Men from English or Germanic backgrounds are, for example, supposed to constantly suppress their emotions and sensuality, as well as any nurturing behavior toward children and the weak. Modern Pagan men can freely express these attitudes and needs without worrying about their masculinity. But Pagan men know that sometimes they do indeed have to be physically and emotionally strong, suppress short-term pleasures, defend the weak, think clearly and logically in times of high emotions, and perform all those other duties of human adulthood that our mainstream culture usually limits to men, whether those duties are politically correct or not in a given culture or subculture.

Dualism

"Dualism," which saturates Christian and Islamic culture, is the belief that everything can be divided into two extremes that are in a state of eternal war with each other: Good and Evil, black and white, male and female, gay and straight, true and false, logic and intuition, and so on. There are no shades of gray, and people who insist on discussing rainbows or sunsets are heretics. Dualists are uncomfortable with diversity and tend to be closed to new ideas until they can assign those ideas to either the good or evil category.

"Pluralism," which is common to polytheistic cultures and what is now called postmodernism, is the belief that reality is complex, multifaceted, messy, and ambiguous. Pluralists are comfortable with diversity and open to new insights and approaches. Pluralists see a thousand shades of gray and millions of other colors. Pluralists still believe in good and evil as appropriate labels, but they are slower to apply them and are likely to use modifying adjectives. Pagans are most likely to be pluralists, with dualism creeping in to the extent that they are Mesopagan.

Exercises

Which way of classifying Pagans makes the most sense to you? Why?

Look back at the list of common Neopagan beliefs. How many of them do you agree or disagree with, to what extent?

How does your gender affect your agreement or disagreement with any of those common beliefs? Why or why not?

CHAPTER 2

Varieties of Modern Paganism

There are many different kinds of Mesopaganism and Neo-paganism being practiced today, almost all of which have men playing major roles in their history, beliefs, and rituals. In this chapter, we will look at the major categories present in the Western world today.

Out of Africa

Africa is a big place, with hundreds of cultures spread across a landmass larger than all of North America. Most of the time when we discuss African Paganism in this book, we'll be focused on Western Africa,* especially the region from which the major-ity of kidnapped men, women, and children were taken in the cross-Atlantic slave trade during the sixteenth through nineteenth centuries. People were captured or purchased from the interior tribes by slave hunters, sold to middlemen, then sold to Europeans

---

*Except for the discussion on Egyptian Paganism later.

for transport to the New World. This was not a pleasant experience for anyone but (some of) the slavers. More than half of the victims (we're talking millions of people here) may have died while being captured, in ships on the way, and after their arrival in the New World from beatings, rapes, starvation, and disease. On arrival, families were shattered, tribal relationships disrupted, and traditional customs forbidden—all to make the victims more helpless and unable to organize resistance.

Not surprisingly, the victims clung to their religious beliefs as long as they could, as one of their few sources of emotional comfort. Though forbidden to keep their ancient faiths, many were allowed (or forced) to practice their owners' preferred religion; usually Protestantism in what was to become the United States and Roman Catholicism elsewhere in the Americas and the Caribbean. Very often, African slaves worked side by side with Native American slaves and Irish indentured servants (men and women who had sold themselves into servitude to pay for their transport from Ireland to the New World), and religious ideas would have been among those communicated between the members of these lowest of the social classes.

Christianity eventually became attractive to the slaves since its theology promised a better life for them after the miserable one they were then experiencing, and over a period of a century or so, distinctly African versions of Christianity were created that still exist today. Some slaves, however, found ways to use Christian religious customs and images in combination with their own remnants of Paleopagan beliefs and practices.

The result was the creation of a dozen major and scores of minor Mesopagan religions, mixing various West African and Native American Paleopaganism with Protestant and Catholic Christianity, then (especially in South America) with the North American religion known as Spiritualism.[1] In South America, the best known of these faiths are Macumba, Candomble, Palo Mayombe, and

Spiritism. In the United States, the best known are Santeria or Lucumi[2] (from Cuba), Voudoun (from Haiti), and Voodoo (from New Orleans).[3]

A growing presence on the current American Pagan scene is Ifa, imported directly from modern West Africa, where it claims to be the original religion from which the other paths diverged. However, it is fairly clear that Ifa (which is named after the ancient Yoruban system of divination) has been influenced by both Christianity and Islam, making it Mesopagan for the purposes of this book.[4]

Ifa, for example, sometimes uses the name Exu or Eshu for the trickster gate opener deity, rather than Ellegua (from Santeria) or Legba (from Voudoun). Exu is the South American name usually associated with images of the Christian Devil. Another example would be the references to Islam now embedded within the Ifa divination system—there are, for example, now-traditional answers that tell questioners to go to a mosque and convert to Islam or else to perform a particular Islamic rite.

Since the 1980s, followers of these African Diasporic faiths have tended to drop the use of Christian saint names and images (such as Saint Barbara, Saint Joseph, or Our Lady of Mercy for Chango, Ellegua, and Ochun) in favor of their original African names and old or new African images. However, monotheistic influences on the original African cultures and their offshoots in the Americas have kept them fairly sexist in their beliefs and habits (at least by modern Western standards).

A "heretical" Ifa priest, who went to Africa to be ordained, told me:

> Most post-Western Ifa puts women in a second-class role.
> But as I have found out, in true Ifa societies the women are
> the key to all things. They are the ones who lay down the
> law of the village and also determine if your opun [the
> divinatory casting tray] gets "fed" [with a sacrifice] each
> year. To the best of my knowledge men in Ifa are there to

serve and protect life, and that means the women—without women there is no Ifa despite what a whole bunch of people in the over-Westernized versions may think. So simple and so easy. The group I was involved with initiated women, most do not. They will do crowning [initiating to the priest/esshood], but no women babalows [diviners]. Which from my research is true BS. Women hold the power to bring life into the world.

In North America, many members of African Diasporic Meso-pagan belief systems can be racist in their attitudes toward people with pale skin wanting to join them. They figure, like many Native Americans and Australians, that "they stole everything else from us, they can't have our religions too!" If you are a white man or boy interested in Voodoo (as I was as a youth), you will just have to put up with the karmic consequences of past crimes by others. Be polite, be respectful, and be patient. Eventually, if the gods and goddesses want you, they will let your teachers know in no uncertain terms.

As far as ritual is concerned, these faiths differ from most Neo-pagan ones primarily in two areas: sex and blood. While some of the African-based systems (such as Haitian Voudoun) can be very earthy indeed in practices and beliefs, others (such as Cuban Lucumi) can be downright prissy about matters of sexuality that would seem ho-hum to many Neopagans. In contrast, because most of the African Diasporic religions are rooted in rural environments where death is a part of daily life, animal sacrifices (seen as giving the spirits a good meal, which may or may not be shared with the worshippers later) are common to many of them— a topic that makes most Neopagans outraged, if not nauseous.*

The overwhelming majority of African Diasporic Mesopagans might never think of themselves as "Pagans" because of the bad

---

*Of course, many Neopagans believe that meat is something that comes in plastic trays at the grocery store. See the discussion later about hunting.

press the term has had for so many centuries, but they clearly fit within the overall category—they are polytheistic, nature-focused faiths with deities who represent both natural forces (wind, fire, fertility, etc.) and human activities (hunting, fishing, blacksmithing, making war or love, etc.). Hardly any of them will have even heard the word "Mesopaganism" (until any Spanish or Portuguese versions of current Pagan books using the term become big sellers), but it is clear to any unbiased observer that their faiths are blendings of Pagan and non-Pagan beliefs and practices.

Since the early 1990s, partly as a result of the drumming movement within mainstream Neopaganism and partly as a consequence of the English-language publication of books about Santeria, Macumba, Voudoun, and Ifa, many American Neopagans have begun to incorporate African divinities in their beliefs and practices, albeit clumsily in many cases. This has created a somewhat shallow "Wannabe Afro" movement that is still growing. Fortunately, it is now common to find genuine teachers of these paths (along with a few clunkers) appearing at Neopagan festivals and presenting well-attended workshops and rituals. Over the next few decades, we should see more and more interaction between these Mesopagan faiths and the Neopagan movement, perhaps leading to the creation of African Diasporic Neopaganisms.

Medicine People and Wannabe Indians

I mentioned briefly earlier the fact that there were Native American slaves in the European colonies. Slavery was just one of the crimes committed by Europeans in the New World. Wholesale slaughter was the most common, along with rape and pillage. Biological warfare was practiced against the native peoples and, even when not deliberately introduced, European diseases such as smallpox and measles killed millions of them. The attitude toward native religions was originally that they were all "savage and barbaric," so that efforts to convert them alternated between murder and enslavement. In the face of this physical and cultural genocide, native peoples tried valiantly to preserve as much of their old beliefs and practices as possible, often altering them to make them more palatable to the European invaders.

It's important to remember that there were hundreds of native cultures throughout the Americas, and scores of language families, each with its own related mythology and cosmology. Most native cultures had very specific gender roles and expectations, but these varied widely depending, in part, on how tough the local environment was and how warlike the neighbors were. Those native religions that survived mixed (willingly or unwillingly) their beliefs and practices with those of their conquerors, creating Mesopagan traditions such as the Ghost Dance (a messianic movement among the Plains Indians in the 1890s) and the highly Christianized Aztec ritual dance troupes, which still perform today. Current Native American rituals and religious teachings are often presented at powwows and other public gatherings as authentically Paleopagan, although that term won't be used, while revealing mainstream monotheistic influences, such as prayers to a Great Spirit.

Members of both the New Age and Neopagan movements developed an interest in Native American spirituality, partly because of the hippie movement of the 1960s and 1970s, and partly in response to the fantasy novels of Carlos Castenada, Lynne Andrews, and others. This interest infuriated some natives and amused others, who called them "Wannabe Indians" and happily sold them bogus spiritual teachings (such as the famous speech by "Chief Seattle" that the environmental movement adopted in the 1980s) and phony religious artifacts (such as "genuine eagle feathers" made from turkeys). Some Native American medicine people such as Sun Bear chose to start their own medicine tribes to bring authentic teachings from multiple tribes to the New Age movement, where they blended it with astrology, ley lines, and even Wicca, creating Neopagan medicine paths that annoyed the heck out of their conservative cousins.

In the 1990s, Neopagans began to do serious research into surviving Mesopagan beliefs and practices among North American Indians, incorporating the results into the stew of their own beliefs and practices. Soon, a Neopagan shamanism movement began to grow. Some did their research well and others simply became the latest members of the Wannabe Indian tribe. At the same time, an increasing number of people with recent native ancestry began to join the Neopagan movement, bringing their own Mesopagan family customs into the mix.

Many Neopagan men have found Native American images and ideals of men as hunters and warriors both satisfying and spiritually fulfilling.

And Now a Word from Valhalla

The evolution of Germanic and Scandinavian/Norse Paganism— which some prefer to call Heathenism to distinguish themselves from other Pagans—is in many ways similar to that of the Druidic and Celtic revivals (see the discussion later on). The original Germanic/Scandinavian Paleopagan beliefs were slowly wiped out by missionaries, then by civil governments aligned with the church. Germanic/Scandinavian Paleopaganism lasted the longest, perhaps, in Iceland, which did not convert officially until 1,000 CE. While Paleopagan folklore and customs survived in bits and pieces, usually highly Christianized, the religions as a whole vanished. Unlike the Celtic peoples whose common Indo-European clergy caste remained strong up to their conquest by the Roman Empire (around 200 BCE to 50 CE) on the Continent and part of Britain, and the Christian conversions throughout the rest of Britain, Scotland, Wales, and Ireland (in the centuries that followed), among the Germans and the Norse the clergy class was comparatively weak even before the Romans showed up. So, there were few clergy of the old religions to become priests, nuns, or monks of the new one and to write the old stories down in manuscript form (as happened in Ireland and Wales).

About 200 years after Iceland officially converted to Christianity, people began to have nostalgia for the good old days, leading to efforts to compose histories of Iceland and to remember the old tales. A historian and skald (bard or poet) named Snorri Sturluson decided to write down some of the Norse sagas and legends and created a textbook of how they were composed for the benefit of student skalds. This became known as *The Snorri* or *Prose Edda*, possibly from a word meaning "poetry." Over the next few centuries, other scholars wrote down skaldic poems that told stories of the deities, famous ancestors, and nature spirits. Many of these were collected in a manuscript that surfaced in the late 1600s, which became known as *The Poetic Edda*. While the Eddas were long taken as authoritative guides to pre-Christian Norse religion, some scholars today believe they were highly influenced by ideas from the Bible (such as the importance given to the story of Ragnarok—the end of the world—which seems to have been influenced by the Book of Revelations in the Bible).

The Scandinavians had an antiquarian movement (people digging up monuments before archaeology was invented as a scientific discipline) a century before those in the British Isles, yet interest in Germanic/Norse Paleopaganism slumbered until the 1800s and the Romantic movement in art and literature fastened on the old sagas and myths as good source material.

These romantic versions of Norse/Germanic mythology and history, Freemasonry and other occult movements, runic research into the magical and divinatory meanings and uses of runes, racism, nationalism, and anti-Semitism merged in the early 1900s to create an ugly stew that a charismatic political leader named Adolf Hitler used to prop up his dictatorship and justify his crimes. He didn't believe in the gods, he just used them for his purposes—ones that the Paleopagans would have despised. Hitler's perversion of Paganism made Germanic or Norse Paganism an unpopular topic for decades after World War II.

It wasn't until the early 1970s that Norse Paganism, then called Odinism or Asatru (the troth of the Aesir), and now commonly called Heathenism, was revived in Iceland (where it is now one of the official religions recognized by the national government), England, and the United States.[*] The revival started out Mesopagan and didn't begin to become Neopagan until sometime in the 1990s, when strong women appeared, including priestesses such as Freya Aswyn, Prudence Priest, and Diana Paxson, who believed there was more to Norse Paganism than just battle stories and macho chest-thumping. They began reviving the "female half" of Paleopagan Norse/Germanic beliefs and practices. Indeed, the history of the last twenty years of Norse Paganism in the English-speaking world can be seen as a tug-of-war between Mesopagans and Neopagans for the soul of Asatru. Unfortunately, you can still find Norse Mesopagans who seem to believe that racism, anti-Semitism, sexism, and homophobia were all part of "Viking religion" and should be practiced today. Even among those on the Meso-/Neo- cusp, however, there is still a strong emphasis on virtues that are usually thought of as masculine[†] (even though the Norse sagas reveal many sturdy and brave women as well).

Diana L. Paxson, a former steerswoman (president) of the Troth, a major Heathen organization, told me:

> Today the major tension is between those who consider themselves "Folkish," and believe that Germanic religion should be practiced by those who are of Germanic descent, and the "Universalists," who believe that the Germanic gods may be worshipped by anyone who is attracted to them.

[*]See chapter 4's entry on Steve McNallen. (p. 64)
[†]See chapter 7 for a discussion of the Nine Virtues of Asatru.

Although women and gay men are more likely to be found as leaders among the latter, there are many women and gay men in the Folkish camp as well.

I'm not sure that a complete overlap can truly be made between the Mesopagan and Folkish categories on the one hand, and the Neopagan and Universalist on the other hand, but I suspect there's a pretty close correlation.

So while the stereotype of Heathens as bushy-bearded, macho warriors waving swords and swigging mead may only apply to a fraction of modern Heathenry, those role models certainly do exist and would-be Pagans who like the idea will certainly find others like themselves with whom to party. Far more common, however, are the quiet scholars, priests, and skalds working to revive what they see as the best of the old faiths in a modern context.[5]

Among the most intriguing aspects of the current Heathen movement is the revival of *seidh,* the ancient Norse system of quasi-shamanic[6] mediumship and oracular divination, with which Paxson has been heavily involved.[7]

I should also mention the Theodish or Anglo-Saxon versions of Heathenism, which have been growing by leaps and bounds since 1976. Garman Lord is the man most responsible for their birth and growth and he is still active in the movement today.[8]

Egyptian Knights

Ancient Egypt was one of the earliest known civilizations and its magic and mysteries have fired peoples' imaginations for 6,000 years. When Islam conquered it in the seventh century CE, it already had 4,500 years of Paleopagan beliefs and practices in dozens of major and hundreds of minor denominations devoted to various deities. Islam did its best to crush them, of course, but fragments survived well into modern times.

One of the first Egypt-related movements that can be called Mesopagan was the Masonic movement, which worked legends about the building of the pyramids into its mythology. While today Masons are predominantly a men's social club and networking organization, in their early years as a mystical movement (during the Renaissance), they created a kind of sun worship connected to the short-lived (less than 100 years) cult of Akhenaten (a monotheistic blip in 4,500 years of Egyptian Paleopaganism) with ties to mystical interpretations of the Bible. Many mystical groups, such as the Rosicrucians (see the discussion later on), during the Renaissance and the Romantic period of European history made reference to Egypt as the supposed source of their teachings. The Romany people, who originally came from India, claimed to be from Egypt as a way to boost their fortune-tellers' reputations, so much so that they were called "Gypsies."*

Following on Masonic concepts, ceremonial magical orders at the end of the 1800s, such as the Hermetic Order of the Golden Dawn (HOGD) and the Ordo Templi Orientis (OTO), incorporated Egyptian symbolism and even deities such as Ra and Isis in their teachings. The OTO in England received an additional heavy dose of Egyptian influences thanks to the HOGD-trained Aleister Crowley, the most infamous magician of his generation. Crowley blended the results of three days of channeled trance writing in Cairo (in 1904) with OTO materials and his reaction against his fundamentalist Christian upbringing, to create an Egyptian Mesopaganism he called Thelema (a word taken from François Rabelais, meaning "will") and a related church he called the Gnostic Catholic Church, both of which are still around today.[9]

The history of Rosicrucianism is complex and controversial. We know that its primary symbol was that of a rose and cross, probably symbolizing the union of female and male principles in an alchemical (and possibly sex-magical) sense. Early Rosicrucians

*Most modern Roms consider the term an insult, hence the quote marks.

mixed Christian mysticism with their alchemical and Egyptian interests. One modern Rosicrucian group, the Ancient Mystic Order Rosae Crucis, founded in 1915, was so obsessed with Egypt that it built one of the finest Egyptian museums in the world at its headquarters in San Jose, California.[10]

In 1970, Harold Moss and the late Donald Harrison (d. 2004) joined with others to found the Church of the Eternal Source as a Reconstructionist Egyptian religion in southern California. They were among the first public Pagans to embrace the term "Neo-Paganism" and to join in councils with other Neopagan churches. This group currently has four consecrated temples and congregations in several states.[11]

In 1989, the Kemetic (Egyptian) Orthodox Faith[12] was founded by Tamara L. Siuda, who later went on to receive a master's degree (2000) in Egyptology from the University of Chicago's Oriental Institute. Her organization is still quite active, with members all over the world.

In 2000, the International Network of Kemetics[13] was founded as "an organization dedicated to the networking and sharing of knowledge among the practitioners of the Kemetic Faith, and to helping facilitate the reconstruction of the Ancient Egyptian religious practices and culture." So, if you have an interest in the deities of Paleopagan Egypt, such as Isis, Hathor, Sekmet, Ra, Ptah, Osiris, and so on, there are plenty of resources available. Some of the newer groups call themselves Neopagan, others Reconstructionists.

Celtic Journeys

The Paleopagan Celts were spread out all over what we now call western and central Europe, although most people think of the "British" Isles as having been their center. On the contrary, there were Celts in Austria, France, Spain, Italy, and Turkey long before those nations existed as such. The terms "Celt" and "Celtic," however, can be tricky to understand. Archaeologists, historians, and linguists use them in different ways. The archaeologists apply these terms to groups of people in central Europe who had bronze, then iron technology, and who shared certain cultural patterns such as particular weapons designs, architecture, jewelry, tools, and so on, that show up in their graves and village sites.

Historians like to limit the terms to peoples who were referred to as Celts (or Keltoi) by the Greeks and Romans, even though these references were often quite vague. Linguists think in terms of those tribes who spoke a particular group of related languages, mostly Irish, Manx, and Scots Gaelic, as well as Welsh, Cornish, and Breton, plus Gaulish (now extinct) and Gallician (nearly so).

The religious beliefs and practices of the Paleopagan Celtic peoples, however defined, closely resembled those of the other Indo-European speaking peoples—no surprise here, since they *were* the western branch of the Indo-European family of languages. So we know that they had a system of social classes or castes, including one for the clergy (the famous druids), one for the warriors, one for the producers (farmers, fishers, and others who supported the upper classes), and one for the serfs or slaves. Actually, they had multiple castes for each of these, because each contained subcastes and sub-subcastes. Among the druids were the ovates (diviners), the bards (musicians/singers), the poets, the judges, and so on. They were polytheistic, with most of the deities having links to the activities and concerns of one, three, or all of the castes.[14]

The Paleopagan Celts were conquered first by the Paleopagan Romans on the Continent and a small part of Britain, then by the church in the rest of Britain and Ireland. Both of these groups (for very different reasons) tried to get rid of the druid caste and its subcastes. The Romans slaughtered them if they wouldn't cooperate in the conquest of their own tribes; the Christians preferred to convert or banish them, but were willing to kill them if necessary.

With the druids went centuries of accumulated wisdom and knowledge, except in Wales and Ireland, where monks wrote down some of their oral history and mythology, although viewed through Christian lenses. References to strong women in the tales, to sexuality in general, or to heroes invoking Pagan deities were usually censored out or described in negative terms. The social and magical power of the druid caste was often described as tyrannical or evil and, of course, all the tales that described magical duels between druids and missionaries ended with the druids being defeated.

Whether we wish to call it Druidism, Druidry, or Celtic Paleopaganism, most of it was lost until the 1600s brought the British antiquarian movement into existence. These early protoarchaeologists, like their colleagues in Scandinavia, began by studying the many stone circles that dot the British landscape. In 1659, one of them, John Aubrey, erroneously attributed to the druids the building of Stonehenge, other scholars of the time promoted the idea, and this became "accepted knowledge" for 300 years (Stonehenge was actually built, torn down, and rebuilt by Neolithic peoples from 3000 to 1500 BCE—long before the Celts arrived in Britain).

In the 1700s, fraternal orders similar to the Masons were created using the name and image of druids. These Mesopagan Druids* dressed in long white robes and performed their ceremonies in stone circles, including Stonehenge, making Aubrey's originally cautious suggestion a self-fulfilling prophecy. Such groups flourished for three centuries in the Isles, France, and Germany, promoting Druidism as a monotheistic "philosophy of nature" very similar to liberal Christianity or deism rather than as a Pagan religion. They claimed that a man (membership was limited to men for the first two centuries) could be a Druid and a Christian or Jew at the same time. Orthodox monotheists were

---

*From this point forward, "Druidism" becomes the name of specific philosophies or religions, and so it and its followers deserve that capital *D*.

not convinced, but many liberal Christians and some liberal Jews were. These groups, some of which (such as the United Ancient Order of Druids [UAOD]) still exist today and most of them (such as the UAOD) did social, cultural, and charitable work rather than esoteric or occult work.

The Mesopagan Druids in America were dying out during the twentieth century until a group of students, mostly young men, at Carleton College in Northfield, Minnesota, began the Reformed Druids of North America (RDNA) as a prankish protest against the college's religious attendance rule. After a year, they succeeded in getting the rule overthrown but found that most of their members wanted to continue doing the rituals they had cobbled together, worshipping the Earth Mother and various Celtic deities, doing guided meditations with materials from a wide variety of religions, and passing around a consecrated cup of *uisce na beath* (Irish whiskey). While the RDNA went in and out of existence at the Carleton campus, its ideas were scattered across the United States by graduates, leading to various offshoots and "branches of the Reform," including the Orthodox Druids of North America (ODNA), the New Reformed Druids of North America (NRDNA), the Schismatic Druids of North America (SDNA), and the Hasidic Druids of North America (HDNA)! The RDNA remained Mesopagan for most of its older members, who insisted that Druidism was a philosophy applicable to all religions, just as their English predecessors had claimed. The offshoots I created (NRDNA, SDNA, and HDNA) were Neopagan from their beginnings, and many of the current members of the RDNA now call themselves Neopagans (without insisting that other members must be).

My own organization, Ár nDraíocht Féin: A Druid Fellowship (ADF),[15] was founded in 1983 as a specifically Neopagan Pan-Indo-European faith based on reconstructed models of Paleopagan Druidism. Then the Henge of Keltria,[16] an offshoot of ADF, was founded in 1987 as an exclusively Celtic group. All these groups after the original RDNA were avowedly Neopagan groups and actively networked with the other Neopagan movements in the United States.

At the same time the RDNA was being founded in America, Ross Nichols (d. 1975), a British college professor and poet, became the chief of the Order of Bards Ovates and Druids (OBOD), a Mesopagan offshoot of the Ancient Order of Druids. His successor as chief, Philip Carr-Gomm, a psychotherapist and author of several excellent books on Druidry and Celtic studies,[17] has since the 1990s taken OBOD firmly toward the Neopagan side of the Paganism spectrum, in the process creating the largest modern Druid organization in the world.[18]

During the 1980s and 1990s, various groups such as Imbas[19] were started by people who preferred to think of themselves as Celtic Reconstructionists rather than Druids. This was because most of them weren't functioning as clergy and/or because they were hostile to the idea of hierarchy in religious groups (in this they have much in common with the Norse Reconstructionists). Other Recon groups, especially in France, used Druidism as a cover for right-wing, ultranationalist, racist, and anti-Semitic agendas—again, like *some* of the Norse Mesopagans and others.

In terms of people practicing Druidism as a spiritual path, the vast majority are now Neopagans and—despite the three-centuries-old stereotype of Druids as elderly men with long gray beards—only half of them are men. "Druidism," by the way, is the term now used by those who see Druids as primarily clergy or members of one or more ancient or modern religions. "Druidry" is the term used by those, such as the members of UAOD and OBOD, who see Druids as individual philosophers and mystics, rather than as clergy or members of any specific religion. "Druidecht," the modern Irish synonym for "magic" as well as the word for what druids once did, is preferred by those modern Druids who emphasize the poetic and magical aspects of being a Druid, such

as Searles O'Dubhain, who leads an online school of Celtic studies and all three forms of Druid practice (Druidism, Druidry, and
Druidecht) at his Summerlands[20] Web site.

Today, you will find Pagan men training to be priests, warriors, artists, poets, and more in these varied Celtic Paganisms.
Different organizations will have different training methods and
ranking systems, but none of them require twenty years of study
before one is allowed to call oneself a Druid (even if that's what
Julius Caesar claimed). While women are treated as equals in all
these modern groups, the superior position they enjoy in most
Wiccan traditions simply isn't there, a fact that makes Druidism
and Celtic Reconstructionism, like Asatru, appealing to many
Pagan men.

Other Ethnic Religions

One of the first of the public Pagan religions in America was the
Mesopagan Long Island Church of Aphrodite, founded in 1938
by Gleb Botkin (d. 1969). Another was the Neopagan group
Feraferia, begun in the 1960s by Frederick Adams. Both these
groups[21] are more or less extinct but in their place stand a number of Hellenic Reconstructionist groups, both in Greece and in
the United States. The Committee for the Hellenic Religion of
Dodecatheon[22] (twelve deities) has been fighting for the rights
of modern Pagans in Greece for several years, with indifferent
success. The Greek Orthodox Church is the official religion of
modern Greece and freedom of religion appears to be very low
on the Greek public's list of important issues. Pagans there have
been subject to persecution and their religious sites to vandalism
in recent years, in an unpleasant echo of centuries past. There has
been no visible response from the Greek government, in violation
of various human rights documents it has signed and the European

Union Constitution and the Charter of the United Nations. A new documentary film about current Greek Pagans, including nasty commentary from government and church leaders, called *I Still Worship Zeus* (in Greek and English, with subtitles) was released in January 2005.[23]

One American Greek Reconstructionist group is Hellenion. Its Web site[24] has links to other groups of Hellenic Recons and Neopagans. Despite the conservative political and social views of its founders, in 2005 its Web site had a notice saying, "Hellenion does not advocate culture wars or bloodshed as a means of advancing the religion of the Gods of Olympus. Nor do we support those Hellenic Pagan organizations which support racism, misogyny, homophobia, or discrimination of any kind." This would seem to imply that some other Hellenic Pagan groups still do, which would match what we have seen with other ethnic Pagan revivals. Generally, the more Mesopagan a group is (the more dualism influences its thinking patterns), the more likely it is to have dysfunctional biases.

One group that has been nonprejudiced from its beginning is Thiasos Olympikos,[25] which was founded in 1990 originally as a men's mysteries group for men attracted to the Olympic deities. Quickly, it plunged into doing public Pagan rituals and today it has both male and female members. One of its founders, the author Ramfis S. Firethorn, tells me that the two things that most distinguish *Hellenismos* (Greek Paganism) from other brands of modern Paganism are the use of both sacrifice as the central ritual and sports as a sacred worship activity. He adds:

> The chief characteristic of ancient Greek worship (in addition to sacrifice) is its variety. Every temple has particular festivals and things that it did which were unique. And that is true of contemporary Hellenismos as well. Though the overall view of ritual is similar, details vary widely. I have

received missives from any number of unaffiliated folks who
assure me that they use my ritual structure, and thank me
for the rituals; but they remain independent, like City States,
and they all put their own spin on things. To Hellenismos in
general, agonistics (literally, "exercises," but taken to have
a tone of competition or argumentativeness) is central and
crucial. Everything is to be considered, debated, argued
about. It is said that the Greeks don't have all the answers:
they have all the questions!

Another Hellenic resource is the Supreme Council of Ethnikoi
Hellenes, an umbrella organization of groups and individuals,
mostly in Greece, who are dedicated to reviving Paleopagan Greek
religions and customs. They are somewhat grouchy Reconstructionists who disdain the use of the word "Pagan," but their
Web site[26] (available in multiple languages) has links to dozens of
other Hellenic Recon groups and resources.

Not surprisingly, there is also a thriving Roman Pagan movement afoot, with the best-known group being Nova Roma. This
Reconstructionist group has dozens of local chapters (provinces)
all around the world and is working hard to revive the worship
of the deities and other spirits of ancient Rome.[27]

But wait, there's more! Romuva[28] is a Baltic revivalist Pagan
movement based in Lithuania. Krug Peruna[29] (Perun's Circle) is a
Slavic one based in Russia. Then there's the Rodzimy Kosciol
Polski[30] (Polish Native Church) and many, many more. In fact, if
you visit the Internet's largest database of Pagan Web sites (The
Witches' Voice)[31] and type the ethnic tradition of your choice
into its search engine, the odds are good that you'll find some
group of people worshipping the Old Gods and Goddesses of
your favorite pantheon.

How authentic are they? That varies considerably. I am unable
to tell whether there really were underground movements of Greek,
Roman, or Slavic Pagans surviving up into modern times, as many

folks claim, but I rather doubt it. I'm just guessing here, but I suspect that, as with most of the European cultures whose native religions were crushed, they probably had revivalist and romantic movements over the last few centuries, leading to various Mesopagan organizations being founded that then claimed to have a direct connection to the ancients. Lithuanian Paganism, however, *may* have a continuous tradition going back to pre-Christian times. The Baltic cultures were among the last in Europe to be conquered and their oral traditions *might* have lasted the two or three centuries between then and the beginnings of a revival.

Some groups are very out-front and honest about not having a direct connection to their Paleopagan predecessors and I tend to trust these groups a bit more. But you will need to examine each group on its own merits before deciding if its claims of antiquity ring true (or if you even care).

In general, for all the groups discussed in this chapter, the more Mesopagan a group tends to be, the more its concepts of manhood and "proper" male behavior will resemble the sexist stereotypes so familiar to us from the mainstream religions. But if you are comfortable with that, such groups might be a perfect fit for you.

But What About Wicca?[32]

"Witchcraft is wimmin's religion" made a good sales pitch for the leaders of the Feminist Separatist version of the Craft during the late 1970s and 1980s, but this popular phrase ignores some pretty important history—including the fact that there probably wouldn't *be* a modern Witchcraft movement if it hadn't been for a number of strong men, most of whom weren't what anyone today would consider politically correct.

In fact, the first influential book of the Feminist Separatist Craft was essentially a rewritten version of the Gardnerian *Book of Shadows.* The *Book of Shadows* was (and is) an evolving text of beliefs and practices, originally put together by Gerald Gardner from bits written by himself or (mostly) other men (including Aleister Crowley, Charles Leland, Rudyard Kipling, Robert Graves, and others), with editing and additions by Doreen Valiente. The feminist rewrite simply had the male deity names and pronouns removed, along with all references to priests and male witches.

From the 1950s through the 1970s, the gender balance in Wicca was probably equal. After the blossoming of Feminist Wicca in the 1980s brought a flood of women into the movement, the ratio may have shifted for a while to something like two-thirds female and one-third male. In the 1980s, I met Feminist Separatist Wiccans who didn't even know of the existence of men in Wicca, since all they had read were books by women who didn't mention them, nor had they gone to public Pagan events where men were present. Thanks to the Internet and the flood of media stories about Wicca in the 1990s, the presence of men in Wicca could no longer be ignored by the separatists. In the first decade of the twenty-first century, the gender ratio now seems to be closer to sixty-forty (female-male) with a general trend back toward a fifty-fifty mix.[33]

Despite the large presence of males in the Craft from the beginning, many books on Wicca assume that would-be Witches are all female. This has been going on for decades.

One Pagan man wrote me:

One of the first books I read on Wicca was Starhawk's *Spiral Dance.* When I bought the book, I was excited, because I thought it would open the way for me to learn about Wicca. But, just about every exercise in the book began with the instruction to breathe into your uterus.[34] Starhawk also made sweeping claims about prehistory, saying that our prehistoric ancestors had been matriarchal. Well, I have a BA in classics and I know that we know so little about the Stone Age that we cannot make that claim.

When I read *Spiral Dance,* I felt excluded. I felt like men couldn't be a part of this religion. We don't have uteruses to breathe into. Starhawk's vision of a matriarchal Stone Age was not utopian for me. It was distopian. I believe in equality between men and women and that means that matriarchy and patriarchy are both wrong. . . . As a man who believes in gender equality, I felt betrayed and humiliated—because I had expended so much passion on women's rights and felt slapped in the face and barred from a spiritual path that I felt deeply called to explore.

Of course, some Wiccan authors choose to use feminine pronouns and adjectives exactly as most authors in English use the male ones, both to empower female readers and to poke male ones in the ribs with their own preconceptions. Nonetheless, if you didn't already know this, let me assure you: you don't need a uterus to practice most forms of Neopagan Witchcraft.[*] The Goddess and the Horned God love their sons as much as they do their daughters.

Most Wiccan denominations/traditions can be viewed on a value spectrum ranging from Orthodox/Conservative or so-called British Traditional (implying a body of belief and practice that has been handed on more or less intact) on one end to Heterodox/Liberal or Eclectic (implying a willingness to combine originally separate beliefs and practices) on the other. As is true for other Pagan paths, the influence of dualism in Western culture causes religious conservatism and liberalism to be usually (but not always) associated with political, social, sexual, and other forms of conservatism and liberalism by both practitioners and observers. Perhaps because of this, the closer to the conservative

---

[*]Any more than you need a penis to consecrate a host—but that's another book.

end of the scale, the more likely a given Wiccan tradition will be to insist that the Goddess is more important than the God and that both genders are needed for effective nonsolitary ritual. It's also more likely to harbor remnants of (or even flagrant) homophobia.

Among those usually on the liberal or eclectic side of the scale are traditions often called Feminist and Fairy Wicca. Groups who consider themselves Feminist Wiccans are likely to have female-dominant (if not female-exclusive) beliefs and practices. These groups may have anywhere from a third to all of their members lesbians with the balance straight or bisexual women. Ironically, most Wiccans who *don't* call themselves feminist probably *are* feminist by the standards of previous generations, if for no other reason than the nearly universal reverence given to goddesses in Wicca.

Fairy Wicca has several related but distinct meanings in the overall Craft movement, usually involving assumptions of spiritual or historical connections to the Faerie Folk. There are several liberal traditions that call what they do "Feri," "Faerie," and so on,* but many of the trads who choose the "Fairy" spelling are specifically for homosexual, bisexual, or transsexual men, playing on the old insult for gay men, "fairy."[35]

Yet, whether we are talking about conservative or liberal Wicca, the vast majority of Wiccan traditions have men as members, leaders, or even founders. What do they do? That all depends on the denomination/tradition and on a man's rank within it. Conservative Wicca places a heavy emphasis on the polarity of male and female energy in balance with each other, so men are expected, at the very least, to individually or collectively generate half the energy in the ritual circle—which can be quite a challenge when you're the only guy with four or five gals to balance! In liberal

---

*See chapter 4's entry on Victor Anderson. (p. 60)

Wicca, each participant is expected to carry his or her share of the magical work, regardless of gender.

Despite the centuries that African Mesopagan faiths have been doing rituals in which both gods and goddesses can possess both men and women, all but a few (usually Fairy) Wiccan trads seem to believe that only women can "draw down" the Goddess into themselves and only men the God. But if you're not acting as the priest of a coven, this is usually irrelevant to a male experience of a Wiccan circle.*

On a social and small-group political level, however, it is a fact of life that many Wiccan traditions are matriarchal, with the oldest and/or highest ranking woman being able to overrule the wishes of the men (and the other women), no matter how experienced and talented they may be. Unless you are unlucky enough to hook up with a weak woman, you will probably never be in charge—get used to it. If you are lucky, however, you will find a strong woman who will accept you as an equal and share power willingly.

There are few (if any) Pagan paths in which males are allowed to exercise the kind of tyrannical power their brothers routinely have in some mainstream religions. Most of the non-Wiccan Neopagan and Reconstructionist paths (and some of the liberal Wiccan ones) are adamantly egalitarian these days, largely in reaction against matriarchalism.

Exercises

Make a list of all the ethnic groups you know you have in your ancestry. Were any of them mentioned in this chapter?

Which, if any, of the paths discussed in this chapter seems ap-

*If you are, see chapter 5 on Pagan men as priests and wizards.

pealing to you? Why or why not? Is your ancestry a positive, negative, or irrelevant factor in your consideration?

What kind of man would be comfortable in the Pagan path
you find most appealing? Are you that man now or can you see
yourself becoming him? Why or why not?

CHAPTER 3

Where Do They Get Those Ideas?

Where do Neopagan and Mesopagan males get their specifically Pagan ideas about what it means to be a man? In this chapter we will look at several important influences, including ancient and medieval myths and legends, as well as modern science-fiction and fantasy literature. We will see that there are many voices telling us that it's okay to be a Pagan man.

European Influences

The major Paleopagan influences on how most Euro-American Neopagans define manhood are probably the Greek and Roman myths and legends.[1] Zeus the divine king, Ares the warrior, Apollo the intellectual, Dionysus the original party animal, Hermes the trickster, and the other Greek gods, along with their Roman counterparts, all showed different ways in which powerful males could act and interact with each other and with females. As works by modern psychologists show,[2] these stories (as well as the others to be discussed later on) provide both positive and negative role models. The mortals and demigods who appear in these tales also

offer different ways of being male. Odysseus's cleverness in out-
witting the Cyclops, Herakles' habit of bashing his way through
problems with his strength and his club, Jason's leadership (and du-
plicity) when searching with the Argonauts for the Golden Fleece,
and so on, all have lessons to teach those willing to study them.

In my own childhood of the 1950s and early 1960s, it was still
normal for American children to at least be somewhat exposed to
these characters. Certainly, for many of the founding fathers of
modern Pagandom, a familiarity with the major Greek and Latin
myths was the result of a normal education.

Other Mesopagan influences on how Euro-American Neopagan men define manhood include the Irish, Welsh, and Norse
sagas, with their mixtures of Christian and Paleopagan concepts.
The Norse tales were sometimes presented in mainstream American
schools to supplement the Greek and Roman myths, but often
they, like their Celtic counterparts, were discovered only by those
students deliberately searching for them. For most Americans,
for many years, mythological books in English were most likely
to cover these five ancient cultures: Greece, Rome, Ireland, Wales,
and Scandinavia (and to a lesser extent Germany). Since these are
all cultures that spoke related (west Indo-European) languages the
stories were filtered through Christian lenses, it should not be too
surprising that these myths and legends depicted similar cultural
ideas about manhood.

All of them expected men to be smart, brave, and/or hard
working, to be tough in whatever way their life path required,
and to defend both their personal honor and that of their tribe.
Except (usually) among the Germanic and Scandinavian cultures,
manly warriors could weep over their fallen comrades before
charging bravely into battle and not be thought of negatively.[*]

---

[*]You can also see this in the Tolkien books and movies to be discussed in a few
pages.

Among the Celts, intellectual men (druids) were honored as priests, poets, and magicians and considered manly for being such, while among the others, these members of the intelligentsia were likely to be depicted as weak and cowardly (an attitude still reflected in mainstream Anglo-Germanic-American culture). I will discuss in later chapters the eternal conflict between "the geeks and the jocks," but the tensions between these social classes are clearly evident in most Indo-European mythology. Certainly, while there were many male occupations depicted in the myths and legends that were neither intellectual nor war related, these other activities (of the producer and servant classes) were usually not considered as manly as those of the two upper classes. Of course, it's important to remember here that the myths and tales were for the most part created by members of the intellectual class to entertain those of the warrior class, so the farmers, fishers, blacksmiths, hunters, carpenters, stablehands, and so on didn't get much space in the stories their "betters" chose to perpetuate, either before or after Europe became Christian.

The Welsh versions of some of these ancient tales appear to have led directly into the romantic literature of the Arthurian mythos, the stories about King Arthur and his noble knights of the Round Table. The romantic triangle between Arthur, his queen, Guenevere, and his bravest knight, Sir Lancelot, seems to have been a late addition to the collection, but became immensely popular, lasting to this very day in dozens of versions and every known form of popular media. In these tales the Christian influences become far more obvious than in those of the earlier sagas, as noble knights are depicted as devout Christians searching for the Holy Grail or going off to the Crusades to fight for the Holy Land. Certainly, knights exhibiting the Christian ideals of self-control and sobriety are elevated over the hard-drinking, hard-loving warriors common to the pre-Christian stories. Even Merlin, the wisest and most powerful of the magic users in the tales, is de-

picted as physically weak and easily bamboozled by women, unlike the druids of the Irish or Welsh sagas.

Perhaps the most important addition to the Arthurian mythos
made to the European concept of manhood was that of a code of
chivalry, wherein knights (depicted as the best of men) were expected to protect the weak and helpless beyond their own neighborhood. Pretty much every human culture expects men to protect
women and children, but usually only of their own tribe/gene pool.
In keeping with the universalism of Christian theology, the ideals
of chivalry expanded the definition of those to be protected to include even the civilians of one's enemies' territories. Insofar as we
can consider human social progress to include an ever-expanding
circle of whom we think of as "people," this was an improvement
over the tribal period in European history, even if the ideal was
seldom followed in medieval times.

When I was growing up, the tales of King Arthur were ones I
was encouraged to read. To this very day, I find the archetypes of
the Sacred King (Arthur), the Perfect Warrior (Lancelot), the
Ultimate Wizard (Merlin), and the Queen of the Land (Guenevere)
so powerful that even when they are treated in radically untradi-
tional ways in modern books and films, they can still affect me
emotionally. If I can find myself tearing up at the end of *Excalibur*
or *The Mists of Avalon,* two of the worst Arthurian movies ever
made (from a historical or Celtic studies point of view), then I
know the myths are still alive, however mutated by modern sen-
sibilities.

Also a favorite of many boys my age were the tales of Robin
Hood and his Merry Men, probably due more to the movie and
television versions of them than the written ones. As with the earlier Indo-European tales of bands of warrior brothers (whether
the Maruts in India or the Fianna in Ireland), Robin and his followers lived in the woods by their wits and skills, fought coura-
geously against evildoers who threatened their tribe (the poor),

and eventually defeated the evil king (John) to restore the good king (Richard). While Robin's romance with the Goddess-of-the-Land figure (Marion—whose name was based on the major quasi-goddess in Christendom) was discrete and delicate (at least in the versions handed down to us) in a proper Christian manner, the rest of his private life tended to be rather Pagan in its rowdiness—the Merry Men were just that, because they drank, feasted, and fought with one another in the classic bonding tests so common to other male groups.

The denizens of Sherwood Forest demonstrated several ways to be manly: the leadership skills of Robin, the musical talents of Alan A'Dale, the loyal strength of Little John, and the wisdom of Friar Tuck. Note, however, that each of these characters—even the priest—was a warrior. Since bows and arrows were their primary weapons, Robin was naturally the best with these, as a leader of warriors would be expected to be. Again, all of these male characters can serve as role models for modern Pagan men who wish to follow a warrior path.*

While these previously discussed myths, legends, and tales may have influenced many of the founders of what were to become the modern Pagan movements, twentieth-century works of science fiction and fantasy also had their effects, not just on the founders but also on many of those young men who would join the rapidly growing new religions. One of the most important authors was J. R. R. Tolkien, the author of *The Hobbit, The Lord of the Rings,* and several other fantasy novels. These Mesopagan tales are rooted in a Christian dualist story-universe in which the forces of Good and Evil are implacably opposed. The prequel to the better-known novels is found in Tolkien's *Simarilion* tales, in which characters very much like the Christian God, Devil, and angels come into conflict in the ages before the Third Age in which

*See chapter 7 for my discussion on Pagan men as warriors.

The Hobbit and *The Lord of the Rings* take place. Sauron, the evil supersorcerer, is in fact a Satan figure, who can only be defeated by the forces of good uniting against him.

Still, most of the characters in the novels are recognizable from the common pool of Indo-European myths. Their cultures are similar to the Celtic and Norse cultures, even to the languages spoken and written. There are wise (Gandalf) and wicked (Wormtongue) counselors, brave warriors (Boromir, Gimli, and Legolas) and monstrous ones (the orcs), sturdy men of the earth (the hobbits), and a sacred king (Aragorn) who must be restored to a throne of order to help defeat the forces of chaos (identified with Good and Evil, respectively, in Tolkien's dualist mind-set). What made Tolkien's version of this ancient pattern different was that his producer-class characters (the simple hobbits) show as much courage as their social betters do. I think this was based on a lesson he had learned during World War I and II—that a farmer or a shop clerk could be as brave and manly as anyone raised to be a warrior.

Indeed, I could argue that *The Hobbit* and *The Lord of the Rings* had more of an impact on the evolution of Neopagan concepts of manhood than any of the older materials did, due to the popularity of the novels in the 1960s and 1970s when Neopaganism was being born and the dwindling of classical standards of education during that period and since. Certainly Gandalf, the brave wizard who sacrifices his life to save the other main characters in *The Lord of the Rings,* is as much a model for modern Pagan wizards as Merlin might be. The bonds of courage, manhood, and friendship so central to Tolkien's vision are an ideal that many Neopagan men try to attain today. Peter Jackson's remarkably effective and spectacular translation of *The Lord of the Rings* into film has brought the archetypes completely to life for yet another generation of young men, who will be looking for spiritual paths that reflect that mythic power.

Yes, Tolkien was a sexist, with his female characters playing mostly supportive roles, but his works affect more than just men. Women are entranced by the magic of Galadriel (the elf queen), the courage of Eowyn (the woman warrior), and the love of Arwen (the elf maiden who renounces immortality to be with the sacred king). These three roles reflect a feminine version of the ancient Indo-European "three functions" of magic/wisdom, battle/force, and fertility/support.[3] Thanks to the amazing Peter Jackson movies, there will be a new generation of Tolkienized young women to match the Tolkienized young men looking for spiritual paths that will honor these roles, and for many those paths will lead them to Paganism.

I'll talk more later about the influences that science-fiction literature and art have had on Neopaganism, but for now let me point out that Tolkien's work led to a flowering of interest in fantasy literature and art, much of which took his core ideas and reworked them in multiple ways, creating many versions of manly heroes (and womanly heroes) depicted in worlds where magic and multiple deities were natural elements. For now, however, let's turn to non-European influences on Mesopaganism and Neopaganism in the Western world.

African and Native American Influences

During the period in which slavery was legal in the Americas, and for several decades afterward, African Diasporic men were affected by some of these tales of the European cultures (depending on what education they were allowed, which wasn't much). They also had the rich Paleopagan myths and folklore of the West African peoples (and various Native American tribes, depending on where the slaves lived) to draw on, with very powerful gods providing, like their Greek, Roman, and Celtic counterparts, both good and bad examples of male behavior. There were brave warriors who sometimes lost their self-control and accidentally killed their friends, wise priests who sometimes reached beyond themselves and caused more trouble than they solved, generous farmers who occasionally forgot to show hospitality to visitors, and other common patterns.

The contrasts between the accepted strong powers of male deities told in these stories, the deliberate efforts to emasculate African American men by the slave owners (and most of later Euro-American culture), and the dualist teachings of the Bible and the Koran, combined to create a confusing stew of mixed dualist messages about the nature of manhood. Is a "real" man a player or family man? Gambler or hard worker? Gangster or cop? These questions still haunt African American and Latino men, whatever their religious beliefs, throughout the hemisphere.

The Mesopagans who practice Voudoun, Macumba, Santeria, Spiritism, and so on today are reviving the West African and some Native American Paleopagan ideals of masculinity in all its many forms, seeing men as potentially priests, warriors, dancers, drummers, workers, healers, and lovers. After all, when the gods can possess their worshippers, they can tell a man directly whether or not they approve of his behavior. And there is no doubt that men play major roles in these religions.

Beyond Tolkien—Other Fantasy and Science-Fiction · Influences

It might have seemed odd that these fiction genres would come up in a discussion of cultural influences on modern Paganism, but what are science fiction and fantasy if not the mythology of our modern age? Certainly, we have to admit that more people of both genders have been brought into modern Paganism (much to the annoyance of the older generation of Neopagans) by *Buffy, Hercules, Xena, Charmed, Practical Magic,* and *The Witches of Eastwick* than by the writings of either the classical mythologists, medieval bards, or even Tolkein himself—let alone by the (officially) nonfiction works of many of the founding fathers (and mothers) of Neopaganism. But don't forget that the scriptwriters of those mass media fantasy works just listed often *were* familiar with the older myths and legends (no matter how much they changed them for dramatic effect) and worked the classic patterns into their plotlines.

Robert Heinlein's sci-fi novel *Stranger in a Strange Land* was partly responsible for one of the early non-Wiccan currents in the Neopagan river—the Church of All Worlds (CAW).[4] This group was named after a new religion started in the novel by its main character, Michael Valentine Smith. CAW was dedicated to a free and open sexuality and sensuality, combined with the philosophy of Ayn Rand and the psychological theories of Abraham Maslow. The founders of CAW, Oberon Zell-Ravenheart and Lance Christie, were the first people to begin using the term "Neo-Pagan" in a positive way.[5]

Other science-fiction and fantasy stories by Heinlein and others during the twentieth century have presented many alternate possibilities for manhood and sexuality, some of which have been based on reconstructions of Paleopagan beliefs and cultures. Whether quasi-historical or completely made up out of thin air, these visions of what religions can be, along with the behavior of the male characters inhabiting these universes, have inspired many men to seek out (or create) their own Pagan paths.

We shouldn't overlook the cultural influences of the *Star Trek* and *Star Wars* universes on the evolution of modern Paganism. *Star Trek* in particular provided two generations of young men with heroes who were both warriors and intellectuals, able to connect to their deep emotions, have real relationships with females—even of other species!—as equals, whip a recalcitrant computer into shape, and do what had to be done physically whenever heroic action was required.

Star Wars, of course, alluded to a "Force" that was obviously the Tao, the underlying power behind the visible universe as taught by Lao Tsu, the founder of Taoism. Like the Tao, it was described as having both a dark and light side, which the films unfortunately equated to evil and good.[6] Obe Wan Kenobe and Yoda, the Jedi masters who taught the young hero how to use this Force, were sci-fi versions of Merlin. They trained their magical apprentice, Luke Skywalker, who went through most of the standard hero's journey (as described in Joseph Campbell's *The Hero with a 1000 Faces* and other works) during the films. So the old stories became new again and the ancient vision of magic and heroism in the service of good became part of the cultural matrix within which Neopaganism would grow and evolve.

Putting It All together

So what's the chain of connection between ancient Pagan myths, medieval legends, and modern arts of the fantastical? And what do they mean for modern men searching for models of masculinity and new faiths in which they can live those models? One link is creativity—not only were these tales invented by creative people, they have been known for centuries to inspire creativity. Whether we think of ancient or modern sculptors, painters, poets, musicians, novelists, or film directors, we quickly see that the stories are eternal, and at least half of them are about men or boys trying to become men or to figure out what manhood means to them.

Another link is intelligence—many of these stories began as teaching tales meant to convey a Paleopagan culture's ideas and ideals from one generation to the next. For every story that glorifies physical violence, there is one that features cleverness and another that revolves around love. Most of these tales disapprove of stupidity and short-sightedness or reveal their unpleasant consequences. Today, tales such as these are sought out by smart people looking for plotlines that don't insult their intelligence.

Yet another link is honor—a two- (or sometimes multi-) edged sword that the tales warn us can lead to terrible consequences when misused or abused but that is ultimately vital if men are to live and work together as men. The heroes in the tales often value honor above all other virtues—including common sense! So the plotlines frequently depend on the honorable or dishonorable behavior of the main characters, whether they are ancient Greek warriors, medieval knights, or *Star Trek*'s Klingons.

So, smart, creative men who are searching for a spiritual path that values honor and other manly virtues may look to these stories and see admirable gods and heroes, many living in a polytheistic past or fantasized pluralistic future, who are worth emulating and giving praise to (whether viewed as real beings or as metaphors). For these men, the idea of reviving a heroic age, along with its religious and cultural beliefs and practices, is a logical and appealing concept. The next step is to find—or create—such a spiritual path.

Exercises

Make a list of all the male deities you can think of, from as many different cultures as you wish. By each name put three words that best describe them.

Make a list of the ten greatest male mortals of history, myth, or fiction. By each name put three words that best describe them.

Pick three of the gods and three of the mortals about whom you know the least. Go search out their stories and learn them.

CHAPTER 4

Founding Fathers

Many men have been important figures in what was to become the Pagan movement of the twentieth and twenty-first centuries. In this chapter, I'd like to give you a *very* brief introduction to a few of them. Some were early folklorists and anthropologists, some were occultists (students and teachers of that which was "occult" or hidden to the mainstream sciences of their day, that is, mostly magical and mystical matters), and some were visionaries. Most have had biographies written about them online and/or offline, including within encyclopedias devoted to Pagan and Wiccan figures.[1]

Please do not assume that I am recommending all these men as role models, for several of them were known to play fast and loose with the truth, especially about themselves and their qualifications, and a couple of them were just plain jerks, as we shall see. Regardless of their characters (and most of them were characters), you should know these men and their works, for they are the seed-sowers from whom modern Pagan men spring.

Let's look at them in more or less chronological order.

Charles Godfrey Leland

Charles Godfrey Leland (1824–1903) was an American folklorist specializing in "Gypsy" traditions, folk magic, and superstitions. His impact on the Pagan revival was primarily through his translation and publication of *Aradia, or the Gospel of the Witches* in 1899. This work was purported to be the secret teachings of an underground religion of (Mesopagan) witches supposedly still living in the mountains of Italy. Its origins and contents were (and still are) controversial, but it was one of the works that Gerald Gardner (see the discussion later on) was to mine for ideas and phrases.[2] Leland was one of the first to insist that witchcraft was a secret underground religion surviving from pre-Christian times, an idea that ultimately led to the creation of Wicca fifty years after his death.

Sir James Frazer

Sir James Frazer (1854–1941) was an early Scottish folklorist, best known for his multivolume work *The Golden Bough,* published in various editions from 1890 to 1915.[3] In this work he argued that there were certain underlying patterns of belief and practice among "primitive" (tribal) and classical (Greek, Roman, Egyptian, etc.) Paleopagan religions. Many of these patterns, such as dying and resurrecting gods, orgiastic fertility rituals, harvest celebration rituals, and so on, found their way, he said, into the so-called "higher religions" (by which he meant mostly the monotheistic ones) in attenuated and disguised forms such as the Christian doctrine of the dying and resurrecting Christ, the monotheistic blessings of the harvest, and so on.

While most of his theories about the ritual sacrifices of sacred kings (that many ancient cultures even up into classical times had ceremonially killed their kings when the harvests got bad or for other religious reasons) are no longer accepted, he was the first to suggest in a widely published academic work that magic might have observed "laws" by which magicians operated. He published extensive discussion and many examples of two of these laws of magic, those of similarity and contagion. The former was the idea that things that had a similar appearance could be used magically to affect each other, such as a doll being used to heal or hex a person. The latter magical law said that things that had been in contact with each other retained a magical connection after they were separated, so that a person's hat or handkerchief could be used to channel a spell toward him or her.[4]

Frazer's importance to modern Pagans is to be found not just in his planting of these seeds of magical theory but also in the *Bough*'s thousands of pages about Paleopagan religious beliefs and practices (many of them reports about tribes no longer in existence) and Mesopagan folklore and customs collected all over the world. The scholarship of many of the reports he collected and printed was often shaky, at least by modern standards, being written by amateur observers (there were no anthropologists yet), who were often Christian missionaries inclined to believe the worst of the Paleopagans they reported on. But the overall patterns, such as those reflecting the various laws of magic and the ways in which Paleopagan religious beliefs and practices are integrated with the agricultural and technological skills and knowledge of their practitioners, become clear to a modern eye (whether that of an anthropologist, folklorist, or occultist). His writings were favorites of Aleister Crowley and Gardner and influenced their theories.

Aleister Crowley

Aleister Crowley (1875–1947), known affectionately to many modern Pagans as "Uncle Aleister," was one of the most important and controversial English occultists of the early twentieth century. He was a brilliant thinker, fluent in multiple languages, a mountain climber, and one of the first writers to attempt to explain magick (which he always spelled with a *k*, to disassociate it from stage magic) in simple language. He loved lurid publicity, presenting himself to the British media as "the Wickedest Man in the World" and "the Great Beast" (a name his fundamentalist Christian mother used to call him). He experimented with alcohol, opium, cocaine, and other drugs during a time when they were legal but disreputable, and wrote amazingly detailed descriptions of the results in his personal journals, along with recording his bisexual exploits and sex magickal experiments. He had a lifetime habit of using people financially, magickally, and/or sexually for his personal gain, then discarding them when they were of no further use.

As one of the leading lights of the Hermetic Order of the Golden Dawn, England's most famous occult society, Crowley knew and influenced (negatively or positively) almost everyone in England's metaphysical community. This included Gardner, who met him during the last year of Crowley's life and who had used some of Crowley's writings in his own ritual workings. Crowley started his own Mesopagan Egyptian religion, which he called Thelema, meaning "do what thou wilt," a phrase he imbued with much deeper meaning than most people then or now have ever understood.

To Crowley, one of the purposes of one's life was to discover his or her own "true will," by which he meant one's destiny for this incarnation, and to follow that will no matter where it took one. Crowley believed that this principle had been revealed to him by Egyptian deities during a three-day series of automatic writing trances in Cairo, Egypt, in 1904. Most modern Egyptian Pagans feel that Crowley completely misunderstood those deities or else filtered them through his own subconscious hopes and fears (as often happens in trance work).

Despite his many character flaws, Crowley is important to know about because he was one of the first voices in the twentieth century to advocate the revival of Pagan worship and beliefs.

Plus, he makes a wonderful bad example for modern Pagan founders and followers to avoid imitating!

Robert Graves

Robert Graves (1895–1985) was a British author and classical scholar. His primary impact on Pagandom was through his magnum opiate *The White Goddess*, published in 1948. This was the book in which he introduced the idea that all goddesses could be seen as either Maidens, Mothers, or Crones. Unfortunately, while this was his least scholarly work, the idea became enshrined in Wiccan duotheology and the book became a sacred text for many members of the matriarchal Goddess worship movement, such as Merlin Stone, Z Budapest, and so on, who were willing to graciously overlook the fact that it had been written by a man. On the positive side, his rather good work of translating Greek mythology was popular in British and American schools for many years and gave some of us our first taste of Olympian deities. Moreover, his highly romanticized version of the Goddess became an image with which many Pagan men fell in love, leading them to look for Goddess-honoring faiths.

Gerald Brousseau Gardner

Gerald Brousseau Gardner (1884–1964), affectionately known as "Uncle Gerald" and "Old GBG," is the father of Wicca. If not for this voracious reader, ceremonial magician, priest of the Goddess, and dirty old man (he had a sweet tooth for women in their teens and twenties, even into his sixties), what is now known as Wicca might never have happened at all. And the larger Neopagan movement would have been a great deal smaller and less evolved than it has become since the Wiccans flooded into it in the 1970s, eventually becoming the majority. He wrote two bad novels called *A Goddess Arrives* (1939) and *High Magick's Aid* (1949), and two (officially) nonfiction books, *Witchcraft Today* (1954) and *The Meaning of Witchcraft* (1959), which introduced his ideas to the world.

Like most founders of new religions, Gardner insisted that his religion of Witchcraft was actually ancient.[5] He created the duotheology of Wicca,[6] with a Goddess who was all goddesses (shoehorned into Graves's triad) and a Horned God who was all gods (but mostly a dark God of the woods and a bright God of the sun). He transformed the idea of the magical circle from a place for solitary magicians to stand within while summoning up critters into outside magical triangles (as in ceremonial or goetic magic) into a place for small groups of people to worship or cast spells. He lifted and transformed Masonic fraternal initiations into priestly ones, converted his personal magical notebook into the Craft's first *Book of Shadows,* and perhaps most importantly, insisted that rituals should be sexy and fun (by doing them nude, using erotic symbolism, and encouraging adult games within the circle). Yes, because he sometimes liked to be dominated by strong women, he made Wicca a priestess-dominated religion, but we can forgive him for that—it was the first new one of those since Theosophy and Spiritualism in the nineteenth century.[7]

Gardner's vision was to create a "native Pagan" religion for England in the form of a revival of its supposed Old Religion of Witchcraft. Moreover, he wanted it to be a Western version of Tantra, a magical and mystical system rooted in India that used sexual activities (among others) as a way to attain spiritual enlightenment and magical power. He faced an uphill battle in getting middle- and working-class Westerners to try doing group sex rituals, but there are many Pagan men today who think that Uncle Gerald's tantric vision was a good one, even if very few Wiccan groups today honor it except in the most symbolic of ways.

Alex Sanders

Alex Sanders (1926–1988) was declared by a journalist to be the "King of the Witches" in England in the 1960s, having started what eventually became known as Alexandrian Wicca. He was also the first to steal a copy of Uncle Gerald's *Book of Shadows* and then make up a story about how his grandmother gave it to him. A showman, a publicity hound, a plagiarist, and an all-around BS artist, Sanders nonetheless is said by his students to have been a good teacher. Since Gardner shared several of these characteristics, Sanders could be said to have been following in the older man's footsteps. Certainly, he managed to start a family of covens that exist to this very day.

Stewart Farrar

Stewart Farrar (1916–2000) was a British journalist who interviewed Sanders in 1969 and was later initiated (along with his wife, Janet) by Sanders as a Witch. This led to a book called *What Witches Do* (1971) about Wicca as taught by Sanders, even though Stewart and Janet had split off from him (started their own, unconnected coven) by then. Stewart went on to become the new grand old man of British Witchcraft after Gardner's death, writing a number of important books with Janet. These include *Eight Sabbats for Witches* (1981), *The Witches' Way* (1984), *The Witches' Goddess* (1987), *The Witches' God* (1989),[8] and others. Through his nonfiction works, Stewart educated an entire generation of Wiccans in both theory and practice.

Stewart was a sweet and gentle man (in both senses) whom I was lucky enough to meet before he died. He adored his much younger wife, Janet, a feisty and fiery woman, and in the years before his death sought out and "fixed her up" with a man younger than her, Gavin Bone, so that Janet would have someone to take care of her after he was gone. The three lived together as partners for several years, writing *The Pagan Path* (1995) and *The Healing Craft* (1998). Since Stewart's passing, Gavin and Janet have married and they are now writing books together, including the excellent *Progressive Witchcraft* (2004). Gavin Bone may not be a Pagan sage now, but he will be someday.

Raymond Buckland

Raymond Buckland (1934–), sometimes called "Uncle Bucky," may be the man most responsible for introducing Wicca to America. An Englishman living in the United States and researching "Gypsy" lore and magic, Buckland made Gardner's acquaintance and became initiated in 1963. He has published many books, some of them more memorable than others, that have brought thousands into the Craft. They include *The Tree: Complete Book of Saxon Witchcraft* (1974), in which he created a new tradition of Wicca he called Seax Wica that allowed men to initiate new Witches without having a priestess. Such a custom had become a necessity for Buckland, since he had divorced his Gardnerian wife, Rosemary, and split off from the Gardnerian tradition, so he had no priestess with whom he could begin his new kind of Wicca.

Perhaps most importantly, the Seax Wica tradition allowed self-initiation as a Witch, thus letting the proverbial cat out of the bag. Before this, the Wiccan belief was that "only a Witch can make a Witch," leading to various Wiccan lines of initiation. After 1974, almost anyone could claim to have initiated him- or herself, which was either wonderful or terrible, depending on whether one was a liberal or conservative Wiccan. In any event, men wanting an entry into Wicca without having an available priestess found Seax Wica a Horned Godsend.

Buckland's best-known books today are *Buckland's Complete Book of Witchcraft* (also known as "the big blue book" and published in 1986) and *Wicca for Life* (2003). My personal favorite is *The Magick of Chant-O-Matics* (1978).

Gavin Frost

Gavin Frost (1930–) is the founder (with his wife and life partner, Yvonne) of the Church and School of Wicca[9] and one of the
most controversial figures in the Craft during the 1970s and
1980s. Most of the controversies were rooted in (1) his very non-
Gardnerian ideas about Wiccan beliefs and practices, including
his monotheistic theology and nonbelief in the Goddess, (2) his
suggestion that young girls be taught how to use dildos before
losing their virginity, (3) his selling of correspondence courses
in the Craft to nonwhite-collar (and nonwhite-skinned) people
through ads in the back of supermarket tabloids, (4) the publication in 1975 of their ideas in a book their publisher decided to
call *The Witch's Bible* (updated and retitled *The Good Witch's
Bible* in 1991), and (5) their insistence that Wicca is supposed to
be a Western tantra, which means actually having sex in the circle from time to time. Of course, none of their critics wanted to
admit that they were racist, classist, or puritanical, so most of the
public pilloring of the Frosts was focused on (1) and (2).

Gavin, however, has simply never cared for popularity, doing
whatever he happened to think was right at the time. Ironically,
America's first Wiccan curmudgeon didn't really think of himself
as a Pagan (since he doesn't worship nature or multiple deities)
until recently, because of these and other differences with most
other Pagans' polytheology. Now, however, he sees himself as
part of the overall Pagan movement, albeit as more of a Mesopagan than a Neopagan. Gavin and Yvonne have produced many
books over the years, including *The Magic Power of Witchcraft*
(1976), *Tantric Yoga* (1989, the first Western book about it to be
translated into Hindi), *The Good Witch's Guide to Life* (1991),
and the excellent *Astral Travel* (1982), based on actual recorded
experiments with hundreds of their students. If you are looking
for a variety of Wicca that definitely isn't matriarchal, let Gavin
be your guide.

Carl Weschke

Carl Weschke (1930–) is the owner and president of Llewellyn Publications, which has published more books (good and bad) about Wicca and Paganism than any other English-language publisher in the world—possibly more than all the others put together! But he's more than just the papa of the 800-pound gorilla of Pagan publishing. In 1971 in a Minneapolis hotel he organized what may have been the first Pagan festival.

Carl was initiated into Wicca in 1972 by Lady Sheba, who claimed to be the Queen of America's Witches (even though no one had ever heard of her) and published her *Book of Shadows*—which was a plagiarization of parts of a Gardnerian *Book of Shadows*. But that didn't matter. Her book was the first widely distributed *Book of Shadows* in America and gave hundreds of people their first ideas about Wicca.

In 1973, Carl hired me to edit his in-house magazine *Gnostica*, which was filled with Pagan and magical materials every month and mailed out to tens of thousands of people. Also in 1973 he organized the Council of American Witches at that year's Gnosticon Festival, the first attempt to unite Wiccans from several traditions (even though almost all of them were just variants of Gardnerianism). The group only lasted a year, but it did approve a general statement of beliefs that can be found in Wiccan books to this day.

In the years since, Weschke has concentrated his energies on producing and distributing books about as many varieties of Wicca and Paganism (real and imaginary) as possible, hoping to push the movement into continual growth and evolution. I have heard it argued that, without Weschke and Llewellyn Publications, the New Age/Pagan/Wiccan section of Barnes and Noble, Waldenbooks, and other major bookstore chains would still be one or two shelves, instead of entire rows.

Victor Anderson

Victor Anderson (1917–2001) is the father of several different Mesopagan and Neopagan Wiccan traditions, usually called Feri, Fairy, Faerie, or some variation thereof. He was a poet and amateur scholar of folk magic systems from around the world (all of which he usually claimed to be an initiate of). As I put it in *Bonewits's Essential Guide to Witchcraft and Wicca*, "He mixed British and Celtic folklore about the fairies, Gardnerianism, Voodoo, Max Freedom Long's [Mesopagan] version of Hawaiian Huna,[10] Tantra, 'Gypsy' magic, Native American beliefs, and anything else he was thinking about at the time he was training the founders of each trad." As a bisexual man, he was sympathetic to gay students, and as a passionate sensualist, he insisted that sexual magic was the strongest kind (far more than that powered by mere chanting or dancing), which was a "scandalous" attitude at the time.

Scott Cunningham

Scott Cunningham (1956–1993) was a wonderful man and the author of many excellent books on herbalism, the magical uses of oils and gems, and related topics. He was also responsible for the explosion of Solitary Wicca in the 1990s, when he published *Wicca: A Guide for the Solitary Practitioner* and an updated version of *The Truth About Witchcraft* in 1988, followed by *Living Wicca* in 1993. These books have remained in print ever since, selling hundreds of thousands of copies and spreading the basic principles of Wicca (without the pseudo-historical claims) worldwide. He represents another sexual minority, by the way, in that he was pretty much asexual and celibate for most of his life. He died much too soon.

Aidan Kelly

Aidan Kelly (1940–) is important to know for three reasons. (1) He was one of the founders of the New Reformed Orthodox Order of the Golden Dawn, the original eclectic (or liberal) tradition of Wicca in the 1970s. (2) He wrote an essay for *Gnostica* in 1974 that spread the "never cast a spell on someone without their permission" taboo among American Pagans. (3) He was the other Pagan scholar besides myself who suggested in the mid-1970s that Wicca was new, not ancient.

He has been in disgrace among Wiccans, especially Gardnerians, for many years because (1) he wrote a snide book about how Gardner created Wicca, called *Crafting the Art of Magic* (1991), filled with many details about how Gardner did it, but marred by constant sexual digs at him, and (2) he was thought to have "outed" many people as Witches (by making available a database of names) at a time when most of them wanted to stay secret. Nonetheless, Kelly was perhaps Wicca's first thealogian and historian and therefore one of the most important men in the Craft's evolution.

Grady McMurtry

Grady McMurtry (1918–1985) is the man most responsible for rescuing Crowley's magical order, the Ordo Templi Orientis (OTO), from oblivion (at least in America). He became friends with Crowley during World War II, and was initiated by him to the highest mystical degree of the system.[11] The "Prophet" Crowley then charged McMurtry to be ready to become his successor or "Caliph" (the title given to the successors of the prophet Mohammed) should the first Caliph, Karl Germer, fail to name a successor (which he did). McMurtry struggled for many years after the deaths of Crowley and Germer to fulfill the obligations he felt to revive the organization in America. After several false starts, he finally was introduced (by my friend, Stephen Abbott, a

Berkeley occultist) to a William Heidrick, a wealthy Californian ceremonial magician who had an interest in Crowley and his work. So, in the 1970s a new generation of Thelemites was initiated by McMurtry, Heidrick, and others. Thus, Crowley's Mesopagan vision* was communicated to a new, mostly young, group of enthusiasts. The organization now has over 3,000 initiates plus hundreds of associate members in over fifty countries around the world, many of whom are also members of other Pagan traditions.

Grady was a hard-drinking, hard-partying, scoundrel guru, with an eye for the ladies and a hearty sense of humor, yet his serious devotion to the writings and visions of Crowley led to the revival of ceremonial magic and Thelemic theory within the larger Pagan and occult movements. I miss him.

Ross Nichols

Ross Nichols (1902–1975) was an English historian, occultist, poet, artist, mystic, and philosopher. In 1964, the Ancient Druid Order (ADO), one of several Mesopagan Druid groups then in existence, had a schism over matters both personal and political, as was not uncommon within esoteric groups then (or now). Nichols, who had been the ADO's scribe for ten years, was elected to be the chosen chief of the branched-off group, which called itself the Order of Bards Ovates and Druids (OBOD). He added the Winter Solstice to the ADO's previous three solar festivals (the Summer Solstice, Spring Equinox, and Fall Equinox), then threw in the Celtic Fire Festivals of Samhain, Imbolc, Beltaine, and Lughnasadh, giving his Druids the same eight holidays that his friend, Gerald Gardner, had settled on for his new religion. Nichols was very much a Mesopagan, mixing Christianity, Buddhism, Sufism, Theosophy, and many other mystical systems with bits of Celtic

---

*Although Heidrick tells me, "Crowley would have gone ballistic to have the term 'Pagan' applied in this way to his work," it is an accurate description.

myth and folklore.[12] Unfortunately, when he died, OBOD dissolved for a few years, to be revived by Philip Carr-Gomm.

While Nichols might not ever have called himself a Pagan of any sort, he did work to unite the British Isles' Celtic and Germanic Pagan traditions. He placed a very heavy stress on the importance of working magically and mystically with the land on which one lives, through the use of ley lines and the stone circles and other sacred sites they psychically connect. Without him, there would be no modern OBOD.

Philip Carr-Gomm

Philip Carr-Gomm (1952–) was asked to revive OBOD in 1988. He eventually turned it into the largest Druid organization in the world (not counting fraternal groups like the United Ancient Order of Druids) and moved it slowly away from Mesopaganism toward Neopaganism. Philip met Ross Nichols when he was young and became an apprentice to the older man, even editing his papers after his death.

Philip tells me that he had "an uncanny encounter with Ross in 1984, in which he asked me to revive the Order. So I feel I was asked first on the inner plane [psychically] in 1984, then when I still hesitated in case I had deluded myself, 'they' [his spiritual guides] arranged an invitation on the outer plane in 1988." Philip is a professional psychologist and applies his knowledge of human nature to his Druidic activities. Under his leadership, an influx of young people in the 1980s and 1990s has led to spectacular growth for the group, with scholars, mystics, and lovers of the Old Gods creating a Neopagan form of Druidry for a new century.[13]

Sveinbjörn Beinteinsson

Sveinbjörn Beinteinsson (1924–1993) founded the Asatru movement in Iceland. In 1972, after a long battle with the Icelandic government, he got Asatru recognized as the first official non-Christian religion there. He was a farmer, poet, and godi (priest). He served as the allsherjargodi (supreme head) of the religion until his death.

Beinteinsson became an expert at *rímur*, the unique sung poetry of medieval Iceland and revived the singing of the Norse epics and sagas, aiming them at younger audiences and even performing them at punk rock concerts! When his singing of the *Elder Eddas* (see the Asatru discussion in chapter 2) was finally recorded,[14] it was by rock and roll music labels, not the classical or folk music ones. He became a beloved father figure to many Asatruar around the world.

Steve McNallen

Steve McNallen (1948–) has been one of the most significant figures in the revival of Norse Paganism. He founded the Viking Brotherhood in Texas in 1972, shortly before graduating from college and joining the U.S. Army. After his tour of duty, he led the Brotherhood, which changed its name to the Asatru Free Assembly (AFA) but fell apart in the late 1980s. McNallen became a school teacher in California, then traveled around the world. In the early 1990s, he revived the AFA, this time as the Asatru Folk Assembly.[15] Through these various groups, McNallen networked scores of solitary worshipers of the Norse gods into a movement, which has grown to include hundreds of Asatruar in several organizations and possibly thousands of independent solitaries.

Harold Moss

Harold Moss (1937–) was one of the first Neopagan Egyptians, founding the Church of the Eternal Source in 1970 and becoming its Priest of Horus. He began publicly celebrating outdoor Egyptian summer festivals in 1963, a tradition he still continues. Under his leadership, the church earned a reputation for both scholarship and ritual skill. Moss actively networked with other early Neopagan groups such as the Church of All Worlds (discussed in the last chapter) and Feraferia (the Greek Pagan group mentioned in chapter 2) in the 1970s. In 1996, he published his first book, *Politics, Religion, and Sex: All the Things You're Not Supposed to Talk About.*[16] Harold was responsible not only for making Egyptian Paganism a permanent part of the Neopagan movement but also for fighting—for over thirty years—for the rights of gay men and lesbians in American Paganism.

Oberon Zell-Ravenheart

Oberon Zell-Ravenheart (1942–) is one of the key figures in the creation of the Neopagan movement in America. Known during earlier incarnations as Tim Zell and Otter G'Zell, in 1962 he was one of the founders of the science-fiction–based Church of All Worlds. It was he who promoted the use of "Pagan" and "Neo-Pagan" as positive terms for our new religions. For many, many years, he published the church's journal, *Green Egg*, which, during its various periods of publication from the late 1960s through the mid-1970s, then from 1988 through the 1990s, was the primary magazine read by American Pagans. It was in the pages of its letters forum that many important issues in Pagandom were thrashed out, including arguments about the history of Wicca, the role of alternate sexualities in Paganism, secular political positions appropriate to Paganism, feminist Pagan theories, and more.

In 1970, he was the first to come up with what would come to be known as the Gaia thesis, that the Earth Mother is a living being composed of Earth's entire biosphere—four years before James Lovelock published his Gaia hypothesis (though there's no evidence Lovelock got the idea from Oberon). In 1973, he met his lifemate, Morning Glory Ferns, to whom I had the honor of handfasting him the following spring. He and Morning Glory added a third partner in 1984, which eventually led to Morning Glory's invention of the word "polyamory" in 1990. Since 1997 they have been in a group marriage involving as many as six people at various times.

In 1980 Oberon created real unicorns, in 1985 he went hunting for mermaids, in 1990 he reconstructed the Eleusinian Mysteries of Paleopagan Greece and began initiating people for the first time in over 1,000 years. Oberon is also justly famous as an artist and wizard and you will find further mention of him in those chapters of this book. Truly, the entire history of the modern Pagan movement would be dramatically different without the presence of this Pagan renaissance man!

These are some of the men who made it possible for us to have the vibrant and varied Pagan movement that we have today. They blazed the trails that Pagan men (and many Pagan women) are following into the new millennium.

Now let's move from what these men did in our Pagan past to what younger Pagan men (and some of us surviving old coots) are doing in the present.

Exercises

Which of the men mentioned in this chapter do you think was the most important? How and why?

Which of them do you think would make a good role model for you? Why?

Which of them could teach you the most about how *not* to be a Pagan man?

CHAPTER 5

Pagan Men as Priests and Wizards

Probably the one activity that most men associate with ancient or modern Paganism, at least after they've studied it a bit, is ritual. When they think of important Paleopagan men, they are likely to think of druids, flamens, godis, or other Pagan priests, or perhaps of Merlin or Pythagoras performing astonishing wonders. Those who feel called to play a responsible role in their religious communities will often think of being priests or wizards of some sort.

A priest, like other clergymen, is an official representative of a given religion who is responsible for leading other people in rituals. However, as distinct from other sorts of clergy, such as rabbis, imams, or ministers, a priest is assumed to have specific spiritual/magical/psychic skills, whether innately and/or by training, that he uses in the course of his duties. Depending on the precise religious, cultural, and historic circumstances involved, the generic duties of priests may include leading rituals, channeling divine wisdom, counseling, divination, mediating disputes, teaching their beliefs, organizing events, representing their community, and so on. A wizard, on the other paw, is likely to be a prestidigitator or an occultist (student of that which is occult or hidden), or perhaps a ceremonial magician. While there are a few stage magicians in the modern Pagan movements, such as the famous Jeff McBride,[1] for most men contemplating wizardry, something a bit more uncanny is what they have in mind.

In this chapter we'll take a look at these two related and very important roles that Pagan men may choose to play, beginning with that of the priesthood.

Some Ancient History

To understand priesthood in modern Paganism, it will be helpful to first look very briefly at the Indo-European origins of many of our modern concepts of priesthood in the Euro-American cultures, for these affect many modern Pagans' views, even when those Pagans are practicing faiths from non-Indo-European cultures.

The Indo-Europeans, as you may recall from earlier chapters, were ancient peoples speaking tongues from related language families such as Sanskrit, Iranian, Greek, Latin, Slavic, Germanic, Celtic, Baltic, and others. Besides having a lot of stories in common, these peoples had other cultural traits they shared such as technology, arts, and sociopolitical patterns.[2]

In the social center of each Indo-European tribe was a king, or chieftain, who was surrounded by classes of clergy/intellectuals, warriors, producers (farmers, fishers, hunters, and artisans), and serfs or servants. Surrounding all of these classes was a vague category of outsiders, which could mean anything from the tribe next door, to the one three valleys away, to the entire outside world.

The Indo-European clergy included the entire intelligentsia of each culture: poets, musicians, historians, astronomers, genealogists, judges, diviners, and, of course, leaders and supervisors of public religious rituals. Various members of the priestly subclasses would be responsible for music, recitation of prayers, sacrificing of animals, divination from the flames of the ritual fire, and other minor ritual duties. Members of the highest subclass (druids, brahmans, or flamens as such) would be responsible for making sure that the rites were done exactly according to tradition.

It appears that in most Indo-European cultures there were cultural and social conflicts between the clergy and warrior classes. This time period (from about 2000 BCE to 500 to 1000 CE, depending on what Indo-European territory you are looking at) is as far back as we can trace the war between the geeks and the jocks that goes on even today. The results of this conflict varied in different places.

In ancient Rome, the warriors became more important than the clergy and made most of them governmental functionaries or political appointees. This seems to have gone along with the historization of Roman myths, whereby various deities became described as mortals in the stories.[3]

In the Celtic cultures, the clergy and warriors seemed to have been in a state of balance (in that neither side was depicted in the myths as more important than the other), at least until the Romans arrived in the first century BCE, which is when we first begin to have detailed knowledge of them. Julius Caesar knew that the traveling members of the druid classes (mostly bards, storytellers, and visiting judges) of Hispania (what we now know as Spain and Portugal) had made the empire's conquest of their Celtic territory harder, by warning tribes further away from the battle lines of what was to come—"Don't trust these Roman guys, they don't fight fair!" Logically enough, when Julius Caesar decided to invade Gaul, he also decided to kill every druid he got his hands on, unless they were willing to become native guides for him and his army.

Over the next century or so, the Romans slaughtered members of the druidic class (throughout Gaul and the parts of Britain that

they conquered) by the hundreds, wiping out the native intelligentsia before conquering the tribes. Later, the Roman Catholic
Church was to wage a centuries-long battle against the Irish and
Welsh druids, finally converting, killing, or banishing them by
600 CE or so.

The Romans weren't able to conquer the Germanic tribes, but
the job of suppressing the clergy class had already been done by
the Germans themselves. That is to say, the competition between
the clergy and warrior classes in the Germanic/Norse cultures
was won by the warriors before the Romans arrived. By the early
medieval period, Germanic Paleopagan clergy spent most of their
time attending to local shrines dedicated to specific deities. The
majority of religious activities were led by the male or female
heads of households or tribal chieftains acting as clergy. There
were *skalds* (equivalent to the Celtic bards or poets) attached to
the households of tribal leaders, much as the *fili* (poets) were in
medieval Ireland. There were some *volvas* (traveling soothsayers/
prophets, usually women), who practiced *seidh* (a form of divination and oracular trance possession). This eventually became
associated predominantly with women and effeminate men,
because the magical techniques usually involved passivity and
receptivity rather than assertive magical action.

The Germanic tribes known as the Angles, the Saxons, and the
Jutes, as well as the Scandinavian Vikings, took these attitudes with
them when they conquered what became the British Isles. Magical
and spiritual matters (other than battle magic) were considered to
be of interest only to women and those weak intellectual men the
warriors kept in their places as poets or bookkeepers.

In northern Europe, like in the south, some Paleopagan clergy
converted to the new religion of Christianity and became monks,
nuns, or priests of the new religion. The rest were banished or
slaughtered, often by the warriors they had served in the past, at the
insistence of their newly converted chiefs. Then followed another
millennium of conflict between the new clergy and warrior classes.

Here is why this history is important: The west and north European warrior classes successfully imposed their attitudes toward clergy and intellectuals (that they were marginally useful parasites) on the masses of their peoples. The church supported those attitudes where they concerned competing Pagan intellectuals and magicians, and opposed them where they concerned the church's clergy. By the eighteenth century, when the church's political and military power was weak enough to allow Pagan revival movements to begin, the German and Norse revivalists were only interested in warrior gods being worshipped by strong, independent, macho warriors.

The Druid revivals in England and France during that same century were also functioning in an environment where being an artist, poet, intellectual, or (worst of all) a clergyman was usually considered feminine. Their solution was to pretend that the ancient druids had never been priests as such, but philosophers catering to the needs of the ignorant masses for deities and worship. Of course, they still wore "dresses" like the Catholic priests did, even if the Druidic robes were white instead of black, so I suspect that this had little effect on the general public's view of their manliness or lack thereof.[4]

One of the major influences on modern Pagan thinking about priesthood is a religious doctrine invented by the German Christian Martin Luther (one of the early Protestant Christian reformers), "the priesthood of all believers." This was not just an attack against the Catholic Church's particular hierarchy, but against the very idea of clergy as something special or needed. Luther believed that any Christian man was worthy to lead Christian worship and that no mortal could or should get between others and God. In contrast, the forty-plus Catholic Churches, believed that certain men had received through their ordinations to the priesthood special spiritual powers to mediate between mortals and God.

When Gerald Gardner was creating Wicca, he took Luther's doctrine and enshrined it into Wiccan duotheology and liturgy as something we could call "the clergyhood of all believers." Every Wiccan was named a "Priest and Witch" or a "Priestess and Witch" on his or her very first initiation into the faith.

So modern Pagan men are presented with conflicting ideas about priesthood. On one side, we know that priests were associated with social and political power at various times in the past, and still have power in some religions today, such as Catholicism and Buddhism—power that they sometimes abuse. On a second side, those of us living in England or the United States are surrounded by a culture that tells us that priests, intellectuals, and spiritual men aren't really very manly, thanks to all that Germanic influence. On a third side, we feel a call from the Old Gods and the Old Ways, pulling many of us to represent them once again and to return magic to a world that desperately needs it.

Modern Neopagan groups, whether Wiccan or not, are thus often ambivalent about having clergy. Certainly, the idea of priests as special rubs many egalitarians (and contrarians) the wrong way, especially in America. We will see this in the pages to follow, as we examine some of the differences and similarities of being a priest in different Pagan denominations.

A Personal Story

Aidan Odinson, a Norse Heathen priest, wrote:

> Priesthood is a state of being. . . . Priesthood is not a job, a title, or something one earns as the result of a course of instruction. Priesthood is not what a person has, but what a person is.
>
> A true call to priesthood refuses to be denied. It will even cross boundaries of denomination and belief system to ensure that the truly called know that they are called.[5]

As a child, I was a devout Roman Catholic. I was an altar boy as soon as they would let me be one, which is where I first got my love of ritual. I spent the second half of ninth grade in a high school seminary, a kind of a prep school for those who would go on to the regular seminary. However, I got in a lot of trouble there, for I had spent half my grade school years in public schools and had read books by Arnold Toynbee and other secular historians about the Church's role in history. Those books did not match the ones being used in the seminary, which depicted the church as a completely benevolent institution that had never erred seriously in 2,000 years.

As a result of my bringing up awkward questions in history class about such topics as the Inquisition and the Crusades, near the end of that first semester I was told not to expect to be back in the fall. I was feeling ambivalent about this, as I was about Catholicism as a whole. This was in part because of the collision of my adolescent hormones with the church's antisexual obsessions, my observations of what I suspected was abuse of the other students by one of the priests, and my fear that becoming a priest would require castrating my intellect.[6] But much to my surprise, on the very last day of school, I was called into the principal's office and told that they had changed their minds and would allow me to return in September. Provided, that was, if I was willing to be one of their unpaid camp counselors during the summer.

"Gee," I said, "that's really nice, but I don't think I want to come back."

"That's too bad," they replied, "did you decide that you don't have a vocation to be a priest after all?"

My reply came to me completely out of the blue. "Oh, no," I said cheerfully, "I have a vocation to be a priest, alright—just not in *your* religion!" Their jaws dropped and I sauntered out to my dad's car and drove happily away, not sure why I had said what I had, but sure that it was somehow true.

A few years later, after investigating other religions, I met Robert Larson, a graduate of Carleton College in Northfield, Minnesota, and an early member of the Reformed Druids of

North America. In October 1969, I was ordained as a Druid priest, knowing that I had finally found my vocation.

Is the priesthood something you can walk away from? I don't think so, at least not based on my own history. I'll quote Odinson again:

> There are those who say that if someone takes down their altar, they never were a priest or priestess. I can attest to the fact that someone who takes down their altar and later knows no peace until their altar is back up again is experiencing the power of the call. It is nearly as impossible to keep a real priest or priestess from being one as it would be to keep a fish healthy and happy out of water!

I can testify to the truth of these words. At one point, when the small-group politics of my local Druid grove in Berkeley, California, blew up in my face (mostly due to my own clumsiness), I swore off magic and Paganism. I sold most of my magical library and purchased books of a different arcane art—computers. I was determined to spend my time doing something that might actually earn me a living.

Even so, only a few years after I had packed up my sickle and put away my mistletoe, I was back leading a Druid group again—Ár nDraíocht Féin: A Druid Fellowship (ADF), which I led as its Archdruid for thirteen years, during part of which I was also running a Wiccan study group with my fourth wife, the Wiccan author Deborah Lipp.[7] I could not escape from my priesthood, although my recent health relapses have slowed me down a bit, so I am satisfying my priestly needs by rituals with my current wife and occasionally performing weddings and handfastings. I know that I will live and die a priest of the Earth Mother and of several other deities (mostly Irish).

Now let's look at different modern Pagan attitudes about priesthood.

Being a Wiccan Priest

Gardner's "everybody is clergy" doctrine got more or less fixed early on, as he realized that the ninety-ten rule worked in covens as much as offices and sports clubs—90 percent of the work gets done by 10 percent of the people. So Gardner came up with the idea of "high priests" and "high priestesses," who usually needed a third-degree initiation rite before they could fully function as such. After a while, it became common for the boyfriend or husband of the high priestess to function as high priest, whether he was a third-degree initiate or not.

Whether or not the new high priest had a personal relationship with his high priestess, he and she were expected to generate and maintain an erotic vibe between the two of them. The assumed inability of gay men and lesbians to do this was one of the reasons for the prejudice against gay and lesbian clergy in Wicca before the 1980s.*

While the "congregation" of a Wiccan priest (or priestess) is rather small—three to five people in the average coven, maybe fifteen or twenty if a few "daughter" covens split off from his original coven—he still has to do the usual things clergy in any other faith do: counseling people, teaching classes, occasionally representing the group to others, and so on. However large or small his congregation may be, a Wiccan priest soon finds out that he has become a substitute "Daddy" to everyone. So whatever issues people have with their own fathers will inevitably be played out with him, whether he wants it or not. This is often colorful and sometimes heartbreaking, so a would-be priest (of any variety) had best be prepared with a little psychological training and lots of patience.

Wiccan high priestesses tend to be rather strong individuals and covens often become matriarchal, with all decisions being

*See chapter 10.

made effectively by the high priestess and the other women. From the most orthodox of the British Traditionalists to all but the most liberal of California Eclectics (who may not have high priests at all), the primary job of the high priest is to support, assist, and "balance" his high priestess. This is not always easy, especially when high priests are feeling subordinate. It can help for us men to remember that, in the deepest Wiccan duotheology, the God is the *source* of the Goddess's power, just as the sun is the source of the Earth's. He gives his power to her out of love, as Hades shares his throne with Persephone. Still, all Hades can do is give Persephone his seeds, which she must take inside herself to nourish. Then he must protect, feed, and support her, until the new life can be manifested in the world above, and guard it afterward until it is grown.

We're not talking twenty-first-century social and economic politics here, we're discussing deep archetypal powers that flow within all men and women, whether it is politically correct to admit them or not today. Granted, some people still prefer to believe that there are absolutely no significant differences between the genders—ignoring the question of how they are defining "significant," and on what levels of reality. Still, on the mythic and archetypal levels, there are definitely major differences that every Paleopagan mythic system shows. Zeus and Hera, Venus and Mars, Thor and Frigga, are very different personalities and it should be logical that they would expect different behavior from their worshippers and clergy.

Thus, the high priest in a Wiccan ritual has as an underlying part of his job the task of role-playing the Horned God, as he understands him (or is inspired by him), often under a particular sacred name and personality. This chosen God usually matches or complements (by pantheon or function) the Goddess that the high priestess represents throughout the rite, but most especially during the "drawing down the moon" phase of the liturgy when the high priestess channels the energy and spirit of the Goddess through her body. In those covens that "draw down the sun," the high priest will similarly channel the God through himself.

Aed, an experienced Gardnerian high priest told me:

> Gardnerian ritual is a lot like pairs ice skating. In the sport, if the man tries to overshadow his partner, out jump her, or otherwise show superiority, they will lose. Your role in Gardnerian ritual is to present your priestess to the Goddess, the God, and the universe. It doesn't matter if you, as a male, are stronger, faster, or smarter than your partner. If you try to overshadow her, you will lose. Learning to leave your ego outside of the circle is difficult.

So a high priest's task can be seen as a combination of high-class altar boy, romantic lover, and hypnotic facilitator. Don't knock the altar boy part—it was my training as a Roman Catholic altar boy that taught me the importance of planning ahead sixty seconds throughout a ritual. This makes sure that necessary items are in your hand and ready to give to your partner when they're needed, while your other hand remains empty and ready to receive the object with which she is done. That, of course, requires the priest to have laid out the altar so that he can reach everything he will need to hand her and that he did the necessary preliminaries such as lighting the incense or charcoal, having the water in the water bowl, and the salt in the salt dish, and so on *before* the ritual begins. Yes, the high priestess or someone else in the coven *could* do all the set up according to a standard plan, but then the high priest would miss the primal male opportunity of building the nest absolutely perfectly.*

A Wiccan high priest needs to be able to see the high priestess with whom he works as the incarnate Goddess she is. When he looks into his priestess's eyes at the beginning of the ritual, he should see Mae West, Marilyn Monroe, Vanessa Williams, Mama

---

*If only there were a way to do it with power tools . . . and yet, what else *are* the high priest's wand and athame and such, if not his power tools?

Cass, or this month's centerfold gazing back at him. Everything he does for her in the ritual should be done romantically, as if he were wooing a lover. By the end of the ritual, he should be seeing a Goddess he is compelled to worship and adore—literally!

During a "drawing down of the moon," one's task as high priest is to assist the high priestess in her effort to invoke the Goddess into herself. This can also be perceived as him *evoking* the Goddess into her.[8] Either way, experience shows that hypnotic trance-induction techniques work very well for this, but need practice by both partners beforehand to get the best results. His voice should be reciting whatever the coven's chosen words are for this trance induction with power, drama, and quiet insistence, while she is repeating them internally. With practice, an entire coven can join in on the drawing, but the high priest has to be focusing the energy and directing it into opening the high priestess's aura to the divine.

If it works very well, the Goddess will speak through the high priestess and move through her body, in which case the ritual may veer off in some totally unexpected direction, according to the Goddess's desires. A Wiccan high priest needs to be able to adapt to sudden changes as well as protecting the high priestess from hurting herself while the Goddess is riding her.

Drawings down don't always work, in which case the high priestess should have a memorized "charge" to dramatically recite to the coven. These often have lead-in text that it is the high priest's responsibility to know and say ("Listen to the words of the Great Mother . . ."), and he has to be alert to her signal (whatever they've decided on ahead of time) that she needs him to say it.

An occasional high priestess may try to dominate her high priest in an unkind manner, but Wiccan men know how irreplaceable good priests really are—and so do most Wiccan priestesses!

Being Other Kinds of Priest

Being a Druid priest (as distinct from being a Druid mystic, artist, bard, or other flavor of Druid) is different from being a Wiccan one. Here, there is no quasi-erotic relationship with a priestess—there may be no priestess at all, or two or three of them plus another priest or two, in any given ritual. Neopagan Druid rites can be done with anywhere from one to a dozen people leading a ceremony. The erotic interplay of yin and yang is irrelevant.

Thus, there are no particular religious jobs that only men or only women can do, and therefore no limits to the "career path" of a Druid priest. Of course, there's no guarantee that your local grove or Druid organization will wind up being led by men either! But for Pagan men who have felt suppressed by strong Wiccan priestesses (not allowed to make decisions, being silenced in discussions, etc.), joining a non-Wiccan Pagan path can be quite liberating, whether or not they decide to become clergy.

In modern Druid ritual (as modeled by ADF) the job of the people acting as clergy is to create sacred space and time, invoke deities and other spirits associated with the cosmology of the particular pantheon being worshipped that day, open the Gates between the Worlds (connect the congregation to the collective unconscious), encourage the generation of psychic energy by the congregation, and channel that energy through the Gates to the special deities of the occasion. Then they must do divination to see what blessings the deities have in mind to bestow, channel those returning divine energies to those present, and perform any rite of passage or spell to be done. This is followed by "unmaking" the energy patterns created during the earlier parts of the ritual and returning everyone to mundane time and space.[9]

Liturgically, a presiding Druid priest can be thought of as a master of ceremonies. He has to keep track of the psychic flow of energies throughout, like any priest, but he also needs to be a bard, poet, dramatist, or drummer himself. He also needs to know how to work other performance artists into the mix, for that is a large part of where the psychic/magical/spiritual energy of a modern Druid liturgy comes from.

Just as important, he needs to have a personal knowledge of, and relationship with, the deities to be honored and invoked. It helps if he knows an appropriate system of divination, just in case no one else is available to be the seer, and knows how to lead successful guided meditations for anywhere from 20 to 500 people. I strongly recommend the development of fluency in one of the Old Languages, for the nature spirits, the ancestors, and the Shining Ones all seem to respond better when addressed in their "native tongues." Thus, modern Druid ceremonies are often done bilingually, with alternating English (or whatever the congregation's usual language is) and Irish (or Welsh, Norse, or Sanskrit) lines.

Norse, Greek, Roman, and other Indo-European Neopagan and Mesopagan priests don't often get the same sizes of crowds that Druids do. The general English-speaking public is somewhat more familiar with the idea of Druids than it is with other Pagan clergy and their pantheons, so they are more likely to attend a public Druid rite. Nor do non-Druid priests need as much of a background in the arts as Druids do, because they don't always use those arts to generate energy and maintain a congregation's focus, but most of the other factors discussed apply. Egyptian priests, however, need to be especially knowledgeable of the deities they will honor in their rites (usually only one per ritual, for the Egyptian gods and goddesses usually get insulted if you invoke more than one of them into the same ceremony). Learning ancient Egyptian is more of a necessity than an option, for many of the rituals have never been translated. On the bright side, very little of Paleopagan Egyptian religion has had to be reconstructed, because there is a wealth of surviving material about it (certainly as compared to many other Paleopaganisms).

Likewise African Diasporic priests usually need to learn Yoruba, besides Haitian Creole, Cuban Spanish, Brazilian Portuguese, or whatever other language their tradition developed speaking. For example, the Lucumi/Santeria Orishas (deities) usually speak Yoruban or Spanish—not English[10]—when they possess someone at a ritual. If one is going to lead a ceremony where they are going to be showing up, one had best be prepared to talk to them in the language they want to use (which may have nothing to do with the language the person they are possessing usually speaks).

By and large, however, priests in most modern Pagan traditions aren't all that different from the priestesses in them. They do the same things and receive the same respect and power—that is, dirty temple floors to clean; candles, incense, and drink to pay for out of their own pockets (except for the African Diasporic religions, where the congregants pay all expenses); late-night conversations with suicidal congregants; crazy mothers of brides to negotiate wedding details with; and so on. They do most of the same things that Catholic or Buddhist priests, Jewish rabbis, or Islamic imams do, only without the regular donations or the perks. But then, they know the job is exhausting and impoverishing when they take it—and now you do too!

Sons of Merlin

The term "wizard" comes from the Anglo-Saxson *wys-ard,* meaning "wise one." This originally may have referred to anyone whose wisdom was respected, or one of those people in the British Isles now usually called "cunning men," whom one consulted for cures of people and beasts, to help find lost objects, or to discover who had bewitched you with an evil spell. During the time of the great European witch-hunts (1450–1750) with their emphasis on female witches, wizard gradually came to mean a male witch, with just as negative a connotation as the female version had.

After centuries of Anglo-Germanic culture denigrating clergy and other intellectuals as unmanly, and the triumph of the secularism of the "age of Enlightenment," the word "wizards" became a term for "crazy old men" beyond the years at which they could be "real men," and matters of magic and the spirit were labeled "ignorant superstition" and "old wives' tales."

Primarily thanks to the writings of J. R. R. Tolkien, J. K. Rowling (the author of the Harry Potter books), and other fantasy authors (as mentioned earlier), "wizard" is now most often used to mean a powerful and wise magician, usually male. This is a figure mostly of myth and fantasy: minor wizards who functioned as tribal magicians or healers, major ones who served as mentors to heroes, or who broke new ground in magical or scientific knowledge.

Now as some people use the term, a wizard may be any kind of modern occultist, shaman, medium, or other user of magical or psychic arts, of almost any religion. But as we'll be using it in this book, a Pagan wizard is someone who tries to teach as well as practice an Earth-centered philosophy as part of his magic.

Robert Moore and Douglas Gillette state in *King, Warrior, Magician, Lover*:

We often mistakenly think that we are very different from our ancient ancestors, with our great knowledge and our amazing technology. But the origins of our knowledge and our technology lie in the minds of men like the old aborigine. He, and all those like him in tribal and ancient societies were accessing the Magician energy. And it is the Magician energy that drives our own modern civilization. Shamans, medicine men, wizards, witch doctors, brujos, inventors, scientists, doctors, lawyers, technicians—all these are accessing the same masculine energy patterns, no matter what age or culture they live in. Merlin, in the Arthurian stories, builds a Camelot of which our technology, psychology, and sociology still dream—regulated weather, an orderly and egalitarian society, the blessings of love and mutuality between people, and the recognized need to go questing for a supreme goal (in this case, the Holy Grail). Obe Wan Kenobe, in the *Star Wars* adventures, seeks to direct a renewal of his galaxy by a combination of his secret knowledge about "the Force" and the application of advanced technology. . . . If we think for a moment about all the areas of our lives in which clear, careful thinking based on inner wisdom and technical proficiency would help, then we realize our need to properly access the Magician.

These Jungian psychologists are discussing magic without actually believing in it as such, but the concept of magic as "secret knowledge known only to a few" is as ancient as humanity. Alongside the village wise woman (or competing with her) stands the wizard, however named, ready to share his wisdom with those willing to listen long and work hard to master it.[11]

Certainly, the Pagan movement is filled with "computer wizards," for it has been a welcoming home for scientists, technologists, and intellectuals almost from the beginning. Here is a community where a man doesn't have to apologize for being smart and where women find intelligence attractive!

It should be noted that another stream flowing into what became Neopaganism was what used to be called occultism or metaphysics. These topics included psychic phenomena, Spiritualism, Theosophy, Rosicrucianism, Freemasonry, various Eastern religions, and so on. The people who attempted to use this knowledge in combination with Renaissance ideas of magic called themselves "ceremonial magicians."

Certainly, many of us thought of ourselves as occultists and/or magicians for decades before we began to think of ourselves as wizards. Perhaps we were waiting for the gray hair and long beards to grow out.

The New Wizardry

Throughout the 1990s and the early years of the new century, a young man named Harry Potter became the most famous student of wizardry in the world. Through *Harry Potter and the Sorcerer's Stone*, *Harry Potter and the Chamber of Secrets*, and all the following volumes, J. K. Rowling brought to life Hogwarts School of Witchcraft and Wizardry in the minds of millions of children and adults around the world. Many, if not most, of those readers found themselves wishing there were an equivalent in what most muggles refer to as "the real world."

So in 2002, Oberon Zell-Ravenheart gathered together some of the best-known minds in the Neopagan movement to form what he called the Grey Council, with the intent of forming an online magical school similar to the fictional Hogwarts of Harry Potter fame. In 2004, the Grey School of Wizardry opened its cybernetic doors with great success. Also in 2004, Oberon and the council published *Grimoire for the Apprentice Wizard*, a book filled with the accumulated wisdom and insight of some of the most experienced magicians, priests, artists, and authors in Pagandom.

The book isn't aimed at just boys and young men, but that's probably going to be its primary readership for a few years (until the girls find out about it). I think Oberon was trying to come up with something for all the young males who were feeling excluded by the teen Wicca movement, most of which is targeted at girls and young women. *He* knows Wicca isn't just for females, but thought that wizardry as a whole would appeal to young men more and give them an introduction to a wide variety of Pagan and magical paths.[12]

This particular project is a brilliant way to revive the archetype of the wise elders teaching the young about magic, heroism, and duty.[13] The *Grimoire* collects in one book a library of wisdom about ceremonial magic, native and Earth-centered magic,

Paleo- and Neopagan religions, the obligations of the wise to protect the defenseless, great wizards and witches of the past and present, and more. If your heart is that of the magician, the way of wizardry may be your path. The *Grimoire* (and its associated online school)[14] will guide you there.[15]

If, however, you prefer to practice your wizardry without subjecting yourself to anyone else's rules or guidelines, as many solitary Pagans and curmudgeons do, you can still find yourself welcome in the various Pagan communities. Not everyone who knows how to lead a congregation or drum circle necessarily knows how to cast a spell or how to use Tarot cards or a crystal ball to divine the unknown. These wizardly skills can be quite useful to people who know their value—and who know that nobody bats a thousand!

How do you learn these skills? There are many on- and offline resources available today, more than at any previous point in human history. Just as some scientists like to point out that 90 percent of all the scientists who have ever lived are alive now, the same goes for occultists and psychic researchers. There are many useful books available about basic divinatory and magical theory, including *Seventy-Eight Degrees of Wisdom* (about Tarot) by Rachel Pollack, *The Only Astrology Book You'll Ever Need* by Joanna Martine Woolfolk, *Taking Up the Runes* by Diana L. Paxson, my own *Real Magic*, Donald M. Kraig's *Modern Magick* and others mentioned in the bibliographies of those works.

Exercises

If you were to become a priest, what kind would you be? Wiccan, Asatru, Druid, Egyptian, Macumba, or some other sort? Why?

If you can't think of a particular pantheon or type of Paganism that you would be a priest of, try closing your eyes and visualizing yourself leading a ritual. Write down a description or draw a picture of how you and the others present would be dressed, then do some research online or in your local public library to see if it matches any known Pagan religion, ancient or modern.

What do you think would be the best and worst thing about being a Pagan priest (of the kind you're interested in)?

What do *you* think makes a man a wizard?

List ten things that a real wizard ought to be able to do. How many of them do you think you could learn to do? How many years will it take you? So, what's your hurry?

What's the difference between wisdom and knowledge?

What are the kinds of magic and divination the world needs the most? Why?

CHAPTER 6

Pagan Men as Artists and Musicians

All healthy religions eventually develop their own artistic views of the spiritual, emotional, ecological, and physical universe(s) in which their members live. The Pagan movements are no different in this from any mainstream religion, except perhaps in their willingness to depict sensual experiences as deeply spiritual, healing the mind/body split that dualism has brought to Western cultures. Pagans write, draw, paint, and sculpt images of deities, humans, animals, and spirits in every conceivable medium and style.

Music is one of the oldest kinds of magic known to humans and is certainly one of the most powerful tools for altering one's consciousness, whether for solitary or group purposes. So it shouldn't be surprising to learn that many Pagan men are actively involved in music (and other performance arts), although they seem to fall into two overlapping categories: bards and drummers. In this chapter we'll take a look at several men who have become known in the Pagan movements as artists and craftspeople, bards, and drummers.

Oberon Zell-Ravenheart

Back in the 1970s, when he was known as Tim Zell and was newly wed to Morning Glory, Oberon Zell-Ravenheart began producing Pagan-centric art, including a pair of pen-and-ink portraits of himself and Morning Glory as Cernunnos (a god associated with the hunt, prosperity, and the Underworld) and Habondia (a goddess of abundance and fertility), two of the then most popu-

"Habondia"

lar names for the Wiccan God and Goddess. These images (one of which is shown here) were published in the *Green Egg* magazine, then the most widely distributed Pagan magazine in the world, and, as large posters, made their way above the altars in many Pagan homes, including my own. He swears he was only drawing idealized versions of Morning Glory and himself, but I'm sure that his picture was also partly a male artist's self-advertising,* which I understand certainly led to a number of Pagan ladies over the years seeking to find out how accurate the picture of him was!†

Seriously, over the years Oberon's artistic talents have proven amazing, a fact that became even clearer when he switched to three dimensions and began producing sculptures of deities and spirits, many of them based on earlier drawings. In 1990, he and Morning Glory began Mythic Images,[1] one of Pagandom's most successful distributors of sacred statues and art, mostly based on Oberon's designs, including the mind-blowing Millennial Gaia, shown here. You have to see this statue up close to believe it, because the amount of detail is incredible.

Oberon says that he wanted to create a sculpture that would be a "sermon in stone" that would convey his Gaia thesis (that Earth's biosphere is a living being) to anyone who saw it. In 1995, he asked a pregnant friend to pose for some photo studies for a proposed statue of Gaia. Over the next three years, he worked intermittently on this figure, first sculpting a detailed relief globe of the Earth for her belly, then gradually building a figure around it, based on several different women.

After tearing apart the entire figure and resculpting the globe to make the location of the *omphalos* (navel) stone of the ancient Greek shrine of Delphi her navel, something happened to him. As he puts it, "I felt my hands were no longer my own, and I found

---

*Morning Glory's depiction, on the other paw, was just the way she has always looked to me.

†No, he doesn't have cloven hooves.

"The Millenial Gaia"

myself almost a fascinated observer as the figure of the Goddess began to form itself through my hands."

He found himself working obsessively on what was now being called the Millennial Gaia, taking the statue everywhere with him, and wearing magnifying glasses to see the tiny details. Finally, in April 1998 she was completed.

Entwined in the statue's hair (with braids representing the double helix of DNA) and tattooed on her skin are tiny representations of every major order of life (lichens, plants, fungi, insects, reptiles, mammals, etc.) on our planet, past and present, linked in the kind of evolutionary trees known in paleontology as cladistic. Together, they present a complete picture of the history of evolution,* from the most primitive one-celled creatures, to the sea and land plants, bugs, fishes, reptiles, dinosaurs, and mammals (including both whales and humans). One breast shows edible fruits and vegetables, while the other is the moon.

What's perhaps the most impressive about this work of art is the incredible detail—I think he used a microscope instead of a magnifying glass! Eventually, the Ravenhearts hope to produce a monumental version of the statue, twice life-size and ten times more overwhelming. Once the first is done, molds will be made and Pagan temples around the world will be installing her in places of honor, then worshiping the Earth Mother through this sacred image.

Why do I spend so much time on one piece of art by one Pagan man? Because Oberon's obsession with artistic excellence is emblematic of many men in our movement who choose the path of the artist, whether they work with words, stained glass, silver, iron, paints, or other media. For them, art is a form of magic and worship, the way in which they share their souls with the world and honor the deities they love. This is how they demonstrate their manhood, their skill, and their courage.

Kirk McLaren

Also known in Pagan circles as "Merlin,"[2] Kirk is a silversmith, sculptor, Tarot reader and teacher, drummer, and local Pagan organizer in his southeastern Virginia home. His first major artistic project began in 1985: "The Tarot Casters," in which he made three-dimensional silver Tarot cards he could either wear as talismans or toss as if he were casting traditional rune stones. The project took him over ten years, during which he also began making

*At least as was known in 1998.

custom jewelry and silver castings, producing amulets and talismans for both individual Pagans and groups. Going back to sculpture, he resumed making small statues and motorcycle accessories out of silver and bronze. He is currently working on two series of statues: "The Drumcircle" (dancers, drummers, parents, and children) and larger versions of the "Tarot caster" pieces, focusing on the Major Arcana (the twenty-two most important) cards of the Tarot. He is also working on a statue of the Dagda, my patron god, for me and has produced silver jewelry from several of my Pagan talisman designs, including "The Druid Sigil" (a sign of the Earth Mother), a "Spells for Democracy" pentacle, "The Dagda's Club" and "The Dagda's Shield"—symbols of this ultimate male Irish god). Here's another one of his designs I love:

© KIRK MCLAREN

"Green Man pendant"

According to Kirk:

Sculpture is where I am focusing a great deal of work these days. I am attempting to bring the images of our "Neopagan culture" into the fine arts. Sculpture has always been my favorite way to express the passions and the daily rituals of life. For me, the act of creation is the ultimate ritual.

One of my favorite sculptures is one he did of Coyote, the Native American trickster god. Here's Kirk's description of the process:

Jamie made a rough sketch of such an archetype, a complete reversal of commonly held ideas of what is correct: shoes on his hands, walking stick in his feet, a playful grin. . . .
   I pushed the idea a little further by balancing him on the top of the world and sculpted him in wax, then cast in bronze, and finished with a sulfur patina. This statue is nearly seven inches tall, fully detailed with a removable staff balanced between paws and tail.

Being a man in the Pagan community is, he says, "a strange feeling. Most of the country is so very male-dominated that when in the company of Pagans it is very easy to feel set apart from the mainstream." Most of the community often seems focused on the Goddess, so even though he tries to keep a balance in his art, he tends to work with more Goddess imagery than God. "I feel that this is only natural in that I tend to notice the female aspect in things rather than the male. However, when working with male concepts I sense a 'corrective' balance in myself."

He told me an amusing story of how he was approached by a festival coordinator on the West Coast to present his work at a women's festival. She explained that only women could go but that his work could be present. Kirk's partner, Tony, let her know that she wasn't interested in taking the jewelry there. Somewhat confused, the woman said that Tony didn't have to feel that she needed to be present and that the work spoke for itself, just as

© KIRK MCLAREN

"Trickster"

long as people understood that a woman had made the jewelry.
The organizer argued that Kirk couldn't have made it "because
of the obvious dedication to the Goddess." Once they convinced
her that he, not Tony, was the artist, there was a bit of laughter,
but he didn't go to the event, nor was he asked again.

Kirk meditated for me about how his faith and his art merge,
coming to these conclusions:

I try to reflect my thoughts and feelings through my art: divinity is invested into the very fabric of being. We have the

capacity to grow and develop beyond our current condition by recognizing what is sacred and treasuring it.

Many of the images I draw on are of the men and women I love and care about. When I work on pieces that characterize sacred ideals, it becomes a combination of several loved ones at the same time, as if their presence shines through the shapes I form. A dancer blessing, a drummer teaching his son to play, a Crone speaking wisdom; these are rituals that hint of eternity.

My work becomes magic when others see beyond the media and into themselves.

Don Waterhawk

Don Two Eagles Waterhawk is a decorated veteran, author, photographer, artist, silversmith, leatherworker, and stained glass creator, as well as a drummer, council facilitator, and a respected Pagan elder. Unlike many Neopagan members of the Wannabe Indian tribe, Don is a genuine Native American in half his ancestry (Tsalagi/Cherokee and Mesquakie tribes) and half German/Austrian, a Red Feather Brother (member of a group of combat medics with native ancestry who served in Vietnam), and a member of the Wolf Clan of the Seneca Nation. This spiritual inheritance informs his physical art (and his drumming, discussed later in this chapter).

His sculptures and ritual tools have been shown on national television and seen in major films such as *Conan the Barbarian, Strange Days, Independence Day,* and *Peter Pan*, and in Pagan magazines such as *Green Egg, Magical Blend,* and *Obsidian*.

He treats the materials with which he works—shells, bones, feathers, hides, horns, wood, crystals, semiprecious stones, and metals—with reverence and respect, often praying or chanting while he works.

He makes Neopagan wands, ritual knives, chalices, swords, scrying (divination) stones, shell bowls, and more.[3]

A drinking horn

A ceremonial knife

Nybor

No discussion of Pagan male artists would be complete without Nybor! Born James R. Odbert in 1936 in Minneapolis, he sold his first piece of art at age six (to a church, for its bulletin). He says he always knew he would be an artist, and went from high school straight to the Minneapolis School of Art (1954–58). He worked as a commercial artist for many years. After getting involved with science-fiction fandom, he published his first professional sci-fi art in *Analog* (then the premier sci-fi magazine) in the late 1960s (for a story that later won a Hugo Award). He is in fact most renowned for his black-and-white science-fiction art, including book and magazine covers and interiors.

At a sci-fi convention in the mid-1960s, Oberon Zell-Ravenheart (then Tim Zell) purchased a copy of a pen-and-ink drawing of a kneeling satyr by Nybor, then went home and put it on the cover of *Green Egg*! Nybor was surprised by this, as he hadn't thought of it as "Pagan art"—or given permission for it to be published! Oberon apologized profusely and received later permission to put Nybor's art in many issues of *Green Egg,* including multiple covers. After doing the "Three of Swords" for a sci-fi themed Tarot deck, Nybor got deeply interested in the Tarot and mythic matters, then into Paganism as a possible spiritual path rather than just as an interesting market for his drawings.

As an artist, Nybor uses almost all of the graphic arts and techniques; he is just in 2005 learning to use a computer as a tool and a technique.[4] Perhaps what's most remarkable about his art is that he is colorblind, yet after years of working in black and white he is now producing magnificent paintings in full color. His latest success has been the release of his highly erotic Tarot deck, the Nybor Tarot, delayed for many years while he searched for a sufficiently courageous publisher.

Together with his lady, Elspeth, he leads a community named Haven, a "loose, widespread group of solitaries," in West Virginia.

They travel around the country (sometimes together, sometimes not) selling art and providing sage advice to younger Pagans on everything from art, to ritual, to relationships, to parenting.

"Welcome"

Bards

The bards were originally a subclass of the druids (discussed in chapter 5) among the Celtic peoples. Their specific jobs were to provide artistic support to the other druids' work, especially in ritual, as well as to the other classes. They had counterparts among the other Indo-European cultures, and the bardic subclass usually had smaller specialties within it, such as poets, ritual invokers, storytellers, and so on.

Many Pagan men find the role of the bard a particularly attractive one, possibly due to its ancient power as a romantic lure to the ladies, but also to their experience of the psychic/magical energies that bardic skills can generate. Pagan men often play instruments, write and sing songs, compose and recite poetry, tell stories old and new, and entertain and inspire their brothers and sisters while invoking (figuratively and literally) the Old Gods. Becoming a bard can get a young Pagan man invited to perform at parties and rituals, sometimes leading to significant responsibilities at public and private religious rites. You will find bards among the Wiccans, Druids, and Reconstructionist Celts, skalds among the Asatruar, and their equivalents in most of the other Neopagan communities.

Contrary to many people's assumptions, however, being a Pagan bard doesn't mean you are limited to doing materials from the British Isles folk repertoire (even if that is my personal favorite). As the Witches' Voice, the internationally known Pagan Web site, puts it:

> Neo-Pagan musicians go way back to the 60s and have entertained us all with their muse and their magick for over 40 years. Stylistically, Pagan music is a tapestry of diversity and runs the gauntlet from ambient instrumental music to hard core Pagan metal. The rule is . . . there are no rules that dictate what Pagan music sounds like. If it's from the spirit and speaks from a Pagan voice, it is real Pagan music![5]

The music section of the WitchVox Web site includes links to over 200 Web sites owned by Pagan musicians (half of whom are men), Web sites of bands, record labels, and radio stations who support Pagan music, a section called "Bardic Circle" with mp3 files of their songs* with stories by the artists on how and why they recorded them, and more.

*Including a couple of my own!

Bardic Circles

While WitchVox's "Bardic Circle" section is an online place for Pagan musicians to share MP3s of their work and the stories behind them, it has an older meaning in the American Neopagan community. Originally, the custom of the bardic circle came into the Neopagan community from the Society for Creative Anachronism (SCA),[6] America's best-known medievalist organization. The first ones were held in Greyhaven,[7] the famous home of the SCA's founder, Diana L. Paxson, and founding members Jon DeCles, Paul Edwin Zimmer, and Tracy Blackstone. As best I can recall, anywhere from twenty to a hundred people would show up with food and beverages, which they would set up in the dining room. Then everyone would gather in a large circle in the living room. One person, usually one of the hosts or hostesses, would begin by reading a brief poem (his or her own or someone else's), singing a brief song (ditto), or telling a brief* story (again ditto). Then the person next to them would perform, then the next, all the way around the circle. No one was allowed to skip performing on this first round, to demolish the audience-performer distinctions immediately.

At the end of the first round, everyone would break for half an hour for food and drinks, then return. On the second and subsequent rounds, at each person's turn, he or she was allowed to pass on performing or to make a request of one of the others present for a particular song or poem. In between each round there would be more breaks, and eventually most would wend their way home and only the hard core would be left. That was when the best stuff was brought out—songs, invocations, brand-new "ancient" sagas, and more.

---

*Why only brief performances on the first round? Well, with a hundred people there . . .

There was usually a fifty-fifty male-female ratio at these events
and many a trembling teenage poet or suave older musician found
himself attracting the attentions he desired from his preferred
gender, at least if his performance was considered good. If it
stank, he was likely to get some good-natured advice (if young)
or some satirical commentary (if older). Either way, those who
wanted to perform had an outlet not found in ordinary mainstream society, especially if what they liked was medieval or pre-
medieval materials. And since many members of the SCA, then as
now, were Pagans, the custom began to spread across the country
and around the world, eventually filling all of Pagandom. Today,
you will find bardic circles occurring at most Pagan festivals and
conventions, whether as a formal part of the program or just in
someone's room or around a campfire.

Gwydion Penderwen

Perhaps the first bard to become well known to Neopagans was
Gwydion Penderwen (d. 1982), one of Victor Anderson's early
apprentices. He became an actor and storyteller, creating ritual
drama, poetry, and music, which he used in Faerie rituals (the
traditions founded by Anderson, described in chapter 4). Because
he felt that the old Celtic languages were beautiful and full of
magical power, he learned to read and write (and songwrite!) in
Welsh. He is perhaps most famous for producing the first Neopagan record album, *Songs for the Old Religion*, released in 1975,
which included songs for all the Wiccan holidays. His second
album, *The Fairy Shaman*, was recorded in 1982, shortly before
his untimely death in a car accident.[8]

He was a frequent pot smoker, a cutting wit, a planter of hundreds of trees, and a lover of many happy women. At his funeral
service, the entire two front rows of benches were filled with
grieving ladies who considered themselves widowed. Unfortu-

nately, it was a mainstream funeral, with the eulogy spoken by a mealy-mouthed idiot who obviously had never met our friend ("He was very fond of nature," the man said, describing an avid environmentalist who literally worshiped Gaia). I will always regret that none of us had the courage to stand up in the middle of the ritual and give our own eulogies honoring the spiritual path to which he had given most of his too-short life. But we all went out to a Pagan circle afterward and sang him through the Gates to the Otherworld.

Many Pagan bards have tried to live up to his example, which has tended to be an exhausting task. But he certainly established the tradition that a Pagan poet, singer, and musician can be as masculine as anyone else, regardless of the mainstream culture's assumptions that all artists are somehow unmanly—which goes back to that whole ancient jocks versus geeks conflict discussed earlier.

My Own Bardic Work

According to my song lyric files, I've been writing songs since I was in my early teens. Perhaps prophetically, the oldest one I've found had a supernatural theme with a religious moral: it was about a surfer who passed up an opportunity to save another surfer from death, died himself shortly thereafter, and was condemned (by an unspecified Power) to surf forever on a wave without end—sort of an early 1960s, southern California version of the "Flying Dutchman" story. Another was an antiwar song about the pitfalls of "winning" a nuclear war in which I made it clear that there were no winners (I've been thinking of recasting it in twenty-first-century terms).

It was only after I became a Pagan in the late 1960s that I began to write songs that weren't so maudlin. The first of these was a love song to the Wiccan Goddess, "I Fell in Love with the Lady," based on the whole Margaret Murray *Witchcult in Western*

Europe nonsense (about witches as survivors of an underground Pagan religion) that, like most Pagans at the time, I believed. In this song, I began my forays into the folk tradition, that is, I stole the tune and title from someone else (in this case, Tim Hardin) and wrote Pagan lyrics to it.

I don't do that from living songwriters anymore except for satirical purposes, as in my "Wizard" song, which is based on "The Gambler" by Don Schlitz and Kenny Rogers (I call it a "country and Wicca" piece). But even my humorous songs can have a serious purpose, which in "Wizard" is revealed by the chorus:

> You got to know when to banish, know when to vanish,
> Know when to back away, and know when to stand.
> You never count your karma, when you're dancin' in the circle;
> There'll be time for counting karma, in the Summerland!

The point of that particular song is to encourage Pagans to use their magical skills when they are needed, instead of making up excuses based in Wiccan beliefs* not to take action, a problem many in the Neopagan community have.

Many of the songs I write are specifically for ritual use, such as "Hymn to Bridget," "Hymn to the Morrigan," and "Hymn to the Dagda," all of which I wrote for use in Druidic ceremonies. As a Druid, I know that one of the purposes of songs is to teach the ancient lore, so unlike many songwriters outside the Pagan movement, I put the results of long hours of research into my lyrics. This also has the advantage that it makes the songs work better in rituals, for the deities appreciate it when they are correctly praised in ways that their earlier worshippers might have used.

---

*See my discussion of the absurdity of most Wiccan theories of magical ethics in *Rites of Worship* and *Bonewits's Essential Guide to Witchcraft and Wicca*.

For example, in "Hymn to the Dagda," I use this ancient Irish God's formal names and titles, in both Irish and English, and I have verses, such as the following, that describe his multifunctional nature:

> You are the flame that burns within
> The royal hearth or an outcast's hovel;
> The sacrificial fire as well,
> The giver and the gift that's given.
> You are the heat of a warrior bold
> When fighting for the tribe's survival;
> The fiery passion of our loins,
> The holy spark of live renewing.

To me, being a bard means merging my left-brain rational skills with my right-brain intuitive ones to create beauty I can dedicate to the gods and goddesses. Since one of my first goddesses was Athena, the matron of scholars, I consider truth to be an important element in my songs. Thus, even when I'm singing someone else's work, such as Charlie Murphy's famous "Burning Times," I change the lyric that says "9 million" women died to "a hundred thousand" died, along with other historical corrections. This has been known to annoy some Pagan women who still have an emotional investment in the Murray-ite myths behind the song (I don't know what Charlie would think if he heard me).

Fortunately, that insistence on historical and mythological integrity has some benefit to Goddess worshippers, because I use it in my songs to Bridget and the Morrigan. The latter especially has been straight-jacketed for far too long by an image of her as "just" a warrior goddess, when she's also a queen, a fertility goddess, and a psychopomp (leader of the dead). I believe my hymn to her was the first written to give her full credit for her glories.

I've two albums out so far, *Be Pagan Once Again!* (1988) and *Avalon Is Rising!* (1992), originally as tape cassettes and now as

CDs, from the folks at the Association for Consciousness Exploration (ACE).[9] At some point in 2006, my third, *She Said!*, should be released as a CD, also by ACE.

Some Other Pagan Bards

There are literally hundreds of Pagan men working as bards within the Neopagan community, scores of whom perform at professional or semiprofessional levels with tape or CD albums released. Here are some of the ones I find most interesting:

Ian Corrigan is well known in Wiccan and Druidic circles as a singer, songwriter, drummer, teacher, and superb ritualist. To him, "A bard is a maintainer and transmitter of lore, a preserver of cultural heritage, an entertainer, to some extent the voice and conscience of a tribe."[10] He takes this role seriously, performing both ancient folk songs and new ritual songs, as well as the occasional satire, entertaining, teaching, inspiring, and amusing his community. His recordings include *Ian Corrigan Live at Starwood*, and *Once Around the Wheel*.[11] Ian is a *big* man—physically, emotionally, and spiritually—who can sing softly enough to attract the Faerie Folk or loudly enough "to keep the wolves awake!" While he is an excellent guitarist, when he leads Druidic rituals[12] he tends to wear a large African drum, which he uses to guide the other musicians and chanters.

Damh the Bard is a British musician, songwriter, storyteller, and poet, who works within the British folk tradition, myth, and legend to create new stories for our times. Many of his works are rooted in his love of the Wiccan Goddess and the Old Gods. While his first guitar teacher was an Irishman who taught him Irish folk songs and dance tunes, he later played drums with a heavy metal band. Then he discovered magic and Druidism, joined the Order of Bards Ovates and Druids, and explored the bardic tradition. A burst of song writing flowed forth, followed by public performances, the winning of a bardic competition in Wessex, and the formation of a Pagan band, Spiral Castle. Currently, he has two albums out: *Herne's Apprentice* (2002) and *The Hills They Are Hollow* (2003).[13]

He tells me:

> As a Pagan man, whose spirit guide is the Stag, I relate directly with the Horned God. To me he is the keeper and quickener within nature, the face in the leaves, the movement in the shadows of the wood, the sleeper beneath the hills, the corn in the fields, and the light of the sun. This love for him is reflected in the words of my songs, and my spiritual practice as a Pagan bard by telling his stories through music. The Faerie gave us music, and when we play, they listen.

Trickster, also known as Loke E. Coyote, lives on a nature sanctuary in eastern Texas. His band, Loke E. Coyote's Wiccabilly Circus,[14] plays country and Wicca, rap, blues, rock, cowboy hip-hop, and metal music, usually with a satirical slant but sometimes with heartbreaking truth. Their albums include *Yipe! Hype!, Druid Four Winds* (a Pagan rock opera!), and *Rhythms of Spring*. Trickster says that he's not a musician, but he "plays one on stage."

Where other bands might strive for musical perfection, Trickster's "I meant to do that" style adds a certain raw charm to his eclectic garage rock sound. Some of his major influences include Frank Zappa, Weird Al Yankovic, Bob Dobbs,[15] and Bugs Bunny. His biting lyrics blur the line between the sacred and the profane—a line he refuses to believe exists in the first place. He tells me:

> I never bought that "it's all love and light" stuff, or the idea that Pagan music has to be worshipful chanting in a minor key. There's a great deal of celebration, partying, and humor involved in the Pagan lifestyle, and unfortunately lots of

politics and somewhat shady behavior in the community.*
Some Loke E. Coyote music is good-time dance tunes, and
some of it rubs a few noses in their own mess. The purpose
of a heyoka[16] [Native American clown] is to shake things
up, expose BS, and open doors to progress. I take my job
seriously, but enjoy the hell out of it at the same time.

Other Pagan bards include James Gagne, who wrote two classical works, *Cantata for Beltain* (1990) and *The Goddess in the
Kingdom of Death* (1991), James Gilchrist of the band Blue Knight
(Celtic/rock/world music), Brian Smith, whose band Coitophonic
does Pagan metal, Todd Alan, who has been a singer-songwriter,
guitarist, and keyboardist for many years, as well as a sound
recording engineer (his albums include *From This Moment On*
and *Carry Me Home*),[17] and many more. Surely, there is lots of
room for new Pagan men to come along and join the bardic
ranks!

Drummers and Dancers

I've been watching and listening to Pagans drumming at festivals
and local drum circles for many years. And, trust me, in the early
years it could be pretty darned awful! Then, in 1990, the folks
who put on the Starwood Festival every year (the largest Pagan-
friendly festival east of the Mississippi), the Association for
Consciousness Exploration,[18] decided to bring Dr. Halim El-Dabh,
a wonderful Egyptian musicologist from Kent State University,
into the festival to teach workshops on drumming.

He taught people that the drum was an ensemble instrument,
not a competitive weapon, that there were many different types
of drums, each of which had characteristic ways in which it was
played, and that drum circles involved customs (such as follow-

*As with any other group of human beings.

ing leaders, setting up the drums in particular patterns, etc.) that had evolved for very good reasons. That very festival the drumming improved tenfold and the graduates of Halim's drum workshops took their newfound skills to other festivals. Every year since then, drummers across the United States have been increasing their knowledge, skill, and art to a point where drum circles are now the highlight of most festival nights for many Pagans around the country and the world.

"One in Spirit"

A year after Halim gave his famous workshop, Don Waterhawk (whom we met last chapter) started teaching classes in Native
American drumming at Starwood (he hasn't stopped since). For
three years after that, the Earth Drum Council was a major presence
there, offering workshops on several different styles of drumming
and drum making. While there were certainly Neopagans drumming long before Starwood, what has become a rhythmic renaissance owes a great debt to Halim and the Starwood crew.*

Now, drumming has become a major art form and spiritual
path for many Pagans, especially men. Night after night at hundreds of festivals, you will find small (or gigantic) fires with
dancers (mostly female) moving around them to the sound of
drummers (mostly male), all night long. Why this gender imbal-
ance exists, I'm not sure, but it seems to have been around for fifteen years or so. Oh yes, lots of women and girls drum, but usually
with each other in women-only or women-majority groups. Do
they have trouble drumming in a testosterone-drenched environment, or is it just more fun to entice some of that testosterone?
My wife Phaedra's theory is that women have more cultural permission to be free and sensual in dancing than men have and
notes that the male dancers tend to be young and good looking.
Perhaps those are just the ones she notices most, or this might be
simply because our younger Pagan men are less inhibited than
their elder brothers and fathers are.

Of course, for many dancers around these drum circle fires,
the dancing is primarily a spiritual activity and the attractiveness
of it to onlookers is not as important as the spiritual energy flow
they are creating. As Waterhawk and Patricia Telesco, the coau-
thors of *Sacred Beat: From the Heart of the Drum Circle,* put it:

> Sacred dance, simply defined, is the spiritual practice of
> putting into motion a physical language that speaks of wor-
> ship, celebration, prayer, and meditation. The entire point of

*And to Jeff McBride, west of the Mississippi.

sacred dance is to connect with the Divine and allow Spirit
to guide one's movements. Unlike professional dance, the
focus here is not on perfecting the outward expression per
se. Rather, fire dancers illuminate the inward transformation
and cultivate the energy of community as it naturally spirals
out through their bodies to the rest of the drum circle.[19]

So why *are* most of the drummers at fire circles male? There
could be lots of reasons, but I guess the most important one
might be the many adventure movies (from *Tarzan,* to *King Kong,*
to *Indiana Jones)* in which mostly male tribal drummers pound
loudly on huge drums while beautiful women dance sensuously.
Whatever the reason, drumming is an activity in which many
young and old Pagan men find deep fulfillment and joy.[20]

Tuatha de Kelti Drum Circle

Tying in to our previous look at Pagan men as artists, the construction of drums is an art form for many. Phaedra has a friend who made ritual objects such as staves, wands, rhythm instruments, altar tools, sacred art, and so on out of found materials—including roadkill! For example, he used to pick up the bodies of dead deer, tan the hides, and use them to make heads for the African-style drums he made. He considered it a modest environmental recompense for the housing projects he had helped to construct as a carpenter, which drove many animals out of their habitats and into the roads. However, he assured Phae that, "I never pick up roadkill on a first date!" Now that's a considerate Pagan male!

Not all the fire dancing that gets done at Pagan gatherings consists of folks dancing around a fire or leaping across its flames.* A new variety of fire dancing has begun appearing throughout the American Neopagan community in the form of people who dance *with* fire, either swinging it on chains, waving flaming fans, fighting with flaming swords, or mixing classic fire breathing with athletic displays. This is done by both young men and women, usually under the careful guidance of experienced dancers.

Being a fire dancer of this new sort, like being one of the bonfire builders or sacred fire tenders, is a powerful experience for any young man as well as for those watching him. Such exercises in controlled exposure to danger are becoming unofficial rites of passage for the current younger generation of Pagan men.

Exercises

Are you an artist? Do you doodle, sketch, or paint? If so, do you find inspiration in natural phenomena like rivers, clouds, forests, or wild animals?

---

*This is often discouraged, see chapter 11.

If not, try making some art anyway—you don't have to show it to anyone if you don't want to.

Try invoking a diety of inspiration like Apollo or Bridget to help you be a better artist, then get to work!

What would it be like to live in a subculture where being an artist was considered manly? How would it be different from the mainstream culture?

How many songs or poems do you know that have a Pagan theme? Include rock, goth, and metal songs.

Try writing a Pagan song, poem, or story—then find a friendly audience to perform it for, or post it on a Pagan Web site.

Go to a music store (or a drum seller at a Pagan festival) with a wide selection of hand drums. Try tapping out a simple heartbeat rhythm on several, until you find one that speaks to you. If you can, buy it and take it home with you (or borrow a similar one from a friend). Try playing along with recordings of your favorite music, when no one else is around, until you feel brave enough to take your drum to a drum circle!

CHAPTER 7

Pagan Men as Warriors and Hunters

Many Pagan men do not think of themselves as priests or magicians, as artists or bards, but rather as warriors, albeit their definitions of this term can vary widely. In the questionnaire that I circulated for this book, one of the questions I asked was about what sort of "warrior," if any, the respondents thought of themselves as. I was surprised to find over two-thirds of the men said they were warriors, although many listed "activist" or "pacifist" as their type of warrior path.

But the field of combat is not the only place where Pagan men have traditionally confronted death. For hundreds of millions of us through the millennia, the quest to put meat on our family's table was a matter of life or death on a daily basis. In this chapter we will look at some of the many ways that modern Pagan men may choose to be warriors or to confront death through the rituals of the hunt.

What Is a Warrior?

Zalon Draconis wrote:

> To me, the role and archetype of the warrior is of the utmost
> importance. It is the biggest factor in my practices, both in
> ritual and in everyday behavior. I think that warrior ideals,
> with their emphasis on family (both biological and chosen)
> loyalty, honorable actions, personal responsibility, and (to
> a lesser extent) self-sufficiency/preparedness, are extremely
> important to modern Pagans. I hope to see a trend leaning
> towards these ideals in the Pagan community, and even the
> mainstream culture, in the future.

Ideally, a warrior is a person who knows how to use violence
effectively, but doesn't fight except when he perceives a genuine
danger to himself or others under his protection. A warrior's duty
is to protect the innocent and defenseless. He tries to use the minimum amount of violence (if any) necessary to defeat the danger
and is willing to risk his life in the process. A warrior wants to
see the face of his enemy and to fight honorably, however his society defines that. While he may enjoy being a warrior and appreciate the thrill of battle, he doesn't disregard the emotional and
moral effects of killing. Warriors will compete with each other,
not just to hone their combat skills, but to emphasize their individual identities. Courage, honor, integrity, and self-awareness
are the characteristics I associate with this image of the warrior,
and I'm certainly aware that many men have been called warriors
by their societies who did not match this ideal closely.

In *The Wiccan Warrior*, Kerr Cuhulain states:

> A Warrior is a person who, through objective and thorough
> self-examination, develops an understanding of his talents
> and limitations. A Warrior then achieves his goals using a
> combination of this self-awareness and his will to overcome
> weaknesses, fears, and limitations. The Wiccan Warrior's
> path is the Wiccan Rede in action: "An it harm none, do

what thou wilt." It is taking responsibility for your actions. It has nothing to do with being a police officer or serving in the military. It has nothing to do with being male or female. It is the process of taking charge of your life.

As we will see in this chapter, there are many Pagan men who are in law enforcement or the military, precisely because they see their occupations as directly related to their warrior path. Cuhulain is a former U.S. Air Force officer, career policeman, and the author of *The Law Enforcement Guide to Wicca* (a guidebook about Wicca and other Neopagan religions for police officers).[1] In this extract, he is not saying that warriors shouldn't be policemen or servicemen, he just wants people to know that his version of the path is not the only one. While the *Wiccan Warrior* is emphatically not just for males, Pagan men will learn much from it about how to integrate their beliefs (even non-Wiccan ones) with a warrior path.

Do we really need warriors at all? Robert Moore and Douglas Gillette, in *King, Warrior, Magician, Lover: Rediscovering the Archetypes of the Mature Masculine,* warn us:

> We can't just take a vote and vote the Warrior out. Like all archetypes, it lives on in spite of our conscious attitudes toward it. And like all *repressed* archetypes, it goes underground, eventually to resurface in the form of emotional and physical violence, like a volcano that has lain dormant for centuries with the pressure gradually building up in the magma chamber. If the Warrior is an instinctual energy form, then it is here to stay. And it pays to face it.

The warrior archetype shows up all over the classical myths and the other sources of modern Neopaganism we looked at in chapter 3, from the Argonauts, to the Vikings, to Robin Hood, to Tolkein's Aragorn, to *Star Trek*'s Klingons. For that matter, we shouldn't forget all those Kung Fu movies that are so popular with many Pagan men. Much of my own ideal of what a warrior is comes from a martial arts perspective, although the only martial art I practice well is Klutz Fu. For many Pagan men, karate, jujitsu, or kung fu opened the way to their discovery of a Pagan path. Thundercloud told me:

> I am a warrior. I have been in the martial arts for twenty-three years and a Pagan for seventeen years. My martial arts have a lot of influence on my Pagan path. Exercise is a large part of the way I worship and thank the gods for my body.

As the ancient Indo-European mythmakers (and their colleagues from most other cultures) knew, a complete society needs more than just artists, intellectuals, farmers, and fishers. It needs people willing to do whatever must be done to protect those who, by nature or training, cannot protect themselves. So if we are going to accept the presence of the warrior path or archetype within modern Paganism, how do we make it as healthy as possible? How do we turn boys and men into something resembling our ideals of what Pagan warriors should be, without encouraging the sort of mindless violence that the mainstream culture seems so intent on fostering?

Barbarians and Knights

Since Norsemen are often seen as quintessential barbarians, let's look at the Nine Virtues of Asatru, a list of Norse Pagan ideals held to by many current Scandinavian and Germanic Pagan groups. Here's a common version of the list:

1. Courage—The bravery to do what is right at all times.
2. Truth—The willingness to be honest and say what one knows to be true and right.
3. Honor—The feeling of inner value and worth from which one knows that one is noble of being and the desire to show respect for this quality when it is found in the world.

4. Fidelity—The will to be loyal to one's gods and goddesses, to one's folk, and to one's self.

5. Discipline—The willingness to be hard with one's self first, then, if need be, with others.

6. Hospitality—The willingness to share what one has with one's fellows, especially when they are far from home.

7. Industriousness—The willingness to work hard—always striving for efficiency—as a joyous activity in itself.

8. Self-Reliance—The spirit of independence that is achieved not only for the individual but also for the family, clan, tribe, and nation.

9. Perseverance—The spirit of stick-to-it-iveness that can always bring one back from defeat or failure—each time we fail we recognize failure for what it is and, if the purpose is true and good, we persevere until success is won.[2]

Now it's true that bravery can turn into foolhardiness, a concern for honor into overbearing pride, loyalty into creedism, racism, and sexism, and so on. For that matter, self-reliance can turn into isolationism—the belief that one has the right to do as one pleases regardless of any negative impact on other families, clans, tribes, or nations. Fortunately, strong Asatru men tend to have strong Asatru women around to let them know when they are getting carried away with themselves! But clearly these virtues, also shared by many mainstream American men, are appropriate for a Pagan boy or man to use in following a warrior path.

The Nine Virtues of Asatru are mostly taken from heroic literature and tend to focus on the ideals of the Norse/Germanic warrior class, ideals that weren't always lived up to back in the days of Viking raids and barbarian invasions. But then, the ideals of chivalry that so many modern men's fraternal orders are based on are also rooted in romantic fiction rather than historical records—for medieval knights were often just thugs with heavy armor—yet those ideals have lasted for centuries.

Now, let's look at a modern Code of Chivalry held to by the members of the Royal Order of the Knights of Herne, a Pagan men's group based in North Carolina:

- Valor—Valor is not the lack of fear, for no one lives without fear. Rather, valor is the facing of one's fears. A true Knight faces his fear, and does what must be done in spite of it.

- Truth—To lie is an act of cowardice, an admission that one is not willing to face the consequences of one's actions. A Knight should therefore seek the truth whenever possible, and should strive to keep the oaths he chooses to swear.

- Loyalty—A Knight remains loyal to the people and the precepts which he has sworn to uphold, ever honoring and defending them, and never forsaking them while there is life left in him.

- Humility—A Knight conducts himself with quiet confidence, never boasting, but letting his deeds speak for themselves.

- Charity—A Knight is generous so far as his resources and means allow, giving selflessly so that the community might prosper. To be a Knight is to be given a power, and with all power comes a responsibility to others.

- Prowess—A Knight should strive for excellence in all endeavors, physical, mental and spiritual. He should dedicate himself fully to the tasks he chooses, and seek always to improve himself.

- Defense—A Knight is sworn to defend those who depend on him—his family, his loved ones, his community, and his nation. He also defends the precepts by which he lives, as well as those who cannot defend themselves.

- Justice—A Knight should serve the cause of justice, taking responsibility for his own actions and, as far as he is able, seeing that others do the same. He must remember, however, that the sword of justice must always be tempered by mercy. As Gandhi said, "An eye for an eye makes the whole world blind."

- Honor—The most important quality of a Knight is honor, for honor is the basis for all of the virtues of chivalry. Honor, in essence, means that a Knight holds to the precepts by which he lives, realizing that though the ideals cannot be reached, striving towards them ennobles the spirit and makes the world a better place for all.[3]

By adding "humility" (a Paleopagan Roman virtue) to the mix of previously mentioned virtues and ideals, these modern Pagan knights come even closer to the idealized warrior described at the beginning of this chapter, even though such humility would seem a strange virtue to ancient warriors, many of whom considered outrageous boasting an art form. The virtue of charity, however, can be seen as a reflection of the Norse virtue of hospitality.

Cops, Firefighters, and Paramedics

If you talk about knights rescuing those in distress in modern times, many people will immediately think of police officers, firefighters, and paramedics—occupations that many might be surprised to find include Pagans in their ranks. The Officers of Avalon[4] (of which Cuhulain was a founder) is a Neopagan service organization linking hundreds of Pagan law enforcement and emergency personnel in the United States, United Kingdom, Canada, and Australia. Certainly, many workers in these fields think of themselves as warriors and risk their lives for others on a daily basis.

One of the questions I asked in my questionnaire for this book was, "In a real life-or-death situation, who is it your duty to try to save, even at the risk of your own life?" Almost half of the respondents checked the boxes for women and children, with most of those adding the elderly and the disabled. Another quarter of the respondents said some variation of "anyone in need." One said, "If I died so that others could live, I would think that an honorable and noble thing." Another said, "As the physical embodiment of the [Wiccan] God, I must stand strong and defend those weaker than myself from those who choose to live without honor."

Such responses would seem to contradict those who think that all modern Pagans are "selfish hedonists" who don't know the meaning of sacrifice.

One man perhaps cut to the evolutionary core of it when he said, "As men, we are expendable." Certainly, from the point of view of the DNA inside each "selfish gene,"[5] once a male has reproduced, his primary role is to make sure that his offspring live long enough to reproduce as well. Earlier human cultures knew this and much of the ancient warrior role, both the positive ("defend our tribe") and the negative ("kill the other tribe's men and rape their women") parts of it can be seen as growing out of this evolutionary need to spread one's genes and protect the resulting children. I hasten to point out here that no modern Pagan warriors approve of rape or any other form of violence against women.

Given such consensus on the need to take care of those who need it, the presence of Pagan men in the law enforcement, firefighting, and emergency medical services (as well as in other caring professions such as nursing and counseling) would seem a logical result, as would the presence of Pagan men (and women) in the armed forces.

Pagans in the Military?

Yes, indeed, there are plenty of them. The Military Pagan Network[6] estimates that there are tens (if not hundreds) of thousands of Pagans who are members of the U.S. military services alone. Many of these people believe that they are following a warrior path by defending their country and/or that they are improving the military system from within by, for example, supporting the environmental cleanup policies that military services have instituted over the last twenty years or so. Some are actively engaged in shooting at other people who are shooting at them, and many are medics or otherwise involved in support services far from the front lines. Some join commando groups such as the Green Berets or the Navy SEALS, because they feel the kind of one-on-one combat these fighters are trained for is more in keeping with ancient warrior ideals.

Many Pagan men in the military keep their religious beliefs private, not wanting to put up with harassment from creedist colleagues or superior officers. Others are out-front about their beliefs, even having "Pagan," "Druid," or "Wiccan" put on their identification tags, and organizing group worship on military bases. Official American military policy recognizes that servicepeople can belong to and practice any religion they like, and some service chaplains' manuals include information on how military chaplains can help Wiccans, Asatruar, Druids, and other Pagans practice their faiths. Nonetheless, as of summer 2005, the many Pagans who have died in combat (or later as the result of injuries sustained in combat) are not allowed to have pentagrams, Thor hammers, or other Pagan symbols carved on their tombstones in veterans' cemeteries.[7]

Being in the military can be a controversial choice for many Pagans, not just because many Neopagans are political liberals, and thus opposed to how the military often gets used,[8] but because there can be significant differences between the activities of idealized warriors as defined at the beginning of this chapter and what many modern soldiers, sailors, and airmen wind up actually *doing* in wartime. Even conservative Pagans can sometimes find themselves gagging at what modern weapons do to distant "targets" that happen to be people. Then there's the fact that the vast majority of casualties in modern warfare are unarmed civilians, thus killing or maiming the very kind of people warriors are supposed to protect.

I have many agreements and disagreements with my colleague, Starhawk, but here is a place where I agree with her 100 percent. In a letter she sent to the Military Pagan Network before the Iraq quagmire began in 2003, she said:

> We may or may not hold differing political views, but I hold respect for you, for the choice you have made to risk your own lives in the service of values you believe in. That choice is a precious gift you give the rest of us. For politicians to take that sacrifice for granted and squander lives for anything less than absolute, last-resort necessity, is criminal. . . . If any of you are contemplating conscientious objection, or refusing orders to serve, I believe you have justification in Pagan thealogy. Should you be ordered to perform acts that go against international law, that target civilians, destroy civilian infrastructure, or contradict your own deepest sense of what is right, I believe you have moral, legal and religious justification to refuse.[9]

All of the acts she mentions near the end are things that a Pagan man in a modern military service could be ordered to do. All a Pagan warrior can do in such situations is ask himself, "What would Thor do? Is what my superior officers want me to do, right here, right now, *really* honorable?" Sometimes it won't be, and then he will have some very difficult decisions to make.

Regardless of our differing opinions of how our modern military services use or abuse our Pagan brothers (and sisters) at the behest of our elected representatives (and the corporations who own them), those who have stayed home should be prepared to greet our Pagan warriors when they come home from war. It should be possible to create and perform cleansing rituals to banish the fear and violence they have been living with and to peaceably reintegrate them within the tribe, just as our predecessors in so many Paleopagan cultures did.

A Hunting We Will Go

Put yourself back in time, whether you are on the plains of ancestral Africa, in the deep forests of Europe, or in the tall-grass prairies of North America. Your children are hungry and your mate looks at you expectantly. It's time once again to go out on the ancient quest for meat. If you are lucky, you will find an animal you can kill, so your children can survive.[10] If unlucky, you may find another animal who would rather kill and eat you instead (today, it might be a drunk idiot with a high-powered rifle).

No "Bambi and bunny rabbits" philosophy here—just the soft footsteps that you hope won't spook the game, the long hours of standing motionless only to burst into frantic action at what you hope is the right moment, the stabbing of your knife, arrow, or spear into the heart of your four-footed kin, and then watching the light die in its eyes. Next comes the long, messy, smelly job of hanging the body up, draining the blood, removing the guts, and hauling the carcass for miles back to your cave/hut/cabin, where you hope your mate will be able to turn it into something edible and wearable.

Century after century, all over the world, this was mostly men's work. Not because women can't do it—they can, especially if they have bows or guns available. But male muscle tissue and glands provide those bursts of short-term speed so often necessary, while female muscles and glands provide long-term stamina and the strength to go through the birthing process. No, this isn't politically correct in a world where some people want to pretend there are no significant differences between the genders (while others want to use real or alleged gender differences to justify discrimination).[11]

While some modern Pagans are vegetarians, most are omnivores. Unfortunately, like most modern people, even Pagan meat eaters are unlikely to know about the horrific lives and deaths of feedlot cattle and factory-farmed chicken, though many seem to know about the miserable and short lives of cattle raised to become milk-fed veal in fancy restaurants.

It's difficult and time consuming to investigate the origins of everything we purchase to eat, which is another reason why spiritual people of all faiths may choose to become vegetarians, while others will eat only free-range and organically fed animal products.

In my home, we attempt to keep our awareness somewhat sensitive by saying a prayer before our main meal:

> We give thanks to the Earth Mother, the source of all nourishment, and to the men and women who work hard to bring food from farm and field to our table, and to the plants and the animals who die, so that we may live.*

Some Pagan hunters and fishers take this awareness of the web of life and death one step further, by taking personal responsibility for the lives they consume. One long-time hunter and fisher named Ravenhawk, who has been a Pagan for over twenty years, told me:

> Hunting and fishing are not against the beliefs of a wizard. The Goddess is a huntress and the Lord of All Animals is the leader of the Great Hunt. It is a very enlightening experience to become a real hunter. It requires the understanding of the prey and it must follow that the respect of the prey is the result. The prey is not a minor form of life for your amusement. It is part of the deity, with whom you become connected by your willingness to pursue, cleanly kill, and

---

*My son Arthur has pointed out that insects and mice, etc. are killed by most kinds of agriculture, so avoiding meat does not, by itself, prevent animal deaths.

consume that prey. The life that is granted to your table is advanced [to its next incarnation] in its pursuit of the clear light. Your responsibility for the taking of that life is to respect it, be grateful for it, and waste not the earthly parts of that life. Organ meats are to be consumed. The hide must be used in a productive manner. The gut pile is to be left for the ravens and other creatures that live on the scraps of life. If you are unwilling to use all that you can from the kill, you are not to take the life of the prey.

Any consumption of meat is to be done with gratitude and a complete awareness of where that meat is from and what it took for it to be part of your diet. Haplessly consuming feedlot meat without regard as to its origin, is to permit the continued feedlot practices of a feedlot society. Know what you eat and how it was raised and treated, and who profits from it. Your purchase of meat is your stamp of approval for the practices that brought it to you.

There are some Pagan men who will only eat meat if they have killed the animals themselves, cleanly and quickly, and others who depend on hunting to feed their families every year (not all Pagans live in big cities, you know). I used to know one man who said that he hunted his deer with a knife! He would run them down on foot, a process that could take hours,[12] but that certainly creates more of a hunter-prey relationship than sitting in a camouflaged blind waiting for some critter to walk in front of your AK-47. Other Pagan men prefer bow hunting as a way to give their prey "a more even chance."

Among the few memories I have of my childhood is that of surf fishing on the southern California beach my family lived on one year. I hardly ever caught anything, but I spent many hours in what I now recognize as having been "nature meditation," becoming one with the water and the sun, rooting my feet in the sands of the beach, trying to telepathically encourage any fish who were ready for their next incarnation to take my hook.

I once met a commercial fisherman who told me that he was careful to invoke the God of the sea (he wouldn't tell me which one) before every trip out onto the ocean. Of course, you won't find many (if any) Western Pagans on factory fishing ships, for we know about the environmental devastation they cause and most Pagans are mild-to-serious environmentalists. But like hunting, fishing can be a spiritual activity, one that appeals to many Pagan men.

Exercises

Are you a warrior? If not, why not?

If you are one, what sort of warrior are you?

Assume that you have volunteered for or been drafted into your nation's military. How would you express your Pagan beliefs in a time of war? What if it's a war based on lies?

Do you eat meat or fish? Why or why not?

If you do eat meat or fish, do you know where it ultimately comes from, that is to say, whether it grew up in the wilds or on a farm, how it was killed, and so on? If you don't approve of its source, what can you do to change it?

Write your own prayer to say before meals, expressing your relationship with the food you eat.

CHAPTER 8

Pagan Men as Fathers

Several of the Pagan warriors who contacted me about this book emphasized the importance of protecting their children. After all, regardless of what religion one belongs to, fatherhood is something that many (if not most) men experience sooner or later. Pagan men are no different from Christian, Jewish, Islamic, or Buddhist men, in that they want their kids to be safe, happy, and healthy. What does make them different as fathers from most non-Pagan men is an ambivalence about raising their children in their religion, as well as a more relaxed attitude about enforcing the mainstream culture's gender roles.

Sharing the Faith—or Not

About a third of the men who filled out my questionnaire told me they were raising kids, either their own or a partner's, or that they intended to. One man told me he had no kids but that he was "a peripheral honorable male role model for other folks' kids." Of those who were raising kids, about one-third said they were definitely raising them to be Pagans, about one-quarter said they were definitely *not* raising them Pagan, about a quarter seemed to be exposing their kids to Paganism regularly (taking them to rituals or festivals), and about half said that they were going to let their kids choose to adopt or reject their parents' Paganism.[1]

I think these particular proportions match what I've observed over the years. Many Pagans are ambivalent about raising their own children Pagan, largely in response to their own childhoods. Many have told me, "My parents shoved their religion down my throat as a child and I won't ever do that to a child of mine!" This apparently dualist reaction (leaping from one extreme to its perceived opposite extreme) produces a spiritual effect known to polytheologians as "throwing the baby out with the bathwater." But then, if you've never had healthy religious education modeled for you, it can be hard to believe it is possible.

In contrast, several responders to the questionnaire told me that their children needed *some* sort of religious upbringing and that Paganism was the healthiest religion they could think of to teach them. A few turned their children's religious teaching over to their local Unitarian Universalist congregation's Religious Education (RE) program. The "UU Sunday school" will give them an unbiased introduction to significant cultural elements that even Pagan kids need to know about other religions, without forcing the children to pick one and only one spiritual path. The fact that Unitarian Universalists also now include modern Pagan religions as well as older Mesopagan ones such as Hinduism and Sikhism in their RE programs is another element that makes the programs so attractive to Pagan parents.

Other Pagan fathers are more adamant about raising their kids specifically Pagan. One young father said he was raising his kids Pagan because "Paganism is cool." Another said, "We believe it to be the best path towards enlightenment. However, at some point our son will decide if he wants to *stay* on that path."

Answers like that are particularly common among members of ethnic-specific Pagan paths, who place a very important stress on family relationships and on connecting to both ancestors and descendants. Children are taught that part of being members of their particular families is being part of the family's religion. But even here, the core Pagan belief in freedom of religion makes it likely that parents will be disappointed but not apoplectic if their children move on to other faiths.[2]

One Pagan father told me how his position on this question had evolved:

> With my daughter from my second marriage, my wife
> and I had agreed that we would not push religion on her.
> Unfortunately I was forced [by her] into agreeing not to tell
> [my daughter] about my beliefs. Never again! She was brow-
> beaten into Christianity through the school system and my
> parents. In my current marriage we are raising our son to
> follow our beliefs. However, we are careful to explain to him
> that there are people who believe differently than us. Those
> other beliefs are to be respected up to the point that they
> show disrespect for our beliefs and at that point to stand up
> for yourself.

Some Pagan paths present unusual parenting issues. Some Pagans, for example, belong to traditions/denominations where rituals are done in the nude. Parents in these groups, especially those that use overtly erotic symbolism or activities to raise psychic energies, will exclude their children from those rituals once they are past infancy. Instead, they create special circles that are child-safe and kid-friendly to bring the children into their faith. This was how we handled this situation in the raising of my own son, Arthur, for his mother and I were practicing Gardnerian Wiccans as well as Druids during his childhood.

My Experiences as a Pagan Father

Arthur was born at home, in our own bed with no drugs and a midwife standing by. Having my son emerge through the Gates into this world and my hands was probably one of the deepest religious experiences of my life. As I held him up, I looked into his eyes and saw a very old soul looking back at me. It was then that I really *got* the doctrine of Original Blessing (mentioned in chapter 1) because it was obvious that Arthur was holy to begin with.

Because of my illness, I wound up being the stay-at-home parent for a few years. Fortunately, I had been a kennel attendant for several months as a teenager, so I was able to handle the messy parts of his incoming and outgoing food without being totally grossed out. He was weaned by the time I could no longer work at a corporate job, so staying home and feeding him was relatively easy. I have to admit that the one part I miss most about his babyhood is holding and rocking him and singing lullabies, sometimes for hours. Eventually, I wrote some new ones with Pagan lyrics, concerned about the images I might be planting in his subconscious mind.

Arthur's Lullaby

Lullaby and good night,
With sigils bedight,
With pentagrams bedecked,
Is Baby's wee bed.

Lay thee down now and rest,
By the Goddess be blessed.
Lay thee down now and rest,
By the Goddess be blessed.

Lullaby and good night,
She has banished all fright,
She has banished all woe,
To your slumbers now go.

Lullaby and good night,
Guardian spirits take flight,
They hover overhead,
They surround your sweet bed.[3]

On a less serious note, there was this one:

PAPA'S GONNA CONJURE

Hush little darling, don't say a word
Papa's gonna conjure a phoenix bird.
And if that bird won't resurrect,
Papa's gonna conjure an ancient sect.
And if that sect it will not chant,
Papa's gonna conjure an Oliphant.
And if that Oliphant won't trumpet,
Papa's gonna conjure a pretty little strumpet.
And if that strumpet she won't dance,
Papa's gonna conjure a prince to prance.
And if that prince he should fall down,
You'll still be the best little baby in town!

To a great extent, becoming a Pagan father was a matter of learning how to nurture—which I managed mostly by reading lots of books on the subject, not passing along the abuse I had experienced during my own childhood (much of which was standard parenting back in the 1950s), and sharing my faith with him in a nondogmatic way.

Arthur knew he was Pagan long before he had words to speak (although he was talking pretty well, pretty early). Before his birth, he attended many rituals in the womb, listening to drums and chanting, and during his nursing period he kept coming to circles with his mother. So for a couple of years, we could put him to sleep at night just by putting Pagan drum and chant tapes such as *Drums of Starwood* and *Bonfire Dreams*,[4] on the boombox—and he slept well at festivals!

When it was time for preschool, we made it a point to tell the school's personnel that Arthur's parents were Witches and that we would appreciate them not putting up pictures of ugly green-skinned ones at Halloween. Not only did they agree, a few months later they asked us if there were any Pagan Yule songs, so we told them about Charlie Murphy's "Light Is Returning," which has become a popular song among Neopagans at Yule.[5] We got to watch Arthur and a dozen other five year olds singing it at the Winter Holiday Concert that the preschool put on!

It was a couple years afterward that Arthur asked for a pentacle he could wear and my friend, Joy, spun him a cord for it out of alpaca hair and her dog Sasha's fur (Arthur had met Sasha and become very fond of him). Arthur proudly wore his pentacle on that cord for many years, until the cord finally broke and he transferred the pentacle to a silver chain like his father's. During these years of grade school, while other Pagan kids were hiding their religion, Arthur's attitude was, "Yes, I'm a Pagan—you gotta problem with that?" Granted, we lived in the suburbs of the New York City region, which is fairly liberal about religious issues, but then, that's one reason why, even after my relationship with Deborah fell apart, we all still live here!

Also during those years, Arthur was sitting in on classes given by his mother, me, and other Pagan teachers about Tarot, Wicca, Druidism, ritual design and performance, Pagan history, and more. At the age of fifteen, he now knows more about Paganism and magic than many who are twice his age.

Yes, we exposed him to other religions. He has attended a number of non-Wiccan and non-Druidic religious rites at Pagan festivals. Deborah's mom is Jewish, so we all attended Passover[6] and Hannukah rituals at Grandma's, and he attended a friend's bat mitzvah. Deb's father is Christian, so Arthur has been to Grandpa's for Christmas a few times, albeit with only secular rituals involved. From time to time, I've had to explain mainstream Christian stories and ritual customs to him, and he enjoys the services at the UU congregation to which Phaedra and I belong. So no, he hasn't exactly been brainwashed into his Paganism, or at least no more than anyone else being raised in his family's faith.

There are some dangers to being a Pagan father, however, that are not immediately apparent. A few years ago at the Starwood Festival, Arthur made the mistake of walking barefoot across the edge of the previous night's fire circle, not realizing that the white ashes were still hot. Ouch! He suffered first- (and a few second-) degree burns on both feet. This being a very well-run festival, he was seen within ten minutes by a doctor, two nurses, and a para-medic* in the first aid booth—not to mention a dozen people waving crystals around and sending him healing energy. For the rest of the festival, including the children's costume parade, we pushed him around in a wheelbarrow and took him back for daily check-ups.

The day after the festival ended, we took him to see his regular doctor at home. He examined Arthur's feet and asked us what had happened and when. We told him and he looked skeptical, "These feet have had at least a week or ten days' worth of heal-ing," he insisted. Then after we left, he called the Child Protective Services (CPS), for he was convinced there was some sort of strange abuse going on. The investigation was quick and profes-sional. We gave the CPS people the phone numbers of the festival organizers, the festival site owner, and the attending physician, as well as a photo of Arthur in his wheelbarrow and a copy of Margot Adler's *Drawing Down the Moon*. A few weeks later I met one of the investigators in a local store parking lot and he said, "I just wanted you to know that everything checked out and we'll be giving you a positive report. Oh, and thanks for the book—we'll be using it in the future!" Shortly afterwards we re-ceived official notice that we'd been cleared of suspicion.

So this particular adventure ended well, but it could have turned out ugly if we hadn't been prepared to deal with potentially prej-udiced investigators. Pagan parents are always at risk of having their children snatched by legal authorities or biased judges, so

---

*All of whom were Pagans attending the event.

it's important to always make sure your parental t's are crossed and i's are dotted.

On a less-stressful, but also annoying manner, there's the issue brought up by one man to me: "I'm a single father. I often receive unsolicited advice from women on parenting matters because they are unable to understand there's a difference between male and female parenting styles." I experienced this myself when taking Baby Art out in public; this is probably an experience common to most single or stay-at-home dads.[*] He may also not be understanding that sharing parenting tips is a common female-bonding activity and that perhaps he's being complimented by being accepted into the club.

In general, however, my main job as a Pagan father is to avoid messing up my child's innate goodness too much, to give him the practical, philosophical, and spiritual tools he will need to have a happy and healthy life, and to otherwise stay out of his way. Yes, I have to nag him to do his homework and chores, but that is a human universal among most fathers of teenagers. Lately, we've been discussing relationships, during which we've thrashed out some of the principles I'll discuss in chapter 11. He is becoming a young gentleman, which he manages to pull off with style rather than smarminess, and the girls seem to like him.

It should be obvious that I am very proud of my son and reasonably happy with the job I've done of fathering him so far. Your own children, or those you wind up mentoring, will present their own joys and challenges, but there is little that will make you feel more manly than the process of being a Pagan father.

Arthur's Experiences as a Pagan Son

Arthur has had to deal with not just the experience of growing up Pagan in a world that is all too often prejudiced against us but

---

[*]And, yes, it's true: babies really are a "babe magnet." ☺

also with having parents who are both microcelebrities—one more notorious than the other—in his religious community. I asked him to write a few comments about how being raised Pagan has affected him:

> So, I'm sitting here, listening to my brand-new mp3 player [a gift from Grandma], trying to fill space until I think of something to write. My dad just sprung this on me today, and said it needed to be done today, too. He'll probably delete this paragraph, but I think it would be more fun if he didn't. And if I sound like a cocky teenage boy in my tone, then it's not just my imagination.
>
> Being raised Pagan has mostly desensitized me to nudity. I have been going to clothing-optional events all my life. I have mastered the art of maintaining eye contact.
>
> Being raised Pagan will probably make it easier to memorize Wiccan ritual scripts. I have been going to ritual my whole life. In one that I went to last night, the high priest forgot a few lines, it being his first time "HPing," as we call it. I knew most of the lines that he forgot.
>
> Being raised Pagan has influenced my views on manliness. No, that's not just shameless self-referentialism. I mean it. I have learned that the mainstream Western pigeonholes that are called definitions of manliness came out of the back end of a male bovine. I know a dancer who is a ballerino. (Read that word again. Notice what letter it ends with.) Let me tell you, he's definitely manly. He's one of three examples I use when talking about my views on manliness. One of the manliest men I know was married to another man for nine years. I also know a man, let's call him "Dave," who is quiet, soft-spoken, and not at all in-your-face machismo. But Dave is a carpenter, a Mr. Fix-it, and really handy with tools. Dave is definitely manly.
>
> I just paused my writing to listen to a sweet electric guitar solo. It is important to remember that being a Pagan man includes not just being a Pagan man, but being a man. And being Pagan.

Arthur banged that out in about fifteen minutes, so apparently the writer genes on both sides of his ancestry have successfully come through.

Exercises

How do you think your father's religious beliefs (or lack of them) affected your childhood?

How would you raise your own child or children, as far as sharing your beliefs are concerned? Why?

What's the single-most important thing you can do as a father? As a Pagan father?

CHAPTER 9

Pagan Men as Brothers

When we meet we do what men have always done. Share maps of places we have traveled and the stories associated with them. Speak of our present problems and the plans for the future. As a group that is truly concerned for each other, we discuss how we can help each other when there is a need, and to share the wealth when fortune smiles upon us. We dine together, drink together, and laugh a great deal. Our rituals are simple and private. When we depart we are confident that even in our solitary paths, we do not walk alone. This is the key, that for all of the rest of it, we express our faith in each other by being the best of friends we can be.

—Kirk McLaren
Tuatha de Kelti

Brotherhood among Pagan men is as essential as Pagan women have found sisterhood to be to them. None of us is an island, and we can all benefit from each other's experience. It's in coming to know each other that we find ourselves. Speaking from my own personal experience, I lost my father when I was only ten years old, and was raised mostly by women. Because of this, I keenly felt the lack of masculine energy within my own life. Becoming

part of the Order, suddenly having mentors, brothers, "male role
models" as it were—this meant the world to me, and has helped
me to grow in ways that I never could have by myself. It's that
need for a sacred brotherhood that brought us all together, and
that we believe is missing in modern Paganism.

—Chris Blackfox,
Knights of Herne

Only a handful of the men I talked to for this book or who answered my questionnaire said that they belonged to a Pagan
men's group, while the vast majority did not. Of that majority,
about half indicated that there wasn't one locally, implying or
sometimes directly stating that they would join one if given the
opportunity. The other half made comments disparaging the manhood of those who join such groups, apparently under the (false)
assumption that such groups are similar to the "men's consciousness groups" that grew out of the feminist movement in the 1980s
and that were widely seen (also falsely) as composed of wimpy
guys apologizing for having Y chromosomes. So I will hazard a
guess that there are probably "only" 10,000 or 20,000 Pagan men
wanting to have specifically Pagan men's groups in their areas.[*]

In this chapter I would like to share what I know about three
men's groups: the Hermes Council (of which I am a member), the
Tuatha de Kelti, and the Royal Order of the Knights of Herne
(mentioned in chapter 7). We'll end with a few words about
Pagan Masons!

The Hermes Council

The elderly folks in the lobby of the nursing home looked up in
curiosity from their wheelchairs as a group of men walked in carrying drums. Some of the men were in their fifties, one (my son,
Arthur) was only fourteen. Their hair length ran from crew cut to

[*]Organizers, that's a hint!

aging hippie. We smiled as we signed in at the front desk, then Bill Seligman (the group's leader) led us through the halls to our destination.

As we walked into his room, the resident (we'll call him "Gene") looked surprised, then very happy. An active sixty-five year old, Gene had been riding his motorcycle a few weeks earlier when a clueless driver had hit him with her car, fracturing one of his vertebras and breaking both legs. The weeks of recovery had been both painful and boring.

"You couldn't make it to the Hermes Council meeting, so we brought it to you!" explained Bill. One of the men pulled a drum out of a bag and handed it to Gene, who slowly but happily sat up to take it; then another started a slow drum beat that the others joined. Soon, a smiling Gene was playing his drum along with the rest of us.

After several minutes of drumming, everyone stopped and noticed a nurse at the door. "We're not bothering anyone, are we?" asked one of the men.

"Oh no," replied the nurse, "everyone's enjoying it. Please continue!"

"We're his music therapy group," I said with a grin. Then everyone started drumming again until Gene's elderly roommate rolled into the room. "Keep going," he said, "I like it."

So we stayed for an hour or so, alternating drumming with periods of quiet conversation about how Gene was doing and a creative project one of us was working on. Finally, it was time to say good-bye and we all left a happy Gene and other smiling residents behind, one of whom said, "You boys come back soon!"*

We took the meeting to a member's nearby home, to continue drumming and sharing the events of our lives as Pagan men.

The Hermes Council was started in the mid-1990s as a counterpart to a women's group within our extended family of Wiccans

---

*The management, however, was not as amused.

living in the northern and western suburbs of New York City. Oddly enough, the women's group faded away within a few months, while our men's group kept going. Perhaps this might have been because Wiccan traditions give a prominent role to women as women, while Wiccan men often find themselves wondering just what their special role as men, if any, is.[*]

The men of the Hermes Council get together regularly for drum circles, BBQs, and other social occasions. At most of these, a highly decorated caduceus (a staff of Hermes, often seen in medical graphics) is passed as a talking stick. Talking sticks are a Native American custom adopted by many Neopagan and counterculture groups to allow each participant in a group to have his uninterrupted say on a topic. While one of the men is holding the caduceus, he is free to talk at length about his life, relationship(s), work issues, creative projects, worries, and concerns. Only after he puts the caduceus down are the others free to add comments, ask questions, or make suggestions. Or as we put it in the Hermes Council, "The one with the talking stick has the privilege of speaking. The rest have the privilege of listening."

Through the years, the members of the Hermes Council have helped each other move house, do home repairs, job hunt, fix cars, and do other practical tasks, as well as perform rituals together, give counsel and advice, and just be there for each other when needed. A year before the hospital visit, the members had organized a coming of age ceremony for my son, Arthur.

Like a bar mitzvah or a Catholic confirmation ceremony, this ritual brought Arthur into the local Pagan community and the Hermes Council as a young man, with the responsibilities and rights of such. It involved a symbolic journey at twilight across the farmland owned by one of the members, during which he was confronted with decisions to be made and childish habits to be set aside (e.g., he was required to give up most of his remaining

*See the discussion in chapter 5.

THE HERMES COUNCIL/BILL SELIGMAN

The Hermes Council's Talking Stick

stuffed animals). Each man he met in the ritual gave him a symbolic object or ceremonial tool; I gave him my oldest ritual knife. At the end of the ritual, we returned to our friend's house, where he was greeted by the women and girls of our tribe as the newest man in the community, teased somewhat, given other presents, and celebrated in a rowdy party in his honor.

Most of the six to eight men in the Hermes Council (the number varies) are straight, a couple are gay, and nobody really cares very much about that particular issue. In all the meetings I've attended over the years, while the topic of their relationships with women may come up, and annoyances with particular women may be mentioned, I have never heard anything that even vaguely resembled sexist complaints or slurs from these Pagan men—a fact that might surprise those Pagan women who are worried about their men joining male-only groups. The women in our extended Wiccan family are all pretty strong, so I suspect that those of us men who might have been uncomfortable with that fact of life didn't stick around very long. The Hermes Council has always existed because of its positive aspects (friendship, mutual emotional support, mutual practical aid, etc.) rather than because of any possible negative ones (such as complaining about women), and we expect it to continue for many years.

One of the firm rules of the Hermes Council, as for most other men's groups, is that conversations within the group stay there. As Kirk McLaren (whom we met in chapter 6 and will meet again in the next section) puts it,

> When you speak of a thing you are giving it the ability of manifesting. If you have invested yourself into a project, do not speak of it—simply do it and be done with it. All things shared within the circle of men (even if only two of you are present) are kept within this circle, giving the man the freedom of speaking his mind. Actually, this is an important aspect that should be respected amongst all close friends; however, by making this "official" it then adds a sense of boundary to the relationship. This boundary defines the sacred space required in a magical working. Within that boundary we can incubate the given problem into a workable solution, knowing full well the safety and security of a solid relationship.

For men to feel free to share their emotions with each other, they have to feel secure that the women and girls in their lives, as well as the non-Pagan men they know, will not be hearing tales of what they've said. In a men's group, we assume that anything one of us wanted to say to an outsider has already been said or soon (perhaps after input from our brothers) will be. As magicians, occultists, anthropologists, and members of other minority belief systems know, *words have power,*[1] both magically and psychologically, to alter reality both creatively and destructively.

If one is busy thinking his way through a problem by discussing it with his brothers, he probably doesn't want the people involved in the problem to hear his half-baked words before he knows what fully baked ones he wants to say to them. The members of a men's magical group, like those of any other, may have special names and titles they use only within the group, and those names and titles could conceivably be used by outsiders to cast spells of a disruptive nature into the group. More importantly, shared confidences can create a strong group consciousness that becomes the spirit of the group.

The Tuatha de Kelti

Kirk McLaren has had a Pagan men's group for several years, as one of several overlapping groups within his Pagan family, the Tuatha de Kelti (Celtic Tribe).[2] There is also a women's group, the drummers and dancers coordinate, the artists and crafters work with each other, and the members of a warrior group pair off to spar. This is in keeping with healthy religious communities of any size, that they are composed of multiple smaller groups (prayer groups, choirs, fund-raising committees, ushers, etc.).

In the beginning, Kirk says, the men found it easier to talk to each other about things "without worrying about the critical commentary from the women folk." They would meet once a week at one unmarried man's apartment to watch a movie and discuss it. Because the larger tribe is spread out over a wide geographical territory, there were only a few men who would attend each meeting, but they found it satisfying to be able to sit for a while in the company of fellow men and be able to speak without being corrected, to watch a movie that their women might not appreciate, and to have a good laugh with each other.

Kirk believes that this is the first building block that makes a successful men's group: "Friendship, a sense of trust that is built with positive experience and a hearty investment of time."

Kirk decided to examine what America's history has to draw from in terms of men's groups and found that successful men's organizations (such as the Masons, Odd Fellows, Elks, etc.) have put their time and energy into community outreach and good works. Aside from the positive investment into one's local community, the group itself gains experience in knowing each other better. His group began to work with others to help those in need, whether they were individuals, families, or even organizations. Their activities have included clearing or gardening land, building barns, helping others to move house, and facilitating gatherings and drum circles. Each project helped them to learn each other's strengths, weaknesses, and capacity for growth both as individuals and as a group.

Once they became conscious that they were doing a "men's thing," the males of the Tuatha de Kelti began to do it "on purpose" and created tasks that would benefit the tribe as a whole. Watching how many of the kinds of organizations that were "men's mysteries" came from actual occupations (such as the Masons or the International Order of Woodsmen), it occurred to Kirk that the group should start making things for their tribe. Since they could all work with various media like wood, metal, and so on, they chose collective works to add to the tribe's camping sites or to their altar, gifts for their women and children, and so on.

As for the "mystery" part of their activities, the group established the same rule that the Hermes Council has, not to discuss what goes on within the men's group outside of it. This holds for both their ritual activities and their private conversations.

Like the members of the Hermes Council, the men of the Tuatha de Kelti have discovered that their meetings are most harmonious and productive when they are run democratically. Each man has his say and then relies on the judgment of his peers. Those who choose to participate in a given project do their best and those who choose to invest themselves elsewhere do so. For the most part, there is little dissent, Kirk tells me. Those not interested in active participation in the group's chosen tasks are generally not invited back; this has become a weeding-out process that keeps the numbers low, which is fine with them as their group dynamics seem to work best in small numbers.

The Royal Order of the Knights of Herne

The Knights of Herne[3] (mentioned in chapter 7) are active in the Triad region (Greensboro, Winston-Salem, and High Point) of North Carolina. They were founded in late 2000 by Gregg B., Joshua B., and others, inspired by an article in *Green Egg* magazine, "Plastic Swords and Pentacles: Chivalry and the Rearing of Pagan Boys," by Sara Reeder.[4]

Chris Blackfox joined the order in December 2000 and became its first knight-probationer (squire). He was kind enough to discuss the order's history and purposes with me. Unlike the Hermes Council or the Tuatha de Kelti, the Knights of Herne were patterned after various orders of chivalry, such as the Knights Templar, and service groups, such as the Knights of Columbus. While mostly focused on the exploration of men's spirituality through Neopagan rituals, they also spend a great deal of time and energy in service to the community.

Why did they find it necessary to found a Pagan men's group? Chris says, "In a nutshell, it's because there's been no such thing up until now. It's an almost entirely unfilled niche."

The founders of the group believed that male deities and men in general are often eclipsed in modern Paganism by goddesses and women and that a Pagan matriarchy was not necessarily an improvement over a Christian patriarchy. So they committed themselves to learning all they could about "men's mysteries," however they might be defined, and creating new, positive roles for Pagan men as men. "We formed the order," Chris says, "because we sought in some way to change that, to restore a necessary balance. We feel that the God, or the gods, and men deserve equal recognition with the goddess(es) and women."

The order is named for Herne the Hunter, a Saxon deity whose name is probably derived from a Indo-European root meaning "horn." To the knights, he represents "the quintessence of manhood, all that we strive to be and to achieve as men." Like other Horned gods, Herne is both the Hunter and the Prey, a Lord of Death and Rebirth, and a sacrificial God, who gives of himself so that others may live.

The order's core philosophy is what it refers to as the Four Pillars of Knighthood: spirituality, service, chivalry, and brotherhood. All of its activities serve to further at least one of these ideas, and usually all of them.

The order focuses on helping its members to research and develop their own spiritual paths, whether as Wiccans, Druids, Asatruar, or members of other Pagan traditions, aiming to make them able to eventually teach these paths to others. This process is begun when a new member first enters the order. One begins as a knight-probationer (squire), and remains so for at least a year and a day before being knighted. During this time, the squire's sponsoring knight mentors him, helping him to research and develop his path as well as teaching him about what it means to be a knight in today's world. The squire must also complete a quest during this time—an act or series of acts of service that betters the squire, the order, and the community. On his becoming a squire and later a knight, the new member takes an oath to uphold the order's Code of Chivalry (discussed in chapter 7), which is based on several historical versions found online, including the Nine Virtues of Asatru.

Like many other spiritual men, the Knights of Herne discovered that an important part of spiritual growth can be found in service to others. The importance of sacrifice for the good of others became an integral part of its spiritual path, as it has in so many other Pagan and non-Pagan groups. Working from the origins of the word "knight" in an Anglo-Saxon term for "servant," its members decided to define themselves as servants of their community, both secular and religious. As Chris says, "We choose to call ourselves 'knights' because we identify strongly with the archetype or idea of knighthood, of a warrior who lives by a code of honor and who stands up for what he believes is right."

In the past, the Knights of Herne has provided security for the Southern Cherokee Powwow and a Bikes, Blues, and Tattoos bike rally, both to benefit the Webbers Falls Native American Reservation, walked in numerous charity walks, done a Vehicle Blessing and Carwash as a fund-raising event for the local chapter of the Covenant of Unitarian Universalist Pagans (CUUPS),[5] Triad CUUPS in Greensboro, North Carolina,[6] and assisted in local Pagan Pride Days and Pagan Leadership Conferences. It has also provided a ritual battle between the Oak King and the Holly King for that CUUPS group's midsummer ritual in 2003 and is a regular presence at the area's Pagans' Night Out events.

Besides these public activities, the members have also provided assistance to Pagan families in need, for everything from extra groceries to house moving. Their private rituals are just that—private—but they don't involve activities that would prove shocking to the average member of the Knights of Pythias or the Knights of Columbus (except for the polytheology involved).

As for the future, Chris tells me:

When we dream of the future, we see Pagan men coming together in brotherhoods across the world, honoring both the many gods of the Old Religions and their own sacred masculinity. We see Pagan women doing the same with their goddesses, in their own groups, and the two genders coming together to honor the gods and goddesses together.

Chivalry is not dead! As one twenty-something man told me, the greatest freedom he has gained from being a Pagan is, "The ability to be more chivalrous, and a belief that might *for* right is what I am able to be part of." In a world in which physical violence is all too often used for evil purposes, may there be many more like this young man.

Pagan Masons

It may come as a shock to some to find out that the oldest known fraternal men's organization, the Ancient Free and Accepted Masons, has Pagan members. Dating back historically to 1717 in England[7] and symbolically (within its own legends) to ancient Egypt, the Masons have been controversial from the beginning, due in large part to their refusal to discriminate against would-be members on the grounds of religion and the roles that many of their local meeting houses (called lodges or temples) played in the birth of revolutionary movements in Europe and the Americas.[8]

While most English and American Masons are required to profess a belief in "a Supreme Being" (however vaguely defined),[9] from the beginning there was a policy against discussing religious matters in the lodge. Christians, Moslems, and Jews could all join, and later Buddhists and Hindus were welcomed (at least in big-city lodges). There is still some slight discrimination in favor of a generic Judeo-Christianity, in that the Bible is the sacred text most often used in rituals, but copies of the Koran and nonmonotheistic scriptures have been known to appear in some American lodges for particular men's initiations.[10]

Early critics of Masonry sometimes called it "pagan," because it did not support the particular religious point of view held by the critics and/or because many well-known Masons such as George Washington and Thomas Jefferson were deists (extremely liberal monotheists), and therefore by either argument Freemasonry was opposed to "real" (conservative) religion, and thus "pagan."

This is our old fiend dualism showing up again, in the equation of religious tolerance with hostility toward the true faith (as defined by the critic).

These definitions of Masonry as "pagan," however, are rooted in the old, hostile definitions of paganism as meaning "false" religion, irreligious, immoral, and so on. Still, an argument using the definitions of modern Paganism can be made that Freemasonry is in fact a Mesopagan philosophy. Much of its inner teachings, as have been published over the centuries, owe as much to the Paleopagan Greek mathematical mysticism of Pythagoras and to ancient Egyptian concepts of sun worship as they do to any monotheistic ideas, however liberal. This is why I often think of them as being Mesopagan, though you will find few Masons who have ever even heard of the term.

While I'm not a Mason myself, I have met at least a score of Pagan men who are, including Wiccans, Druids, Celtic Reconstructionists, Asatruar, Native American religionists, Voodooists, ceremonial magicians, and others. Many told me that they had been surprised to find out that a belief in monotheism is not an absolute membership requirement in most North American grand lodges (state or provincial jurisdictions) of Freemasonry (although it sometimes is a de facto requirement in more rural, local lodges). In city lodges, the Masons have been accepting Hindus and Buddhists as members for a century. When I asked my local Masonic lodge secretary about the issue, he asked, "Do you believe in God?" When I said, "I believe in lots of gods," he replied, "That works!"

As some readers may know, the general organizational structure for Masonic organizations includes a series of degrees of initiation. As I understand it, most Masons go through the first three, then later there may be a thirty-second-degree initiation and an honorary thirty-third degree. The degrees from fourth to thirty-first, however, tend to be used for initiation into various subgroups within Masonry, some of which are special interest groups (SIGs) for specific religions, magical exploration, artistic groups and so on. One of those in-between degree numbers I've been told is now being used for a Wiccan SIG in one state, and an Asatru one may not be far behind.

Other Fraternal Organizations

The Independent Order of Odd Fellows recently started to admit women due to a possible lawsuit in Canada, but the overwhelming majority of members are still male. Alan Salmi, a Pagan Masonic friend of mine told me, "They require a belief in a higher power/supreme being but they aren't that picky" about the precise details of members' beliefs, and they have been making major efforts to bring in new, younger members, before their current leadership dies of old age.

The Knights of Pythias are based on a Greek myth of brotherhood between two members of the Pythagorean brotherhood (a mystical Paleopagan Greek movement). It has some very Pagan mythological origins, although it was formed shortly after the first American Civil War.

The Patrons of Husbandry, also known as the Grange, could potentially be a very Pagan-friendly group for Pagan men (especially those of a conservative political persuasion) to consider joining. Three of the members of each Grange hall have to be female, since they play the roles of the Three Graces (of Paleopagan Greek myth) in the initiation rites. The first four degrees of its rank system are focused around the symbolism of the four seasons, and its final big degrees done at its national convention are a reenactment of the Paleopagan Greek rites of Demeter, the goddess of the Earth. Alan tells me, "They own a building in Washington, D.C., and have a requirement that you have to be interested in agriculture—as one of them put it: if you eat, you are interested in agriculture!" They are a largely rural organization, but could easily have members in urban areas, especially with Pagan families wanting a group with a friendly infrastructure. It might also be easier for Pagan men to "fit into" city halls, since the influence of conservative monotheists would be less than in the rural ones.

Granted, these fraternal groups may think of their Pagan influences as "just symbolic," but it would be hard for them to turn away prospective new members just because we happen to think those ancient deities are real!

Sadly, these groups, the Masons and other fraternal organizations, seem to be falling on hard times. Many men who joined them for the purpose of gaining business contacts are using other means of networking. The rampant selfishness of American culture since the 1980s has led to a loss of membership in most charitable organizations, including fraternal ones. Now, the average member of a fraternal lodge is likely to be in his sixties or seventies, with far fewer younger men getting involved than in previous generations.

Perhaps a flood of Pagan men into what could be called Mesopagan men's organizations could revitalize them. Certainly, the centuries-old commitment of the fraternal movements to masculine fellowship, spiritual exploration, and community service is a shining star that many new Pagan men's groups could well use to guide them into their future.[11]

Exercises

If you were to join or start a Pagan men's group, what sort would it be?

When was the last time you spent several hours together with other Pagan men? Did the womenfolk complain? If so, how did you handle it?

Have you ever thought about becoming a Mason or joining some other fraternal society? What stopped you then and is it still stopping you now?

CHAPTER 10

Pagan Men as "Queers"

I title this chapter with a certain amount of trepidation for, while there are plenty of Pagan men who proudly claim the term "queer," there are plenty of others who find it offensive. "Queer" is a reclaimed word, that, the *American Heritage Dictionary* warns us, "is a word that was formerly used solely as a slur but that has been semantically overturned by members of the maligned group, who use it as a term of defiant pride." In recent years, gay men, lesbians, bisexuals, transsexuals, hermaphrodites, and others whom we shall meet in this chapter have taken to using "queer" as an appropriately vague term to cover them all.

In my questionnaire, I asked the respondents "On a scale of 0-to-10, where 0 is totally Het and 10 is totally Gay, how do you usually think of yourself?" While I expected the vast majority to say that they were on the heterosexual side of the scale, and was not disappointed, what I found fascinating was that very few respondents listed themselves as either a 0 or a 10—indeed the majority of those who answered this question were at least willing to consider that they weren't 100 percent gay *or* straight. This might not be news to most gay men, but it is a remarkable sign of how comfortable Pagan men can be with a little sexual ambiguity. These responses are also "queer" in the old-fashioned sense of being unusual, at least in Western society.

A gay, bisexual, or transgendered man growing up in one of the mainstream religions is likely to feel unwanted by the Divine and condemned by his fellow religionists. Wicca, Druidism, Asatru, and other modern Pagan faiths, like their Paleopagan predecessors, clearly have space (some more than others) for members of sexual minorities looking for a religious home. In this chapter, we will look at some of the issues involved and see why minority-sexual Pagan men can feel so comfortable in polytheistic religions.

Sexual Minorities in Mainstream Religions

All but the most liberal of spiritual authorities in Judaism, Christianity, and Islam are agreed that maleness and femaleness are dualistic absolutes, that only heterosexual behavior (usually within specific limits) is permissible, and that the behavior of sexual minorities is not just sinful but demonically evil. Much of this goes back to the prohibitions listed in Leviticus, many of which were designed to discourage Jews from engaging in behavior associated (rightly or wrongly) with the Paleopagan religions of the ancient Near East. From the Babylonian *Epic of Gilgamesh*'s homoerotic relationship between Gilgamesh and Enkidu, to the Egyptian homosexual relationship between Set and Osirus, to the homosexual and transgendered priests of Astarte (herself sometimes depicted as a hermaphrodite), Ishtar, and Cybele, Middle Eastern Paleopaganism recognized the existence of gay and bisexual relationships as part of the divine and mortal universes. Not surprisingly, worship of homosexual or bisexual deities could sometimes involve homosexual or bisexual actions (from cross-dressing to same-sex intercourse), and since some of those actions could be pleasurable, the authors of Leviticus were anxious to discourage their people from participating in rites that might "seduce" them from Jehovah's path and/or cut down on the growth of a specifically Jewish population (by encouraging nonreproductive behaviors).

Conservative Christians and Muslims usually incorporate selected Old Testament laws into their beliefs and practices, especially those related to sexuality, despite those laws having been supposedly superseded by the later teachings of Jesus and Muhammad. The influence of dualism, discussed earlier in this book, set up a war between "the spirit and the flesh," leading to all forms of sexuality other than married heterosexuality being condemned and, for many years, punishable by death for one or all participants involved. In Europe, these attitudes merged with the warrior caste's condemnation of passive homosexuality as "unmanly."

Most varieties of Buddhism are not as condemnatory of homosexuality as conservative Judaism, Christianity and Islam are, but consider it (as well as other kinds of minority sexuality) a form of lust that is likely to interfere with attaining enlightenment. Monks, nuns, and priests are supposed to avoid both homo- and heterosexual activities. The Dalai Lama, the spiritual leader of Tibet's Buddhists and widely revered by members of many other Buddhist communities, has spoken in favor of civil rights for homosexuals.

Some Hindu teachers believe that homosexual couples can gain the same spiritual benefits of marriage that heterosexual ones can, while others condemn homosexuality as a form of sinful lust equivalent to premarital intercourse or adultery, both of which are seen (as in Buddhism) as threats to marriage. In India, however, you can still find members of the Hijras caste, who are transgendered or transsexual men, hermaphrodites, or intersexed people with ambiguous genitalia. They religiously identify themselves as a "third sex," and a place has been made for them in India's culture and law.

Paleopagan Polymorphous Perversity

Also present in Hinduism are deities who don't seem to be quite as puritanical as some modern Hindu teachers would have us believe. Ishvara is a creator god/dess, usually depicted as both male and female, and probably is popular with the Hijras. Ganesh, the elephant-headed god of breaking through obstacles, is also androgenous, with heavy breasts and a phallic trunk, and is sometimes worshiped with homoerotic rites. Krishna, the blue-skinned god of love, seduces both men and women to worship him.

Besides India and the Middle Eastern cultures previously mentioned, Paleopagan religions all over the world have been known to include homosexual, bisexual, or even zoosexual deities. Ancient China worshiped a homosexual rabbit-god named Wu Tien Bao, and Chinese mythology and folklore are filled with tales of deities, humans, animals, and nature spirits engaging in both gay and straight sex with one another.

In the Americas, the Mayans had a dwarf god named Chin, who was said to have introduced homosexual relationships to the Mayan noblemen, who took lower-class youths to be their lovers and spouses. Xochipili was an Aztec god who was the patron of homosexuality, as well as of flowers, dance, art, music, and shamanic trance. Among many Native American tribes, homosexual or bisexual people were considered natural shamans or medicine people and given special training and often special treatment as respected members of their societies.

Among the Norse and Germanic peoples, passive/receptive homosexuality was looked down on by the warriors, while active partners of such men were given free rein. It was "unmanly" to be passive and receptive,[1] which is why the seidh system of shamanic divination was considered an unfit occupation for males (despite the story about Odin being taught seidh by Freyja[2]). Diana L. Paxson, a leader in the Norse Neopagan community, has these important notes to make in the essay "Sex, Status, and Seidh: Homosexuality and Germanic Religion":

Late Norse homophobia seems to be inextricably connected to late Norse misogyny. Femaleness and Magic were both severely repressed and thrust into the dark, chthonic realm of the unconscious, which therefore became a place of horror and fear. This represents a major shift from the situation in most Pagan cultures, which recognized and valued chthonic [underworld] and liminal [borderline] power, and saw in it a necessary balancing aspect of spirituality. Perhaps the degree to which horror of "woman's magic" is expressed in the Saga period provides a measure of the prestige in which women's spiritual power was held in earlier times. . . .

Clearly in a traditional culture the criminality of sexual behavior depends less on the gender of the partners than on their relative social status—their freedom to refuse. Whether any act (of sex or magic) is considered shameful depends on the status of those with whom it is typically associated in that society. If women are defined by a culture as submissive, and if one considers women inferior, then it becomes shameful for a person of socially superior status (a male) to submit sexually.[3]

The situation in Paleopagan Greece (at least for a few centuries) was quite different, although here, too, we see a power-status aspect involved in social attitudes. Ancient Greek society seems to have been completely at ease with homosexuality—at least when it didn't cross class lines in the "wrong" direction. It was perfectly okay for an upper- or middle-class Greek man to have active gay sex with a passive Greek youth of the same or a lower class, a situation that is clear from surviving Greek documents and art. In fact, far from destroying its civilization (as modern homophobes claim always happens when a society tolerates homosexuality), the time period during which public homosexuality was common turned out to be what later generations of historians, philosophers, and others would call Greece's Golden Age.

Many (if not most) of their philosophers were gay or bisexual men, as were scientists, mathematicians, artists, historians, political leaders ("inventors of democracy"), priests, and warriors. The Spartan army encouraged male lovers to train and fight together, "for no man would abandon his love on the field of battle!" Athenian men were quoted as preferring, "A wife for children, a hetaera[4] for conversation, and a youth for pleasure." Of course, this was a time period when fourteen year olds were considered old enough to be married, so a philosopher in his thirties having a teenaged lover (of either gender) wasn't particularly shocking.

They were following the examples of the Greek gods in their behavior: Zeus turned into an eagle to snatch up a handsome youth named Ganymede to become his cupbearer (and bed partner). Hera's annoyance at this seems to have been no worse than her ire at his heterosexual exploits. Apollo had sexual relationships with men, including the youth Hyacinth. Artemis was depicted in intimate embraces with her nymphs, and Pan was shown having sex with men, women, satyrs, nymphs, goats, sheep, and anything else that didn't run fast enough to get away!

Pan wasn't the only one—there is a great deal of zoosexual activity going on in ancient Greek myth. Zeus turned into a swan to seduce Leda and into a bull to seduce Europa (I suppose we could include the eagle getting Ganymede story here, too). A mortal queen named Pasiphae mated with a white bull, giving birth to the Minotaur. Many of the half-human/half-animal creatures of Greek legend, such as the *silenoi* (two-legged horse-men), the *centaurs* (four-legged horse-men), and the *satyrs* (two-legged goat-men), are implied to have had both animal and human ancestry (impossible as that is from a genetic perspective). Other pantheons included animal lovers, too. In Sumeria, Baal is said to have sired a bull god by impregnating a cow. In India, there is a story about Brahma having sex with a bear (now *that* would take courage!) and in Vedic times there was a royal inauguration ritual involving a queen and a (dead) horse having symbolic intercourse.[5]

But let's omit any zoosexual S&M and refrain from beating

this dead horse. The point I'm making in this discussion is not that most readers might want to imitate any of this behavior, but that some Paleopagan cultures had plenty of room for members of sexual minorities.[6] Neopagan religions, drawing on Paleopagan cultures from around the world, have the option to be open to sexual minorities as well, and most traditions in fact are.

"Downright Jolly!"

Even Wicca, in which the heterosexual love between the Goddess and the God is central to its symbolism and the exchange of erotically tinged magical energies between the priest and priestess to its practice, is no exception, as Christopher Penczak[7] tells us in *Gay Witchcraft: Empowering the Tribe*: "Witches honor the masculine and feminine within all beings, regardless of physical gender, sexual orientation, or identity. Everyone embodies both the divine feminine and the divine masculine within, but we each contain a unique balance of the energies."

Anyone who has gay and lesbian friends knows how quickly most of them can flip between masculine and feminine vibes when they need or want to. The fact that this can be used for magical purposes, even in spiritual systems that use divine heterosexuality as a prime metaphor, should come as no surprise. In his book, Penczak discusses coming-out as gay and Wiccan, gay handfastings (weddings) and handpartings (separations), and so on. There's even a chapter on "Queer-Positive Deities," in which he adds names to some of the ones listed earlier. Penczak's work celebrates an evolutionary change in how some Wiccans think about homosexuality.

The first book to discuss Witchcraft from a gay perspective was Arthur Evans's *Witchcraft and the Gay Counterculture* in 1978. It focused on a (sometimes shrill) discussion of the similarities between the persecution of gay men and lesbians in Europe and that of supposed witches past and present. It was one of the first works to point out that whether they were accused of witch-craft or not, many gay men and lesbians were burned at the stake in medieval Europe.

For many years, some Wiccan traditions on the conservative-orthodox side of the spectrum I described in chapter 2 were either actively hostile or subtly resistant to the participation of gay men and lesbians in the Craft. This changed as they became more Neo- and less Mesopagan, and as the invention of Feminist Wicca brought many lesbians and other women comfortable working in all-female circles. Meanwhile, the overall American culture was becoming more comfortable with the public presence of homo-sexuals and bisexuals, and this has influenced American Paganism beyond Wicca as well. We still have Pagan homophobes, just as we still have a few sexists, racists, and creedists, especially in the more Mesopagan parts of the Pagan movement, but they are becoming a dwindling and increasingly irrelevant presence.

None of this is to say that gay men and lesbians don't have different sexual energies in a ritual space than straight men and women (or bisexuals or transgendered people) do. As a magician and psychic, I've been aware of those differences for years. But since 99 percent of all modern Mesopagan and Neopagan traditions never actually do any sexually powered magic or worship,* it simply doesn't matter.

I remember years ago at a Pagan festival someone asked me if a couple of my friends there were gay, as she had never heard of gay Pagans before. "We're not just gay, honey," one of them told her, "we're downright jolly!"

Gay-Friendly Pagan Traditions

Although arguments can be made in favor of gay Wicca, many Pagan men find themselves more comfortable in Pagan denomi-

*Sex magic is like the weather, everybody talks about it but . . .

nations in which their sexuality is either irrelevant or actually celebrated. The best example I can bring up is my own Neopagan Druid tradition, Ár nDraíocht Féin: A Druid Fellowship (ADF). Now, occultists and Pagan clergy all know that almost anything that generates emotional excitement also generates the psychic/spiritual/magical energies that we use in magical and religious rituals.[8] Paleopagan religions have used music, chanting, poetry, drama, dancing, storytelling, sublimated (or not) sexuality, and the presence of death to raise this energy for ritual use.

When ADF made a conscious decision to use music, poetry, and other performance arts as its primary energy-raising techniques, rather than sublimated sexuality as in Wicca, it made the sexual preferences and gender identities of its members utterly irrelevant to their ritual participation.

I probably shouldn't have been surprised when this decision resulted in a significant inflow of gay, lesbian, bisexual, and transgendered people into the organization. They kept telling me, "At last! A Pagan tradition that doesn't care what I am, just *who* I am!" Eventually, some of these folks organized the People of the Purple Feather[9] as a special interest group within ADF and made me an honorary member for having provided them a friendly "place" to be themselves.

While the Church of All Worlds (CAW), discussed earlier, is very pro-sexual in its beliefs and rituals, and borrowed some magical techniques from Wicca, Oberon Zell-Ravenheart, Morning Glory, and the other early founders also chose to honor a famous Wiccan phrase attributed to the Goddess: "All acts of love and pleasure are my rituals." For the CAW members, as for the liberal/heterodox Wiccans, this principle makes all forms of ethical sexuality potentially appropriate for Pagan worship and celebration.

If you go to the Web sites of the major Neopagan organizations today, whether Druidic, Egyptian, Norse, or Roman, you will find that almost all of them (even those that used to discriminate) now have nondiscrimination policies in effect that include sexual orientation and gender identity alongside race, color, and place of planetary origin. The situation with Mesopagan groups is more complex.

Even though some of the gods were ambisexual in their proclivities and shown as such throughout Greek literature and art (as we have just seen), many Hellenic Mesopagans in modern Greece attempt to keep a wide distance between themselves and gay or bisexual Pagans looking for a home. There are several Greek Neopagan groups around, however, mostly outside of Greece, who welcome gay and bisexual men,[10] but oddly don't seem to get many of them these days.

The Norse Mesopagans used to be known for homophobia, along with racism and sexism, but seem to be growing out of this as they become more Neopagan (and as more strong women become prominent in the Asatru movements).

As for African Diasporic Mesopaganisms, their attitudes on this topic, like that of race and gender, varies wildly from group to group even within a given system such as Santeria or Macumba. Some Santeria houses (local groups/initiatory lineages) may have no gay men or lesbians at all, or refuse to initiate them to the highest levels, some may simply not care, and others may have a majority of such people as members. You have to find out from whomever your contacts or prospective teachers may be what their particular attitude is.

Exercises

How weirded out, if at all, were you by this chapter?

Do *you* have any erotic tendencies (or at least fantasies) that you would rather not see described on the front page of your local newspaper? Welcome to the club. If you feel safe doing so, write a few down.

How did your childhood religion, if it wasn't Pagan, feel about such ideas?

How important is it to you to belong to a faith that doesn't want to kill or imprison you for your desires?

CHAPTER 11

Pagan Men, Pagan Women, and Sex

In this chapter, I would like to share some of the responses that I received from Pagan men when I asked questions about Pagan women and their relationships with them. I discovered widespread and deep wounds in many Pagan men's hearts. Moreover, I found that confusion about what is or is not "proper" for a Pagan man to do with (or want sexually from) his partners was often a source of the wounds in both genders.

Are Pagan Men Feminists?

Lots of people assume so, due to all those female-dominant clichés, but I wanted to find out for sure, so I asked in my questionnaire: "Do *you* consider yourself a 'feminist?' Yes, No, Why?" and "Do the *women* you know consider you one? Yes, No, Why?" The results were fascinating.

Many of the Pagan men who answered my questionnaire said "yes" and many said "no" to either or both questions without giving any explanations. Others preferred to offer alternative terminology that in fact amounted to feminism, in its earlier sense of "political, economic, and social equality for women," without calling it that. And many, especially among the older respondents, had a conviction that feminism means female supremacy or even tyranny, probably as a combination of the mainstream's dualism and the matriarchal rhetoric of past years in the Goddess movement. It's ironic that the majority of these Pagan men *would* have been considered feminists by women of previous generations, and by many today, whether they (or their current female friends) consider them to be such now.

In fact, Pagan men are often more feminist in their political and cultural views than mainstream, non-Pagan women are. As Bill of the Hermes Council told me:

> As a member of a matriarchal religion, I have naturally become more concerned with women's issues. My teachers were women; my high priestess is a woman; I am a male teacher of women. To be a witch is to try to look at the world holistically (and maybe other worlds as well . . .), and to see the connections between an individual's behavior and society's behavior.
>
> The conventional societal view is that a person's experience in religion, in the workplace, and at home can somehow be separated. I don't think so. If I am to work with women as a student, as a high priest, and as a teacher, I must have some awareness of their personal lives, and some awareness of their lives outside the ritual circle.
>
> But some moral urge inside me wants women and men to have the same practical opportunities, even if they can't share the same biological realities. As I listen to my teachers, my circle mates, and my students, I perceive that our Western society does not offer equality in the workplace, equality under the law, even equality in social behavior to women.
>
> So I guess this makes me a feminist.

Ironically, there are plenty of Pagan women who are not feminists themselves, or who decline the label and foolishly assume that feminist males must be unmanly or weak.

Pagan Women Hurting Pagan Men

No, I'm not talking about leather-clad dominatrixes. When I asked questions about "What's the best" and "What's the worst thing about being a Pagan male," the answers surprised me. About half of the respondents answered some variation of "Pagan women" to *both* questions![1]

I found it astonishing how many, especially young Pagan men, told me they had been insulted, denigrated, and pushed away for wanting to love the Goddess—by the very sisters who should have been welcoming them! Said one man, "A Dianic [Feminist Witch] once told me I couldn't connect with 'The Lady' and could therefore not do 'real magic.'" Another said, "You're afraid to open your mouth half the time because something you say may be taken as 'sexist' or chauvinistic." An older man told me, "I've been told that I cannot be worthy before the Goddess—which is not what she has told me!"

I suspect that most of this is female abuse victims passing their abuse along, as happens so frequently in many other cultures and subcultures, and I sincerely hope that these women do not represent the majority of Pagan women. Still, it does mean that male newcomers, especially in local Pagan communities where Wiccans and Goddess religion women are in the majority, need to get in the habit of carefully observing the emotional territory (as revealed by the body language and voice tonalities the women are exhibiting toward males) before speaking or acting in a way that even vaguely resembles traditional mainstream male words or behavior.

There is an important pattern that I see here, however, one that my Pagan sisters would do well to notice. The vast majority of Pagan men *accept* female equality, some of the older ones perhaps grudgingly, but the younger ones enthusiastically or matter of factly. As with all those young mainstream women who don't call themselves feminists because they grew up with feminism as a negative stereotype even while it was transforming the mainstream culture, for most young Pagan males *feminism is part of the wood-work*. As far as the subculture of Neopaganism is concerned, as well as much of Mesopaganism, the battle has already been won. Yet, many Pagan women are still fighting it, deeply hurting the men who would willingly be their comrades and equals.

This seems especially true with young men and women in their teens and twenties. Since they associate mostly with their age-mates, many of the young ladies coming into Pagandom from the mainstream *assume* Pagan guys will be just like the sexist non-Pagans they are used to, and come in with chips on their shoulders. And perhaps far too many young Pagan males *assume* that the females will accept them as nonsexists, just because they are Pagans.

Then there's the added factor of women in their thirties and forties discovering the Goddess, joining a community where women can have power, then realizing that they enjoy cracking the whip over a community of men who are "not allowed" by the rules of the game to object (because if they do they are being sex-ists or bad Pagans). Which brings me to a story sent to me by a Pagan male whom I will call "Joe." I've also changed a few other details about times and locations to protect the guilty. It is, how-ever, a true story as far as I know and certainly resembles similar events I have witnessed.

Once upon a Time . . .

A festival was taking place in a rural area. It was an annual all-invited, open to the public, weekend campout, with days of ritual and workshops, and nights of singing and storytelling around the campfire. One man, let's call him "Jack," had brought a bunch of firewood, made a good firepit, and as night fell began experimenting with some rubbing alcohol. When Jack was done, he tossed it in the fire—whoosh! A big gout of flame erupted, there was spontaneous applause from all the men, and a chorus of boos and gasps from the women. The high priestess of the event stomped over to have a long talk with Jack about the nearby trees and how he could have started a fire, and so on. Later, the fire spinners came out (most of whom were women) and the high priestess said nothing. Afterward, she explained that "they have licenses and know the dangers." She hadn't asked if the man who threw the rubbing alcohol into the fire had that locally prescribed fire-handling license, but he did.

At the next year's festival, Jack and Joe arrived early. Jack carefully set up his campsite and firepit away from all trees and possible overhead fire dangers, then put five-gallon buckets of water and a couple of fire extinguishers nearby. When evening came there were a number of somewhat tipsy adults gathered around the big fire. Since part of the festivities the next day would involve jumping the fire, some of the younger men asked permission and began doing practice runs over his firepit. Then someone mentioned the "gout of flame blasting skyward" from the previous year and they spent about twenty minutes pleading with Jack.

He made sure that everyone knew he had a fire-handling license, warmed up a frying pan full of rubbing alcohol, and tossed it into the fire. This produced a gout of flame blasting upward for about two seconds—impressive, but not long enough for anything flammable to warm up (rubbing alcohol, as special effects people know, burns very coolly). The young men arranged things with him, and returned to practicing their jumps with Jack tossing in the alcohol in such a way that the blast of flame would envelop them for about a second as they hurtled over the firepit.

"All the women in camp were up in arms," Joe recalls, "shouting and booing, and so on. And this time both the high priestess and the high priest went to have a long talk with him. He was so disgusted, he didn't come back the next year."

But Joe did, and some of the young men came to talk to him, so he agreed to do something. On the day of the fire jumping, Joe, who had one of those fire licenses, made a big fire in a firepit that was at least thirty feet away from any overhanging branches and made sure that shovels and buckets were handy. As evening fell and everyone—man, woman, and child—had already had the thrill of jumping over the fire, the young men gathered for their own ritual of fire-jumping, calling it "the flame-gate dance." As they jumped over the fire, Joe squeezed a bottle of rubbing alcohol in such a way that about a half-second gout of ten-foot flames surged up from the fire. This went on for about three runs each, when the high priest came over and asked Joe to stop, without being able to fully explain why. This confused Joe, since all the fire-jumpers were consenting adults. Says Joe now,

> There is something about "pushing the envelope" that men need to [do to] clean themselves out, at least once every few years. Maybe women need it too, but the jumpers and askers were all men in their twenties, and the gaspers and shouters were all women in their forties.
>
> I guess there's a directness, almost foolishness, to men that I find easy to be and easy to deal with, even when we don't agree; and a circumspectness/worry in women, particularly Pagan women, who, regardless of how an event is going down seem to feel that they, ultimately, are in charge of everything. This I find difficult to deal with and/or explain to myself.
>
> Would the high priest have interrupted the flame-gate dance if no women had been around? I'm not sure, either way.

Perhaps what is going on in such situations, and I have seen many of them, is that the women are treating the men as if they were children, which is not what I would consider respecting their inner deities. This maternalism is, I suspect, a form of sexism, just as the common paternalism of older males in the mainstream culture is.

But just as there are those who believe only white folks can be racists, there are women who believe that only men can be sexists, or that it doesn't really count as sexism if it's done in the name of the Goddess. Unfortunately for all of us, it does.

So the advice I would give to Pagan men on this issue is to always remember that many of our sisters are wounded birds, trying to recover from a lifetime of suppression and abuse, and that some of them will lash out without thinking, while others will take revenge on any available targets, including you. *You don't have to hang out with them while they recover and you don't have to accept abuse from them.* There are plenty of healthy Pagan women and girls (now that we are finally getting multigenerational Pagan families) who will take you at your word and give you the chance to demonstrate your character. Treat each one as the unique Goddess she is and don't assume that you'll be snapped at or insulted for being a guy. You might be, but then you can always go find someone else to spend your time with.

I would repeat to my Pagan sisters, *the war against sexism in Pagandom is over—you won.* There may still be a few unrepentant male chauvinist pigs in the movement, but the social pressure is now against them and for you. Most Pagan men, especially the younger ones and the boys growing up, *want* to treat you as equals, or at the very least have accepted that that's the way things are. So please think before you attack. Treat each boy or man as the unique God he is in the here and now, not as a stand-in for ones who have hurt you in the past.

And just because you're middle aged doesn't mean that you have a license to suppress harmless male risk-taking.

And Now a Few Words About Sex

Near the beginning of this book I mentioned some of the things that most Neopagans believe and practice. Some of those are directly relevant to this topic:

- Divinity is both immanent (internal) and transcendent (external)
- Ethics and morality should be based on joy, love, self-esteem, mutual respect, and the avoidance of actual harm to others and ourselves
- People are meant to lead lives filled with joy, love, pleasure, beauty, and humor
- Sexual ecstasy is a divine blessing and it can be a major source of spiritual growth and enlightenment
- We must practice what we preach

By putting these principles together, we can arrive at good advice for Pagan men on this most delicate of topics. By the way, after the previous chapter, I hope you won't assume that I'm only discussing heterosexuality here, even if I do phrase most of the discussion that way.

Basic Principles

Often, when I am speaking about Pagan sexuality, I begin with the First Law of Sex: Nothing should ever go crunch!* If something does, then whatever you are doing, it's not sex. This usually gets a good laugh, but the underlying idea is sound. Our body parts, when engaging in sexual activities, are not designed to break anything. Our spirits, when having sex, shouldn't be breaking anything either.

*Discovered by Deborah Lipp and John Franza in the 1980s (personal communication).

Anti-Pagan accusations have frequently revolved around the idea that "Pagans have no morality—they do anything they want and simply don't care." For many years, one of the dictionary definitions of "pagan" was "immoral," rooted in the dualist idea that people with different moral codes are obviously part of the forces of evil.

Certainly, there are plenty of examples from Paleopaganism of people doing things that don't seem to show much in the way of caring (e.g., raping, looting, and pillaging), but then there are plenty of examples in the history of non-Pagan religions that show the same lack of caring for others (including the raping, looting, and pillaging parts). And as we have seen, in many Paleopagan religions some sexual activities were considered perfectly normal that monotheistic religions find horrifying—homosexuality, zoosexuality, and polygamy among them (although ancient Jewish patriarchs were, and modern Muslim men are, allowed multiple wives).

You won't find too many Neopagans who will admit to having amorous interests in four-legged animals, but we have, as this book has made clear, plenty of gay men and many practitioners of polyamory—the idea that some people are capable of loving more than one other person at a time. What's more, there's a sizable "leather" contingent of Pagans who think that various forms of sexual bondage, discipline, and sadomasochism are okay among consenting adults. So exactly where and how do we modern Pagans draw our lines?

Do as I Say, Not as I Did?

I will grant that, during the early days of the Neopagan movement, there were plenty of people who believed dualistically that "anything the mainstream religions don't like must be okay," myself among them. In the 1960s and 1970s, we assumed that anything we wanted to do sexually was okay, regardless of the mainstream culture's opinions—the old "if it feels good, do it" philosophy. Being Pagan seemed to provide us with a green light to indulge ourselves in every way possible, with anyone willing to allow us to do so with them, whether or not it was classy, kind, or worthy of us. Truly, testosterone (and estrogen) poisoning can be an ugly thing.

Between the alcohol and other mind-altering substances I was consuming at the time, and the L-tryptophan poisoning I suffered in 1990, I can't remember much of my teens and twenties, yet I have a nagging suspicion that I did a few things that would make me cringe today. It was only gradually, as I became more aware of the spiritual issues involved (and perhaps as the testosterone levels in my bloodstream dropped), that I began to think clearly about my sexuality.

I suspect that my feet of clay go up at least as far as my belly, so this is one of the reasons why I am uncomfortable being presented as a "spiritual leader," rather than just as an author and teacher, within the Neopagan movement. It took many years for me to mature as a man (assuming I've done so, opinions are divided), and much of that time was spent in a dualistic reaction against my Catholic childhood of sexual abuse and confusion.

I would guess that it was the combination of an honest reaction to the legitimate complaints of the feminist movement of the 1980s,* my own growing interest in developing a systematic approach to polytheology (i.e., in making my beliefs and practices mutually support each other), time spent in "twelve step" programs, increasing devotion to several goddesses, and the influence of many good Pagan women that ultimately made me change my ways. As Morning Glory and Oberon Zell-Ravenheart have said for many years, if "Thou art God" and "Thou art Goddess" are true, then *we are godlings* and had best start behaving as such.

---

*Although I never did swallow the line that the sexual revolution was a patriarchal plot against women.

A Simple Rule

There's a very nice Pagan online community[2] I joined while writing this book, and it has only one rule. It started out with this one rule, then added all kinds of other detailed rules to control people's behavior in the forums, and finally realized that the one rule it had started out with was sufficient: "Respect your fellow community members." In the same way, *respect for the immanent deities of others* will tell you whether the sexual escapade you have in mind is appropriate or not.

When you look into the eyes of someone you are thinking of having sex with, search for his or her immanent god or goddess. Make that connection and ask that deity if it is okay with him or her if you and his or her incarnation have some fun together. The god or goddess will tell you, rather bluntly if you are listening, whether you are connecting to an equal or exploiting someone who, by age, experience, or current state of mental health, is not able to make that healthy connection. If the god or goddess in the person says, "Back off," *just back off*.

However, if the person's immanent deity thinks it's okay, then it is. If the man, woman, alien, fairy, or German shepherd you are attracted to wants you to cover him or her in whipped cream and lick it off, to tie him or her up with silk cords and make him or her beg for mercy (or vice versa), to pull you into bed with his or her spouse(s), or to have you give him or her multiple orgasms until he or she is unconscious—then go for it! As long as your actions are "based on joy, love, self-esteem, mutual respect, and the avoidance of actual harm to others and ourselves," then whatever sexual activities you and the other party(ies) want are moral by Neopagan standards. As my son, Arthur, speaking strictly from theory, puts it:

> If all parties concerned give their consent in their right mind,
> and perform the act in their right mind, and nobody is
> forced by anyone or anything, then it's okay. This policy

functions very well most of the time. However, it does mean that public sex is not okay, because the people watching have not given their consent. By "public sex," I mean something like sexual acts done in, I don't know, a portion of Central Park that people go through regularly. In addition to excluding exhibitionism, this policy vetoes voyeurism. The exhibitionists and the voyeurs can hook up [and do their thing in private], and then it's okay. Otherwise, no dice.

A Pagan man or youth should *never* force, browbeat, manipulate, trick, or blackmail another person into sexual activity. But once informed consent is fully given, by both the other party and his or her immanent deity, *no one* has the right to stop you (although you may want to pay attention to the relevant laws in the local jurisdiction).

What about the charisma factor? If you become a famous high priest, or a talented drummer or artist, or some other sort of grand high poobah, you will find yourself attracting many people, especially females. This has to do with core DNA programming that urges men to choose "good breeding stock" (which explains traditional sexual attractions to youth, wide hips, and healthy breasts) and women to choose "powerful" males (however defined in the culture or subculture involved) to protect the future offspring. This is definitely *not* politically correct, but it does seem to be an awkward reality. So where most men are subconsciously attracted to "sex objects," most women are likewise attracted to "power objects."

There is nothing in Neopagan polytheology that requires you to reject this reality—on the contrary, Earth-based religions encourage you to accept realities of every sort—so there is no ethical reason why you should push away potential partners who are attracted to you for less than enlightened reasons. Just be happy that in the Pagan movements there are many different kinds of sex and power "objects" that can be found attractive.

Avoiding Harm

The avoidance of harm issue naturally includes paying attention to matters of contraception and disease control, as well as the possibilities of doing emotional or social damage to others (or yourself). A Pagan man is expected to take care of (on multiple levels) any children he knowingly or carelessly sires. That can range from holding a woman's hand at the abortion clinic, to helping her through nine months of pregnancy, to raising the offspring, so no, we are not casual about the issue.

Not too surprisingly, Pagan men are expected to know what condoms are and how to use them. Pagan women (and other Pagan men) know all the excuses for not wearing them and simply won't accept them. Pagan men are also expected to practice safe sex whenever requested, which will be most of the time (outside of trusted closed relationships) if you and your partners are wise.

There are reasons why there still isn't a cure for AIDS and why so many millions of people are still dying from it. Judeo-Christian-Islamic worldviews that see AIDS as divine punishment for sinful behavior provide some of those reasons. If there was some other disease that didn't have a sexual component to it ravaging as many people as AIDS has done and is still doing, billions of dollars more would have been made available for treatment and research for a cure, as well as honest public education on the topic. But no politician in a monotheisticly dominated culture dares to vote for the money to be appropriated, especially when the majority of the victims now dying are poor people in distant lands. Then, too, the virus involved is complex and constantly mutating, so even if the research gets fully funded, it will take years to find a cure or a vaccine.

I mention all this to stress to my younger readers that *AIDS isn't over!* You can still get it, even from "nice" people, in the

twenty-first century. And there are plenty of other sexually transmitted diseases you should study up on as well, some of which
are making comebacks after having been supposedly wiped out
decades ago. Maybe our grandsons will be able to stop wearing
condoms someday, but we and our sons won't.

Common sense and a little emotional sensitivity toward your
sexual partners can help you avoid most kinds of emotional and
social harm. You don't have to be a "sensitive New Age guy" to
do this, you just have to avoid acting like a jerk. When in doubt,
ask an older female friend or read a few books on how to have
healthy relationships. This isn't something that comes naturally
in a culture as sexually confused as America, filled with hundreds
of mixed messages about sex every day ("You want it," "It will
kill you," "Cool people have it," "It's sinful and evil," etc.).

Be aware that you are allowed to say "no" to a sexual invitation, even if the other party tries to convince you that you are
being "un-Pagan" or "unmanly" by doing so. Not every Pagan
man is a sex machine, nor wants to be! An old friend of mine,
who came to Paganism late in life, told me, "I have never partic-
ipated in the amorphous sexual glow of the Pagan community,
except for dancing at festival rituals, where a 'safe' [not sexually
aggressive] male who dances is often a welcomed partner."

Some of us older Pagan men just can't keep up with the
young'uns, so let's not hurt ourselves by trying! And even young
Pagan men sometimes need sleep or food more than romance. . . .

You Always Hurt the One You Love?

How does the avoiding harm issue work with partners who want
you to beat, brand, or humiliate them? That's become a tough
question for Pagans since the 1980s, when bondage and discipline (B&D), sadism and masochism (S&M), and domination
and submission (D&S), all became more popular than they had
been in years in the mainstream society. This popularity was due

in part, I suspect, as a solution to the "how do we have sex without having sex?" question posed by the AIDS epidemic, and then filtered down to the sexually adventurous members of the Neopagan movement.

Personally, I have always believed that pain is nature's way of saying, "Ouch! Don't do that!" I suspect that most of these leather (as the BDSMDS subculture is often called) activities are rooted in adult reactions to dysfunctional childhoods, but I'm told that they can be very therapeutic for the people involved. Of course, I've always had trouble keeping a straight face while trying to do the sort of role-playing these activities require, but maybe that's just me.

How does a Pagan man handle the sexual ethics of these sorts of activity, should he choose to do so? "Just don't do it in the street and scare the horses!" In other words, if you and your friends are going to be cracking the whip all night at a festival (or just making lots of noise of any sort), make sure the hotel door is closed or your tent is far away enough that you won't be turning the stomachs of people—especially kids—who wouldn't find your personal predilections amusing. Otherwise, you are dragging onlookers or listeners into your sexual adventure, and that's a kind of disrespectful assault itself.

Love Can Count Higher Than Two

"Polyamory" is a word coined by Morning Glory Zell-Ravenheart[3] to describe a "lovestyle" in which each of the participants is willing to accept that he or she will not be the exclusive sexual or emotional partner of the others and that he or she will have the freedom to fall in love with more than one person at a time. It's not quite the same thing as polyfidelity, which is the creation of closed group relationships. Both of these can be found in the Neopagan movement, though they are still quite a minority.

Polyamory and polyfidelity[4] are definitely not for everyone, because they require making both major and minor changes about how you think about relationships and what sacrifices you are willing to make to try something new.[5] Presentations on these topics have been occurring with increasing frequency at Pagan gatherings since the mid-1990s, with some unexpected side effects.

There's a cultural pattern I have noticed, in which a minority group (whether racial, religious, sexual, artistic, or other) begins to gain some of the equality it has been wanting, sometimes for centuries, only to provoke a negative reaction from the previously (and usually still) dominant group that the minority is "going too far" and that it is "asking for special privileges" and "discriminating against us!" This has happened in the mainstream culture with the backlash against affirmative action, the antifeminist movement, and the constant complaints by fundamentalist religious leaders that freedom for members of religious minorities constitutes oppression of the fundamentalists.

Something similar to this has happened in the Pagan movement, in reaction to the public arrival of BDSMDS practitioners and the polyamorous Pagans. As these two groups of Pagans have appeared publicly at festivals and conventions, holding workshops, playshops, and private parties, some monogamous and vanilla (non-BDSMDS) Pagans have complained that there aren't any workshops or special parties for *them*—as if the new arrivals[6] were somehow preventing the majorities from doing what they wanted!*

So I've received complaints from monogamous men that they are being pressured to become polyamorous by the public discussion of the topic. The question becomes, are they really being pressured, or are they being encouraged to reconsider their beliefs about a very personal matter, something they might not

---

*I will prophesy that after a summer or two of my doing workshops based on this book, there will be complaints about a lack of workshops for Pagan women!☺

want to look at too closely? That's impossible for me to judge from a distance, but I would suggest that both polyamorous enthusiasts and the people they are talking to need to be careful before jumping to conclusions.

One of the most difficult things for many modern Pagan men to do is to overcome mainstream-indoctrinated attitudes of jealousy and possessiveness. Whether they are polyamorous or not, Pagan women will *not* be owned, and you had better get used to it. Fortunately, this gives you the right not to *be* owned in return, though (again) respect for your mutual immanent deities implies that you had better work out what the rules for your relationship are going to be before opportunities for involving others are encountered. Some Pagans are monogamous, while others find the whole concept laughable. You had best figure out what your own psychological needs are, and why you have them. Then make sure your potential partner is agreeable *before* you enter into a relationship—but that's true for members of any religion or none.

And no, just because someone is Pagan and sexually active doesn't mean he or she necessarily wants to sleep with *you*. Conversely, just because you're Pagan and sexually active doesn't mean you have to accept every offer someone makes to you. I have known Pagan women who insisted that any Pagan man they wanted was obligated to worship them sexually. Sometimes I did so and other times I just laughed. . . .

When Do We Get To the Good Stuff?

What about sex magic and Pagan orgies? Well, as lurid as those sound, you'll find they aren't—alas—very common anymore.[*] Oh sure, plenty of Pagans do magic for sexual purposes (mostly to attract appropriate partners), and this can be ethical if one is

---

[*]Back in the good old days, we really knew how to party, not like these young'uns today. . . .

careful to "aim" them generally at a preferred type of partner, or onto yourself, rather than specifically at a particular person. But despite the ideals of many of the founders of Neopaganism, it's very seldom that sex is used for magical or religious purposes, except for the reinforcing of relationship bonds. As for orgies, a combination of herpes, feminism, and the AIDS epidemic pretty much killed them long ago, except within polyfidelitous relationships (group marriages).

So if you are thinking of becoming a Pagan man because you hope to achieve a wild sex life, the odds are that your Pagan sex life will be satisfying, both physically, emotionally, and spiritually and may indeed involve several people sequentially or together, but it's unlikely to make a good porno film (people connected sexually, staring motionless into each other's eyes for hours, just isn't good cinema). However, you may wind up having a heck of a lot of fun and giggling helplessly into the wee hours. . . .

The bottom line? Pagan men who are willing to treat Pagan women as the incarnate goddesses they are will find that they can be warm, friendly, and loving, often in astonishing and imaginative ways. Gay men will find plenty of other gay men to enjoy as well, but mutual respect is obviously just as necessary here.

Oh, we still have some puritanical people (usually female) in our communities, but if you stand up honestly for your principles they will usually back down. Most of them are abuse survivors and have good reason for being a bit paranoid. Convince them that you are being chivalrous and honorable and they will usually get out of your face. If you can't, consider that perhaps you aren't being chivalrous or honorable and rethink your intentions. Be aware that we also have men and women in the Pagan community who practice what is perhaps the most bizarre perversion of all: celibacy. Grit your teeth if you have to and respect it as the choice of their internal deities.

But for most other Pagans, remember what the Goddess says— all acts of love and pleasure are her rituals. As long as your pleasure is liberally sprinkled with love for her, as well as affection and respect for your partner of the moment, you are worshipping her and your ecstasy is a religious experience. Pray often.

Speaking of rituals, in the next chapter we will look a bit at what sorts of rituals Pagan men do.

Exercises

How do you make sure that your prospective partners or play-mates are in synch with your needs and desires?

How many different ways can you think of to pleasure some-one else (of your choice)?

Do some research on safe-sex techniques and pick a few with which you might enjoy giving or receiving pleasure.

True or false: jealousy equals love? Why or why not?

True or false: jealousy equals fear? Why or why not?

CHAPTER 12

Pagan Men and Ritual

In this chapter, I will present a ritual for creating a sacred men's space, using the metaphor of building a temple so popular with fraternal organizations and Western occult traditions. I'll also include instructions on setting up a home shrine to your forefathers and a visualization useful for psychic/magical protection on a daily basis.

But First, Some Technical Background

There are many, many books on magic and ritual, some of which I've written! For the purposes of understanding the following rituals, it is only necessary to be aware of a few things:

Magic can be thought of many ways. My favorite definition is, "Magic is a collection of rule-of-thumb techniques designed to get your gods-given natural psychic talents to do more or less what you want, more often than not, you hope." It's an art form as much as it is a science or philosophy, and is at least as reliable as drawing, music, or poetry usually are. Fortunately, a little hard work can make most art forms function effectively to change your (or other people's) reality.

Worship is not a matter of groveling, it is a matter of showing respect. In the case of these rituals, worship is showing respect to other people and spirits. Worship rituals are designed to put mortals and immortals in touch with each other, so they can exchange love and strength.

A ritual is just an ordered series of steps designed to produce a particular desired result. A pancake recipe, the rules for baseball, the score for a symphony, or the script for a play are all rituals. In magical and religious rituals, however, the ordered sequence of events, actions, and/or directed thoughts is meant to produce specific altered states of consciousness that make it easier to use your psychic powers and/or contact the gods.

Is there anything that's particularly different between the ways that men and women do ritual? Yes! As I put it in *Rites of Worship:*

> There appear to be two major approaches to generating and releasing mana [psychic/magical/spiritual energies], which can be correlated to a male/female polarity. The "masculine" approach seems to be one of building up energies higher and higher until they can't be contained anymore, then releasing them in a sudden burst of power, usually in a particular direction. The "feminine" approach seems to be one of generating and building continuous waves of energy, which are released, built up again, then released again, in a series of waves of energy sent in all directions. Does this remind you of anything?

Beyond this gender-specific energy manipulation difference, I've noticed that male rituals tend to be rather wordy and left-brained, while female ones are likely to be nonverbal and right-brained. I have also noticed, however, that men's drum rituals can often follow the female pattern just mentioned, in that they go on all night, creating waves of energy, and are usually nonverbal too. Perhaps this is because the ones I've attended at Pagan festivals involved both genders and the energy was in large measure being generated for and guided by the female dancers.

The following rituals, however, fit the usual male patterns. . . .

Building the Temple of the Gods

This ancient men's ritual* may be done by a single† man or by a group of men. It reflects a common worship pattern as discussed in my other books, especially *Rites of Worship,* which will be useful to explain the underlying structure.

It is best done in a rectangular room (though it may be performed outdoors) with enough space to measure 8' x 13', 9' x 14.5', or 10' x 16' on the floor or ground. These proportions are close to what the Paleopagan Greeks called "the Golden Rectangle"[1] and that they used to design the Parthenon and many other temples. If possible, the rectangle should be oriented along an east-west line, so as to mimic the path of the sun, and the room's height should measure the same as its short side, so as to make the resulting psychic structure be composed of four golden rectangles and two squares.[2]

The leader of the ritual is the magus, which is a word based on the old Persian‡ term for "priest." He may be assisted by one or more men, whom we will logically enough term "assistants." In the following script, M will mean "Magus," A will mean "Assistant," and "All" will mean. . . .

There should be a simple altar near the eastern side of the rectangle that should have on it a sword (unless the magus is wearing one), a dish of loose incense or sweet oil (with a dipping ladle), a large horn or drinking cup filled with an alcoholic or herbal beverage, a container of spring or ocean water, and a sprig of leaves. Also on the altar, in a brazier or at the eastern edge of the rectangle, should be a small fire made from woods considered

---

*It goes back to 2760 AUC in the Roman calendar, or the fourth year of the 695th Olympiad, and is based on the rites of the *Thiasos Hermou,* the *Boulê Hermou,* the erection of the Parthenon, and possibly other sources.

†Or married . . .

‡One man's Mede is another man's Persian.

sacred by those gathered. Either on the altar, on a stand some-
where in the rectangle, or at a participant's belt should be a horn,
gong, flute, or other musical instrument.

After appropriate prayer and meditation during or after a cleansing bath, and dressing in what the men consider appropriate garb,
the participants gather in the temple-to-be.

---

*The magus or one of his assistants makes a sound on the musical
instrument, three times.*

M: "We are here to honor the gods, the ancestors, and
     the spirits of nature! Now let us turn within to greet
     our innermost god, our genius, that he may inspire us
     to perform this rite of Art properly."

*All pause and do so. The magus takes the Sword of Art to
the northeast corner and placing it on the floor or ground
traces the shape of the sacred space, repeating as needed:*

M: "I charge and consecrate thee, oh rectangle of power,
     that thou shalt be a firm foundation for the temple we
     shall erect on thee, and a protection against all chaos
     arising from the Underworld."

*Drums may be played throughout this and subsequent steps
of building the temple. At his return to the northeast corner,
the Magus uses the sword to similarly trace a vertical line up
to as far as he can reach or the ceiling of the room, then
across the edge of the ceiling, then down to the floor at the
southeast corner, repeating:*

M: "I charge and consecrate thee, oh rectangle of power,
     that thou shalt be a strong wall for this temple we now
     erect, and a protection against all chaos of air arising
     in the east."

The magus then traces the next wall likewise, drawing the sword in a line from the floor up to the top of the southeast corner, across the edge of the ceiling, then down to the bottom of the southwest corner, repeating:

M: "I charge and consecrate thee, oh square of power, that thou shalt be a strong wall for this temple we now erect, and a protection against all chaos of fire arising in the south."

The magus then traces the next wall likewise, drawing the sword in a line from the floor up to the top of the southwest corner, across the edge of the ceiling, then down to the bottom of the northwest corner, repeating:

M: "I charge and consecrate thee, oh square of power, that thou shalt be a strong wall for this temple we now erect, and a protection against all chaos of water arising in the west."

The magus then traces the next wall likewise, drawing the sword in a line from the floor up to the top of the northwest corner, across the edge of the ceiling, then down to the bottom of the northeast corner, repeating:

M: "I charge and consecrate thee, oh square of power, that thou shalt be a strong wall for this temple we now erect, and a protection against all chaos of earth arising in the north."

Finally, the magus uses the sword to cast the roof of the temple, beginning in the top northeast corner and continuing along the edge of the physical or visualized ceiling to the southeast, southwest, northwest, and back to the northeast, repeating:

M: "I charge and consecrate thee, oh square of power, that thou shalt be a strong roof for this temple we now erect, and a protection against all chaos descending from the heavens."

Drums stop. At some point where it is appropriate, either in the west wall or (if indoors) at the place where an opening into another room physically exists, the magus cuts a symbolic door and shuts it with his hands.

M: "Who will guard the door?"

An assistant volunteers to do so and is given the sword of the magus or unsheathes his own. If none volunteer, the magus lays his sword across the door.

M: "I call on you, guardian of the threshold, to keep this
       door safely shut against any who would seek to spy on
       or disrupt these holy proceedings—so be it!"
ALL: "So be it!"*

The magus now sheaths his sword (or returns it to the altar) if he has not left it at the door, and stands in front of the altar speaking to those others present, saying:

M: "We now stand as in a temple of the ancients, built by
       men's hearts and hands and hopes, protected from
       chaos and all danger. Neither tornado, nor wildfire,
       nor tidal wave, nor avalanche may assault us, nor me-
       teor descend, nor miasma arise. So be it!"
ALL: "So be it!"
M: "Now let the temple be cleansed by the waters of wis-
       dom!"

An assistant takes the sprig of leaves, dips it into the container of water, and sprinkles the altar, the magus, all else present, and the floor of the temple.

M: "Let us become one in our intent and in our brother-
       hood. If any man here be in a state of enmity with any

---

*All these exclamations of agreement should be said, according to Russian tra-
dition, in unison, by this rite's workers.

other, or bear ill will toward him for real or imagined
injury, let him honestly give and receive forgiveness, or
else leave this place."

*All grasp hands with one another, greeting each other quietly and
in good fellowship. If any leave, the guardian of the threshold or
another assistant shall open, then shut the symbolic door behind
him. A song of unity may be sung.*

M: "Let us now return in our hearts to those ancient times,
       when men would gather to honor their gods, their an-
       cestors, and the spirits of nature. Today, we shall do
       likewise, particularly honoring _____ because of
       _____."

*Magus announces the special being(s) to be worshiped (hereafter
referred to as the "spiritual guest(s) of honor" and represented
by the short blank line), and why. If this ritual is being held for a
particular purpose, such as a rite of passage, a seasonal celebration, a spell to be cast, or a council to be held, this, too, is mentioned.*

M: "This temple is erected in the center of the world, in
       the shadow of the home of the gods. Within these
       walls our words may be heard by those whom we wish
       to hear them, and none else. So be it!"
ALL: "So be it!"

*The magus (or an assistant) goes to the altar, takes a large pinch of
loose incense (or a ladle-full of the sweet oil), and places it into the
fire, saying:*

M: "As the smoke rises to the sky, is carried across the
       land, and sinks into the waters beneath the earth, so,
       too, do our prayers travel through this flaming Gate
       between the Worlds, to reach those whom we would
       praise. Let the guardian of the gates make this be true,
       now and always. So be it!"

ALL: "So be it!"

M: "Now see in your mind's eye the face and form of the one(s) we shall honor above all."

The magus or an assistant now gives a vivid description of the spiritual guest(s) of honor.

M: "Let us praise _____!"

Each participant, beginning with an assistant, now throws a bit of incense (or pours a ladle of oil) into the fire, offering his praise to the spiritual guest(s) of honor. The magus should offer and speak last, gathering the energies in the temple and focusing them into the act with a dramatic exclamation. After a pause, he continues:

M: "In the ancient times, people worshiped _____ because of the blessings they received. We, too, may receive such blessings if we ask for them with an open heart. Think now of what you truly need from _____."

The magus takes the cup or horn of beverage and holds it up, saying:

M: "I call on you now, oh ancient one, _____, to consecrate this, that your blessings may be transmitted to those who have asked for them."

The magus channels the return flow of energy from the guest(s) of honor into the cup or horn.

M: "There is no part of me that is not of the gods!"

He sips, then passes the cup or horn to an assistant, saying:

M: "May you never thirst!"

A: "May you never thirst!"

He sips, and passes the cup to another man, saying:

A: "May you never thirst!"

If there is a mortal guardian at the door, he partakes last. The magus waits until all have partaken, then speaks:

M: "Each of us is a man among men. Here within this temple we are a band of brothers. Look at one another and see the bonds of fellowship and honor that link us together."

All do so.

M: "Is there any more work to be done here now?"
A: "No, for we have praised _____, received blessings, and shared them."

Or:

A: "Yes, for we are filled with the blessings of _____ and would share them by _____."

Assistant reveals the rite of passage, celebration, spell casting, or council to be held.

SAID SPECIAL EVENT IS THEN PERFORMED

When the special event, if any, has been finished, the magus resumes direction of the main rite.

M: "We have praised _____, received blessings, and shared them with one another. Now let us thank _____."

The magus (or an assistant) throws more incense into the fire, saying:

M: "_____, we thank you!"
ALL: "_____, we thank you!"
M: "Now let the fire of knowledge be mere fire, and the waters of wisdom be mere water, and the door of our temple be merely a door. Guardian, we thank you!"

ALL: "Guardian, we thank you!"

If a mortal guardian be present, he sheaths his sword or puts it back on the altar.

M: "We have done as our ancestors did and as our grand-sons will do, meeting in fellowship and joy to honor the spirits. Let us once again remember ourselves and our mundane lives, and think on how we shall manifest the blessings we have received here in our lives outside this temple."

Assuming that the place in which this rite has taken place is not a permanently dedicated structure, the magus says;

M: "Now [as the ceiling, walls, and floor of this temple dissolve back into the energies that created them,]* release whatever excess power you may be feeling is beyond your limits back into the Earth, our Mother and final resting place."

M: "These rites are ended, yet eternal. Go!"

The magus or one of his assistants makes a sound on the musical instrument, three times.

Pagan Men, Death, and the Ancestors

A man faces the chance of death whenever he goes out to the battlefield or the hunt, or—if he's poor or lives near a terrorist target—into his own neighborhood. A woman, however, confronts the chance of death every time she gives birth—much less so if she is middle or upper class in a wealthy nation, far more if she is poor or lives in the Third World—or goes into that same bad neighborhood, or near that same terrorist target.[3] So it shouldn't be sur-

---

*Skip bracketed text if temple is permanent.

prising that our relationships with death and the dead should be important in our lives.

While the evidence for survival after death, whether through an afterlife of some sort, reincarnation, or preservation in Carl Jung's collective unconsciousness, or my switchboard theory,* is all circumstantial, it is also substantial. You will find that most human cultures have some sort of ancestor worship practices, at least in the sense of showing honor and respect toward one's ancestors.

Setting up an ancestor shrine in your home and stopping there to honor them regularly is thus a perfectly appropriate thing for a Pagan man to do.

Your ancestor shrine may be a wide shelf or a shallow box hung against a wall. It should be decorated with photos, drawings, statues, or other items that remind you of your ancestors and your ethnic heritages, whatever they may be. Do some genealogical research as best you can. Perhaps, you will be able to put together enough information that you can write an ancestor invocation such as the one I use:

ANCESTOR INVOCATION

I, the son of James Edwin Bonewits
and Jeanette Marie Charlebois
(born Marie Sedrida Quesnel),
call to my ancestors, known and unknown:
I call to my father's parents:
James Emmons Bonewits and Persis Mae Harbin.
I call to Emmons's parents:
Peter Bonewits and Sadie Florence Indiana
    Alexander.
I call to Peter's parents:

*See *Real Magic*.

Jacob Bonewitz and Nancy Caroline Myers.
I call to Jacob the Younger's parents:
Joseph Bonewitz and Sarah Franks.
I call to Joseph's parents:
Jacob Bonewitz and Eve Rosanna Specht.
I call to Jacob the Elder's parents:
Johann Adam Bonnawitz and Juliana.
I call to Adam's parents and grandparents,
of the Germans and the Wends.
I call to my grandmother Persis's parents and grand-
     parents,
of the Irish and the Scots, the Welsh and other tribes.
I call to my mother's adoptive parents:
Amable Charlebois and Marie Églantine Portelance.
And to her blood parents and grandparents:
of the French and the Bretons,
And of the native peoples of the Six Nations.
Spirits of my ancestors,
Hear and answer me!

You will notice that my list is primarily of my father's ancestry. I would have more of my mother's information except the relevant records are all in French, a language I do not speak. Generally, you can always be surer of maternal ancestors (the mother of your mother of your mother, etc.), since (until the rise of DNA testing) all recorded paternal lines rest on faith, while a mother always knows who her children are. Nonetheless, for use in men's ritual, you might want to focus on your father's line, using the short names they used. In my case, for example, if I were asked who I was in men's ritual, I might say, "I am Isaac, son of James, son of Emmons, son of Peter, son of Jacob, son of Joseph, son of Jacob, son of Adam!"*

---

*Ironic as that last name is for a Pagan . . .

An ancestor altar should have a candle burning when you are talking to them, and you should try to spend at least ten minutes a day communing with your ancestral spirits. You will find that when your ancestors become to you friendly spirits you expect to join someday, much fear of death will evaporate and courage will be easier to come by in times of need.

The Shield of the Dagda

This is a self-protection meditation, based on what is now known as the Shield of Saint Patrick, but was probably a druidic incantation long before him. I have rewritten it to feature my personal patron deity, with references to his mythic adventures and multiple activities as the omnifunctional God of Ireland. You could write a similar incantation, around the qualities and powers of your patron, with the appropriate mythic and cultural references. However, I would recommend that you keep the pattern of the section that begins "Dagda be with me," for this is the peak of the visualization that surrounds you with the protection of your patron.

When you arise in the morning, find yourself a quiet place where you won't be disturbed for ten minutes or so. This is one of the few times I suggest doing magical work before your first cup of coffee or tea in the morning, so that your mind will still be partly in the dream state, and your internal gates of perception will be most clean. Alternately or additionally, you can do this ritual just before going to bed, so as to drift from it into your dreams.*

Begin by feeling your connection to the physical world around you. As you say the words, see your patron in your mind's eye, standing before you, listening to your words. Feel his power surrounding you, flowing in and out of you with your breath, guarding you on all sides. When you come to the "Dagda be with me"

---

*Or perhaps to provide a pleasant surprise to your partner!

part, visualize a round shield coming into position around you
on each side, with the six of them merging into a sphere of energy, then sinking into your skin as you finish the incantation.
Offer a word of thanks, then go about your day or night, secure
in the knowledge that you are filled with divine power and protection.

The Shield of the Dagda

I bind unto myself today, the strong name of the Dagda,
By invocation of the same, the Three in One, the
    One in Three.

I call this day to me forever, the Dagda's many arts:
His mounting of the River Women, his siring of the
    God of Love
His fury on the field of battle, his druidry so strong
His majesty as High King, his sympathy for the despised.

I bind unto myself today, the Good God's mighty seed
His eye to watch, his might to stay, his ear to harken
    to my need
His wit to teach, his hand to guide, his shield to ward
His fire to enflame my speech, his mighty club to be
    my guard.

> *Dagda be with me, Dagda within me*
> *Dagda behind me, Dagda before me*
> *Dagda to my left, Dagda to my right*
> *Dagda beneath me, Dagda above me*
> *Dagda in quiet, Dagda in danger*
> *Dagda in the hearts of all that love me*
> *Dagda in the mouth of friend and stranger.*

I bind unto myself the name, the strong name of the
    Dagda,

By invocation of the same, the Three in One, and
   One in Three,
The mightiest of all the Gods, Father of the Queen
   of Arts,
The Supreme Knower, Lord of Fire, and King of
   Druids.
So be it!*

Useful Spells for Pagan Men

In most Pagan religions, ancient and modern, the polytheological line between "prayers" and "spells" is broad and fuzzy. Neopagan religions in particular, perhaps because of the heavy influence of Wicca, are often classified by religious scholars as "magical religions." Modern Pagans, men and women alike, often find themselves interested in doing magic for both spiritual/psychotherapeutic ("theurgical") and practical/mundane ("thaumaturgical") purposes. "Spells" as such are usually considered to fall into the latter category.

This isn't the place to explain what magic is or how it works,† so I will limit myself here to saying that a (working) magical spell is a multi-media psychodrama you perform for yourself. You do this in order to convince your inner child to release the psychic energy that he controls, perhaps with some divine assistance, so your conscious mind can direct it toward a particular target, in order to achieve a specific goal.

Spells don't always require invoking divine assistance but getting that kind of help always puts more power into your efforts. Doing your homework here is vital. Learn which deities from your favorite pantheons are most appropriate for what sorts of

---

*I have designed a silver talisman of the Shield of the Dagda for use with this meditation. Visit my Web site, www.neopagan.net.

†That's why I wrote *Real Magic*!

spells. Many deities are multi- or even omnifunctional. Cernun-nos, for example, can be used for hunting, prosperity, fertility, and lust spells.* To someone attracted to Irish deities, the Dagda is good for almost any activity that men may be involved in.

For these spells, I'll be using deities and cultural elements with which I'm familiar and comfortable. You should use ones that work for you and adapt my examples to your personal needs.[4] Each of these spells uses a similar format that many people have found to be effective. Obviously, your concentration and deter-mination are vital to their working properly.

For each spell, I'll list one or two suggested deities, whose pic-ture(s) or statue(s) you should have if you can manage. I'll also list what colors would be appropriate to using in choosing can-dles or in decorating your altar or working area, what kind of candles to use, incense you might want to burn, etc.

Many spells work better if you have "figure candles" which are ones designed to look like men or women; however, if you can't find figure candles, use regular tapers or votive candles in the ap-propriate colors. "Knob candles" are ones that consist of several flattened spheres of wax above a similar base; they are usually used in spells where you burn one knob's worth of wax per day. If your working area does not have a fireproof surface, you should obtain a plate or stone that is so, upon which to burn all your candles. *Candles should not be left burning without someone in the room paying attention!* By the way, if your home has smoke detectors (and it should) be sure to turn them off during each spell and back on again after the incense smoke has cleared.

"Dragon's blood" is a kind of incense made from a plant resin; it isn't an extract from unlucky komodos. Feel free to substitute appropriate incenses and herbs for the ones recommended.

---

*Just don't confuse the latter two categories or you may wind up being a father, when all you wanted was a hot Saturday night!

To Make New Pagan Friends

Deities: Gaia, the Goddess of Nature.

Colors: Blue and green.

Candles: One figure candle to represent yourself and one or more to represent others. Score all of them lightly with a sharp blade to mark three equal sections.

Incense: Ones with a woodsy or oceanic scent.

Time: During the new crescent moon and two nights afterwards.

Talisman: A symbol or image of the Earth Mother.*

Intro: One of the biggest problems that men and boys joining the Pagan movement encounter is the difficulty of finding other Pagans with whom they can study and worship. Unless you live in a college or university town, or perhaps a technology center such as Silicon Valley in California or the Triangle region of North Carolina, you probably won't see many people running around with noticeable pentacles or Thor hammers. In most parts of the Western world there is still a great deal of creedism (religious prejudice) against minority belief systems, though this is thankfully growing less every year as people abandon various fundamentalisms and more information about Paganism becomes available in the mass media and the Internet.

Practical Steps: First, do some searching at Witchvox.com and yahooGroups.com for Pagans who are in your physical area or who worship the deities in whom you are most interested. Send them email or join the e-lists. If this doesn't provide sufficient contacts, the following spell will help you to connect with other Pagans.

Procedure: In front of your image of Gaia, place the figure candle representing yourself in the middle of the fireproof surface. Place

---

*Oberon has a magnificent one based on his Millenium Gaia statue available at www.mythicimages.com.

the other(s) as far from this one as possible while remaining on the altar/plate/stone. Light the incense, wave it in front of the deity image, place it in its holder. Light your figure candles, then the others, then take the talisman and pass it through the smoke and flames while saying:

Gracious Goddess, Mother Earth
Bring me new friends of true worth
With whom I can both laugh and pray
And honor you both night and day.

Repeat this for a total of nine times while visualizing yourself surrounded by new Pagan friends both online and in real life. Let the candles burn about one third of the way down (keeping an eye on them for safety's sake), then snuff or blow them out.

Do all this again for two more nights, each time moving the other candles a third of the way closer to the one representing you. On the third night, let the candles burn themselves out completely, watching carefully to prevent any accidents.

You should have made new Pagan friends by the next full moon.

To Attract New Pagan Lovers

Deities: Eros (as a young man) and/or Aphrodite, the Greek deities of lust and love. If you are looking for a lover who follows a specific Pagan path, or who belongs to a specific ethnic group, choose corresponding deities from that path or ethnic tradition.

Colors: Purple and red for Eros, pink and gold for Aphrodite (vary as needed for other deities).

Candles: One figure candle to represent yourself and one or more figure candles to represent others of your preferred gender(s). Score all of them lightly with a sharp blade to mark seven equal sections.

Incense: Musk and rose.

Time: On the first Friday night of the new moon and six nights afterwards.

Talisman: A seven-pointed star in copper, silver, or gold.

Intro: Just making new friends isn't always enough. Many men join Paganism because they hope to find a lover with whom they can share their life, including their beliefs. Having similar religious beliefs is usually crucial to making a relationship work, no matter what the religions involved are. Certainly mixed Pagan/non-Pagan relationships have a lot of problems. So it makes sense to want someone with whom you can worship happily.

Practical Steps: First follow the advice given in the previous spell. Then take a shower, comb your hair, clean your fingernails, etc. Dress nicely in comfortable clothes of the sort you would wear on a date. Meditate for a while on exactly what sort of lover(s) you are looking for, creating a clear visual image without picturing a specific person. Then do the following spell.

Procedure: This is very similar to the preceding spell, but more intense. In front of your deity images, place the figure candle representing yourself in the middle of the fireproof surface. Place the other(s) as far from this one as possible while remaining on the altar/plate/stone. Light incense, circle it around the deity images seven times, then place it in its holder. Light your figure candles, then the others, then take the talisman and pass it through the smoke and flames while saying:

> *Lady and Lord of love and lust,*
> *In you I place my hope and trust.*
> *Let my spirit a magnet be*
> *To those who search for one like me.*
> *Lovers kind and loyal bring*
> *That we may all your praises sing*
> *Together in your temple bright*
> *With our joy both day and night.*

Repeat this for a total of seven times while visualizing yourself surrounded by an aura of golden light. See the images of potential lovers you visualized earlier floating within your aura, saturating it with loving and erotic feelings. Let the candles burn about one seventh of the way down (keeping an eye on them for safety's sake), then snuff or blow them out. Pick up the deity images and let your feelings flow into them with thanks for the blessings you know they are sending you.

Do all this again for six more nights, each time moving the other candles a seventh of the way closer to the one representing you. On the seventh night, let the candles burn themselves out completely, watching carefully to prevent any accidents.

Wear the talisman whenever you leave your house and keep it next to the deity images at night.

For Courage and Protection Before Battle

Deity: Mithras, the Persian deity of soldiers.

Colors: Red and orange

Candles: One figure candle to represent yourself, one or more shorter taper candles to represent the "enemy."

Incense: Dragon's blood and myrrh

Time: On a Sunday afternoon or whenever needed.

Talisman: A small sword to be worn on a chain around your neck or a combat knife.

Intro: Whether we are unlucky enough to be going off to a war zone to fight for higher profits for Exxon and Haliburton, getting ready to play a rough sport, or just facing emotional battles ahead, we can all use a little extra courage and protection from time to time.

Practical Steps: First dress or visualize yourself as you expect to be dressed when going into battle. Do whatever physical exercises are appropriate to the type of battle expected. Once you've worked up a good sweat, do the following spell.

Procedure: You can place the smaller candles in a line "facing" the figure candle or in a circle around it, depending on how "surrounded" you expect to be. Light the incense and offer it to the deity image. Light the candles. Visualize Mithras watching as you stand facing the enemy. Then slowly recite the following poem ("A Song to Mithras" by Rudyard Kipling)[5] passing the talisman through the smoke as you say:

*Mithras, God of the Morning, our
    trumpets waken the Wall!
'Rome is above the Nations, but Thou art over all!'
Now as the names are answered, and the guards are
    marched away,
Mithras, also a soldier, give us strength for the day!*

*Mithras, God of the Noontide, the
    heather swims in the heat,
Our helmets scorch our foreheads, our sandals
    burn our feet.
Now in the ungirt hour, now ere we blink and drowse,
Mithras, also a soldier, keep us true to our vows!*

*Mithras, God of the Sunset, low on the
    Western main,
Thou descending immortal, immortal to rise again!
Now when the watch is ended, now when the wine is
    drawn,
Mithras, also a soldier, keep us pure till the dawn!*

*Mithras, God of the Midnight, here
    where the great bull dies,
Look on Thy children in darkness. Oh, take our
    sacrifice!*

Many roads Thou hast fashioned: all of them lead to
  the Light!
Mithras, also a soldier, teach us to die aright!

See the power of Mithras flowing into the talisman as you hold
it up, then use the talisman to snuff out the taper candles, just as
you will use your battle skills to defeat your enemies. Carry the
talisman with you when you go into battle and the blessings of
Mithras will strengthen and protect you.

To Improve Your Hunting (or Fishing)

Deity: Cernunnos (or Neptune)

Colors: Brown and green (or blue and green)

Candles: Two short (three-inch) tapers, one to represent yourself,
  one to represent the beasts (or fish) you are after. Carve an
  image of your quarry on its candle with a sharp knife or
  icepick.

Incense: Pine and dragon's blood for hunting, or lotus and sea-
  weed for fishing.

Time: Before going out to hunt or fish.

Talisman: A miniature bow, rifle, or rod and reel. A keychain
  decoration bought at a sporting shop will do.

Intro: Many men find hunting and fishing an important part of
  their life and we all know the vital role that "luck" plays in the
  processes. Most Paleopagan people believed that the coopera-
  tion of the deities was necessary for success in these activities.

Practical Steps: First learn how to use your weapons and/or tools
  properly, so that you may kill your quarry as quickly and pain-
  lessly as possible (to make an animal suffer needlessly is insult
  to the Gods and they will not bless your efforts in the future).
  Study where your quarry is most likely to be found, how to
  sneak up on it, and any other skills appropriate to reduce the

necessity for luck as much as you can. Dress or visualize your-self as you will be dressed when you go out to hunt or fish. Then do the following:

Procedure: Light the incense and offer it to the deity image. Light the candles. Visualize Cernunnos or Neptune watching as you pass the talisman through the smoke while you say:

Lord of the hunt (sea) hear my cry
Grant me success when next I try
To feed my family, that's my quest.
When in your realm I next am guest,.
Grant me cunning, luck, and stealth
So I may share of your great wealth.

Repeat this over and over until the candles burn out, creating a rich visualization of your success, then take the talisman with you when you go off to hunt or fish.

To Get Your Power Tools Returned

Deity: Hermes, the Greek deity of thieves, liars, businessmen, and lawyers.

Colors: Gold, red and black (SKIL™) or orange and black (Black & Decker™) or whatever colors your missing tools are.

Candles: One short taper to represent yourself, scored in thirds.

Incense: Frankincense, machine oil.

Time: On a Sunday, Monday, and Tuesday.

Talisman: Little drawing or photos of the missing tools, gold-colored thread.

Intro: We've all had it happen. A friend borrows our power drill or saw, uses it for a while, then forgets to bring it back. Usually they've borrowed other tools in the past and not returned them. You mention it to them, but they keep forgetting. Eventually, assuming we don't want to destroy the friendship, it's time for some magic.

Practical Steps: Obviously, this spell should only be done after you have exhausted other means of getting your tools back.

Procedure: Using a needle, attach each photo/drawing to one end of several inches of thread. Place your candle in the middle of the fireproof surface, with the tool talismans six inches away. Wind an inch or so of the threads around the base of the candle. Light the candle and the incense, offer the smoke to the deity image, and tighten the lines between the candle and your missing tools. Say the following:

Mighty Hermes, hear of my lack:
I lent my tools and I want them back!
Bear this message to my friend
The time to keep them is at an end.
Of this thought let him not be free
Until my tools come back to me.

Repeat this chant a total of three times. Let the candle burn one-third of its length, then put it out. Repeat this for two more nights, each time bringing the tool talismans closer to your candle. When the candle is almost gone, burn the talismans in the flame (without putting it out, if you can avoid it). Let the candle extinguish itself. Your tools should return within a week or so.

To Prevent or Cure Impotence

Deity: Priapus, the Roman god of penises. Any carved or painted phallus will do, if you can't find a Roman icon or statue.

Colors: Whatever color your wand is at full arousal (usually a purplish version of your regular skin color)

Candles: The thickest nine-inch taper you can get (any more would risk hubris).

Incense: Musk.

Time: During the dark of the moon and for eight nights afterwards.

Talismans: A small phallic charm (winged penis, Italian "figa," or piece of horn), a few really hot erotic images, some condoms.

Intro: The most important "power tool" to most men is the one between our legs. Unfortunately, sometimes the batteries run out or a bit gets bent out of shape. This spell will help you to get your wand back up and running smoothly.

Practical Steps: First, check to see if you have any medical conditions that could be causing your problems. Get plenty of rest and spend some time thinking about your partner and whether you *really* want to be making love to her/him (even Viagra™ doesn't work if you really don't want to be there).

Procedure: Carve a rounded head and tapered shaft into your candle so that it looks like a giant erect penis. Score or paint a mark every inch. Set the candle in the center of your fireproof surface, surrounded by the images and condoms. Light the incense, wave it around the deity image and your candle. Stroke the candle lovingly, as if you were masturbating it, then light it. Slowly repeat the following nine times:

> *Priapus, great god of the rooster*
> *Give my magic wand a booster!*
> *Heal all weakness and all curve*
> *So that my lovers I can serve.*
> *Lord of stiffness and of strength*
> *Increase its straightness and its length!*
> *Thrusting out from 'twixt my thighs*
> *To every challenge let it rise!*
> *And let it remain petrified*
> *Until my lust is satisfied*
> *And my lovers, filled with bliss,*
> *Thank me with a final kiss.*

Blow the candle out lovingly after it reaches the first line, say thanks to Priapus, then repeat the spell every night for the next eight nights. Carry the charged condoms with you or keep them by your bedside.

Note: Setting up a shrine to Aphrodite and Eros in your bedroom and lighting its candles and incense before lovemaking will also help you in this department.

CHAPTER 13

To Be a Pagan Man

To my mind the goal is to be the Avatar of your god, to be a clear channel so that to which you are devoted may become real and manifest. This can be done with every little task throughout the day whether you are making your bed or opening a door for someone. By making every greeting a blessing, a simple edict your ritual devotion, polite words incantations of blessings, you may harness your daily life as a constant rite.

—Kirk McLaren

Advice from Our Elders

Some of us Pagan guys have been around for a while. In the process of writing this book, I asked several of my older friends and colleagues what they would like to say to men about being Pagan, what they would say to Pagan women about their brothers, and anything else they wanted to share from their years of experience.

Skip Ellison is one of my successors as archdruid of Ár nDraíocht Féin: A Druid Fellowship and is the author of *The Druids' Alphabet*[1] and *The Solitary Druid*. A retired electrical engineer and a grandfather, he is working on new books about runic and other forms of divination:

As followers of Earth-based religions, we should think first
of the Earth and how she is treated. Do you recycle, drive a
fuel-efficient car and work to protect the environment? If
not, then doing any one, or better yet, all three will make a
difference to the world.

He went on to mention the importance of religious tolerance,
sharing your faith openly with the curious, and letting your local
elected officials know that you are Pagan and you vote!

Fred Lamond is the author of *Fifty Years of Wicca, Religion
without Beliefs,* and *The Divine Struggle,* and was one of Gerald
Gardner's last students:

I would tell any Pagan man: You are an incarnation of the
masculine divine or God, however you choose to name him.
Behave as such and radiate divine masculine energy to all
those whom you meet. Be proud of your body and keep it
fit, healthy, and attractive. Be proud of your feelings, mind,
and abilities. Enjoy and make the best use of them, both
professionally and in your private and family life!

Interestingly, as with some of the other sages I consulted, his
advice for Pagan women was nearly identical!

Searles O'Dubhain is a follower of the Druid Way and one of
the hosts of the Summerlands,[2] an online Pagan community with
over 1,500 members. He currently teaches courses in Celtic traditions and the use of ogham for divination. He has nine books in
varying stages of completion that serve as an introduction to
Druidism, Druidry, and Draíocht:

I'd tell future men in the Pagan movement to look within
themselves to discover just exactly who they are without
all the programming and biases that have influenced them
in modern life. I'd also tell them to ignore any gender
differences in the initial process (because most will discover
that they have what is considered masculine and feminine

personas in their many lives and existences). For the self and spirit, there is no gender difference in the ultimate analysis.

He went on to discuss how technology has changed gender roles from those of pretechnological times, as well as Pagan women's backlash against often innocent Pagan men. His advice to Pagan women is similar to Pagan men, with an extra suggestion that "keep in mind that the Pagan males of today can be your best allies in redefining and gaining the goals that you consider to be inherently due to you and your sisters."

Ramfis S. Firethorn is a science-fiction and murder-mystery writer, who has authored *Blindfold on a Tightrope: Men's Myths and Men's Mysteries,*[3] and is the founder of the Neopagan Greek temple Thiasos Olympikos, mentioned in chapter 2. When I asked him for some wisdom, he said:

> Why would anyone conceive that the Great Goddess would accept some sort of weakling or wimp as Consort? Surely, the Great Goddess must have as a Mate a Great God! Your role model must be that of equal, not subservient. Seek a partner, not a mommy.
>
> As for our sisters: Try to understand the positive side of men's passions. The desire to help and defend is a form of nurturing. It is hard for men to trust in a world where they have been taught by experience that they will always be betrayed.

The way to a man's heart, he added, "is not through his stomach, but through loyalty." Honor, a topic we have seen much discussed by men in this book, is "a quotient of trustworthiness." I would agree and add that honor is not just an obsession of men but, in Paleopagan times, was something that was just as important to women. The fact that the term has been severely twisted in monotheistic cultures (usually as an excuse for violence, often against women) does not mean that we Pagans cannot create our own codes of honor. Indeed, in this book we have seen Pagan men doing just that.

Oberon Zell-Ravenheart has been mentioned several times in this book. His thoughts were, as usual for him, long and complex. I hope he'll forgive me for boiling them down to their essence:

> Your Pagan sisters are the living avatars of the Goddess we all worship. So are all women, of course; but Pagan women are actively *conscious* of this fact, which makes all the difference in the world. . . . An essential teaching of Paganism is the value of diversity, and the cherishing of that which is different from yourself. Know that all that you are as a man—as the living avatar of the God—has its complement in your sisters, precisely because they *are* "other" than you.

He went on to emphasize the importance of partnership between male and female, yin and yang, each reflecting the immanent deity within the other. He talked about the deep inner need that women have to be "valued, cherished, respected, consulted, and listened to," whether their relationship to a man is romantic or not. "Women long to be loved, of course, but they also need to feel validated, seen, and appreciated." Respecting the inner goddess of every Pagan woman you interact with is the key:

> For here is the tragic inner secret of women: Deep within, nearly all of them do not know or believe that they are beautiful. . . . Thus the greatest gift you can give the Goddess— and the truest worship—is to invoke Her in the women you relate to. Be a mirror into which they may look to see the Goddess within them. Remind them constantly of who they truly are, and call them to manifest their divine essence.
>
> And through this, you will discover a depth and breadth of relationships and wholeness—with women, with the Goddess, with yourself—that is unimaginable to those who do not know this mystery.

Not surprisingly, his advice for our Pagan sisters was very similar: that they should see and appreciate the inner god within each of us, know that Pagan men are *conscious* of their inner gods, work with them as partners rather than as competitors, and so forth. "Men need love, too, of course, but they also need to feel needed, useful, and heroic."

Our tragic inner secret? "Deep within, nearly all of us do not know or believe that we are worthy," spending our lives trying to prove ourselves. The greatest gift our sisters can give the God is, naturally, to invoke him in the men they relate to, with the same benefits to be gained for the women who do so as for the men.

Is he working within a very heterosexual, Wiccan paradigm? Yes. But our species is composed of two major genders and most of his advice is easily adaptable to other erotic preferences and other spiritual paths of Paganism, for we all have divinities within us. Usually, deities whose gender matches our body's gender are the easiest to manifest and the easiest to worship. So whether you are Wiccan, Druidic, Asatruar, a Greek or Roman Reconstructionist, or a Buddheo-Pagan, Oberon's advice is well worth pondering.

Real Men, Real Pagans

What does it mean to be a man? Here are some of the questionnaire responses I received:

"To be born having male organs and to have the male spirit. To protect the women and children." (from a teen)

"Physical strength, fortitude, analytical thinking, protection, some aggression, stewardship, hunting, leadership."

"To be a man is to stand up for your values and to be loyal, protect and support your family, whether blood-related or chosen."

"The ability to have strength and knowledge and great enough wisdom to know the difference."

"Honor deity, avoid evil, live in courage. As the physical embodiment of the God I must stand strong and defend those weaker than myself from those who choose to live their lives without honor."

"Being a good husband and father. Representing the divine aspect of the father/warrior/hunter/sage."

"Chivalry and fatherhood." (another teen)

"The Nine Virtues of Asatru, to be loving, compassionate, to *think* before acting, to take full responsibility for all actions without flinching or making excuses."

"Is this a trick question?"

It certainly seems to be. We've seen these ideas repeated throughout this book, from many other men. A Pagan man named Daven offers these suggestions:

It takes a real man to admit he is wrong. A real man is a daddy, any fool can be a father. A real man keeps his commitments and honors his responsibilities. A real man makes his child laugh more than his child cries. A real man can fold his wife's underwear.[4]

Apparently, this list came to him while he was in a Laundromat, doing the family clothes, and noticed some of the men there looking at him in sympathy because he was folding bras and panties, "as if that somehow made me less of a man." He realized just how much time, effort, and energy most men invest in their illusions of macho.

Except for the polytheological references, however, most of the points mentioned earlier could be made by men of many different religions or none. Many Pagan and non-Pagan women would agree with most of them too. What can I add to this list of characteristics from my personal perspective as a Pagan man?

My Own Thoughts

A real man can change a diaper as easily as an oil filter, and sing a lullaby as easily as a patriotic anthem. Being able to nurture our sons and daughters shows our strength, not weakness.

A real man isn't afraid of homosexuals because, "if he doesn't like it, he can't have any."* Someone else's sexuality (or lack of it) does not affect my own and really is none of my business if I'm not planning to sleep with him or her.

A real man isn't afraid of feminists either, because he *is* one, in that he is willing to treat women as his equals in most situations—whether all the feminists he meets can figure it out or not. Of course, he may also expect them to change their own tires or take out the garbage now and then.

A real man gets his ideas of manhood from the gods—not from the mass media, his high school gym teacher, or his army drill sergeant. Whether his patron deity be Agni or Ptah, Apollo or Dionysus, or any of the other gods we've met in this book, *they* radiate his manhood within him.

A real man isn't afraid to say, "I don't know!" when he doesn't, or "I know the way!" when he (really) does—although I have learned never to say, "I know this road like the back of my hand!"† There's nothing unmanly about looking up information you don't currently have.

A real man loves strong women, whether as lovers or just as friends, because weak ones are boring, often parasitical, and make the worst exes.

---

*One of Oberon Zell-Ravenheart's best sayings.
†The last time I did, I had a head-on collision a few moments later!

A real man uses violence only when it is absolutely necessary to protect the helpless or the innocent, not for the convenience or profit of himself or others, and uses the minimum amount necessary to solve the problem—no more and no less.

A real man will risk his life to save a child, a handicapped or elderly person, or a woman who can't save herself, and do it quickly, effectively, and with minimum fuss.

So with all that said, what is a real *Pagan* man? My answer, and your indwelling god may tell you differently, is that it's any real man who worships the Gods, honors the Goddesses, and is willing to fight for truth, justice, and the Earth-centered way.

Changing Faiths, Changing Men

How will becoming a Pagan man change your ideas about manhood, compared to your earlier ones? One man told me, "I have started to take responsibility for my actions and have more respect for the world around me, as I see myself not being separate from nature but a part of it." This key Pagan belief will lead him to take more conscious action to preserve and defend the Earth Mother.

A Pagan teen said to me, "I now understand that there are 'men' well into their old age who aren't men—manhood is spiritual, not physical." We don't become men just by aging, but by deepening our spirituality in our daily life.

One man told me he had learned two major lessons by being a Pagan man. The first, "It's not necessary to adhere to some standard of intellectual or physical perfection." This alone can lessen stress on Pagan men and perhaps extend our lives. Since there are so many ways to manifest our indwelling gods, we have multiple options to show our different strengths. Nor do we need to be supermen of any sort. He added, "As a general rule, women will respect men who are reasonably sincere and reasonably mature. So will other men."

The second lesson, he explained, was that he was not required, "either by my own definition of manhood or by that of any woman I've met, to solve other people's problems for them." We don't always have to *fix* things for other people; people often want a sympathetic ear more than a solution. "When I was younger," he said, "I thought it was manly to fix people. Now I think it's manly to listen to them, and let them 'fix' themselves." There's another load off our backs!

Members of other faith traditions are often taught that being personally virtuous and praying for good things to happen is all they are expected to do. Pagan men learn that magical and spiritual rituals are hard work and require learning and practice to do effectively. Moreover, Pagan men learn that even the most powerful words must be matched with physical deeds and that sending vaguely positive energies out into the world does not stop war, heal broken ecosystems, or feed the hungry.

There is an old occult saying, about what magicians or wizards need to be able to do: "To know, to will, to dare, and to keep silence." Pagan men are updating this for an age in which they no longer need hide in fear from the forces of oppressive religions. Now, Pagan men *know* what they believe and why, and they study their particular Pagan paths well enough to be able to teach them to the curious or defend them to the hostile. It is their *will* to make their lives, the lives of their loved ones, their community, and the world at large better. Pagan men *dare* to take whatever actions are necessary to protect the innocent, to stop the forces of civil and environmental evil, and to defend their rights as Pagans and as men. Lastly, Pagan men *break the silence* that has long stifled Paganism, mainstream and minority sexualities and lovestyles, and the patriarchal "men's conspiracy" to suppress our sisters' freedom.

What Freedoms Do Pagan Men Gain?

I asked my questionnaire respondents this question and their answers were illuminating. Many emphasized the freedom of thought they had gained, saying things like, "Freedom from monotheist Christian tyranny" and "A freeing of my mind and soul." Others celebrated the weakening of what they had experienced as oppressive mainstream restrictions on their very souls. One said, "I have gained the freedom to explore not only my manhood but to see that there is an anima[5] as well." Another commented that he now had "some freedom to express my artistic/feminine side more without worrying that someone will think I'm gay." One gay man said he had, as a Pagan, gained "freedom from the oppressive Christian mind-set that characterized me as a second-class person when it afforded me personhood status at all."

As Kirk McLaren put it:

How we feel about the role of men in our society has changed a great deal over the last forty years. As women assert themselves in the workplace some men have responded as if threatened by their presence. At Pagan gatherings the opposite is true. In fact many facets of diversity are accepted. It is this positive reception that allows men and women alike to seek their true nature as themselves rather than to reduce their lives to a gender role. Men have much more to offer than the typical stereotype.

One man perhaps combined all of this when he told me that the greatest freedom he had gained as a Pagan was that of "knowing deep down that the children I've not had yet will be free to think for themselves and love as their hearts and minds choose."

What's the Best—and Worst—Thing About Being a Pagan Man?

I feel it's only fair to mention the downside as well as the upside of Pagan manhood. When I asked this question of Pagan men, I received many positive responses similar to those in the previous section. Others emphasized the fellowship of other Pagan men, the knowledge and wisdom gained in their Pagan studies, and the many enjoyable activities, including "meditation, fun, quietly contemplating the mysteries of the universe, folklore, divination, stories, music," and more.

Certainly, many Pagan men feel that the sexual freedom-with-responsibility they gained was a great benefit to their lives. One said, "By learning to honor the goddess in each woman, I find that I am surrounded by goddesses." Another was simply relieved that he no longer had to deal with religious dogmas about sexuality, but could steer his own path with the help of his inner god.

And the worst part of being a Pagan man? Most men who talked to me or answered my questionnaire mentioned the difficulty in finding other Pagan males except at festivals and conventions, the public perceptions of all Pagans as women, and the lack of books about Paganism for men. One rather philosophical man noted that he had "no 'revelation' to hide behind when making moral choices—I am a moral agent charged with full responsibility for all choices."

I discussed in the previous chapter some of the responses I received from many Pagan men about the negative ways they have been treated by some Pagan women. For the next ten years or so, until all the chips have been worn away from the shoulders of those carrying them, Pagan men will just have to be aware that we must *earn* the trust of certain Pagan women—or at least leave them alone to work out their issues while we get our own spiritual growth attended to.

One teenager told me that the best thing about being Pagan was "no clearly defined roles." He then said that this was also the worst thing to him! I hope that this book has helped to show some "clearly defined roles" that this lad and those who will follow him may explore.

Notes

Introduction

1. Copies were handed out at a large Pagan-friendly festival and a downloadable version was posted on my Web site, www.neopagan.net.

What Is Paganism?

1. From "We Won't Wait Any Longer," in *Wheel of the Year: the Music of Gwydion,* by Gwydion Penderwyn.

2. See Kerr Cuhulain's book, *Witch Hunts: Out of the Broom Closet,* for a discussion of several of these authors.

3. Some writers use a hyphen after the prefix and capitalize the second half, as in "Neo-Pagan."

4. A good argument can be made that Christianity itself started out Mesopagan, since it was a blend of monotheistic Judaism with Paleopagan ideas from Mithraism, Greek philosophy, and Gnostic dualism.

5. See my essay "How Many 'Pagans' Are There?" at www.neopagan.net/HowManyPagans.html

6. See www.gc.cuny.edu/faculty/research_briefs/aris/key_findings.htm for details.

7. These descriptions of Neopagan beliefs are highly condensed from my other works, including *Rites of Worship*.

Varieties of Modern Paganism

1.Spiritualism was started in New York in the nineteenth century as a blend of liberal Christianity with the results of rituals in which the dead were summoned to speak with the living through séances. This religion still exists today and can be seen as a Mesopagan religion in its own right (or rite), since it mixes Christianity with ancestor worship and necromancy, both Paleopagan customs.

2. See www.church-of-the-lukumi.org and www.orishanet.org for details.

3. Visit www.Voodoospiritualtemple.org (The Voodoo Spiritual Temple) to learn more.

4. See Lillith Dorsey's *Voodoo and Afro-Caribbean Paganism* and www.ifafoundation.org (Ifa Foundation of North America) for details.

5. One of the best resources for Heathenry on the Net is www.thetroth.org.

6. The ancient Norse peoples didn't have shamans as such, being agricultural and pastoral peoples rather than hunter-gatherers, but they apparently picked up the practices from the Sámi and other Finno-Ugaritic peoples.

7. See www.seidh.org for details.

8. See *The Way of the Heathen* by Garman Lord for details.

9. Visit www.oto-usa.org for details about these two movements.

10. See www.egyptianmuseum.org for details.

11. See www.cesidaho.org for more about CES.

12. See www.kemet.org and www.netjer.org for details. "Khem" was the ancient Egyptian name for Egypt, and "netjer" for deities.

13. See www.inkemetic.org for more. Kemet OnLine at www.kemetonline.com is also interesting.

14. For details see *Bonewits's Essential Guide to Druidism*.

15. See www.adf.org for more of this history.

16. See www.keltria.org for details about this group.

17. Carr-Gomm's books include *The Druid Renaissance, Elements of the Druid Tradition*, and *The Druid Way*.

18. See www.druidry.org for more about the OBOD.

19. See www.imbas.org for you know what.

20. At www.summerlands.com.

21. See Margot Adler's *Drawing Down the Moon* for details.

22. Their Web site is at homepage.mac.com/dodecatheon.

23. See istillworshipzeus.com/ for news and clips.

24. At www.hellenion.org.

25. At home.pon.net/rhinoceroslodge/thiasos.htm.

26. At www.ysee.gr.

27. See www.novaroma.org for details.

28. See www.romuva.lt.

29. At krugperuna.narod.ru—you'll need Russian to read it!

30. At www.geocities.com/gnievko/ and for this one, Polish.

31. At www.witchvox.com. Trust me, this one you will want to bookmark or even put on your browser bar!

32. There are hundreds of books now available on Wicca (a good fraction of which are worth reading), so I'm not going to spend much space here defining it, but will refer people to my book *Bonewits's Essential Guide to Witchcraft and Wicca* (or it's earlier incarnation, *Witchcraft: A Concise Guide*) for a useful overview. Most of the terms I'll be using in this discussion are self-explanatory.

33. These percentages are guesses, based on my research and personal experience—there are no reliable sources for Wiccan population figures and gender ratios, due to the underground nature of the movement for so many years.

34. *The Spiral Dance* doesn't actually have every or even most of the exercises beginning this way, but there are a couple near the front of the book that do. Certainly, the book is woman-centric.

35. See *Witchcraft and the Gay Counterculture* by Arthur Evans for the early arguments for this.

Where Do They Get Those Ideas?

1. An argument can be made that these were really Meso-pagan, because almost everything we *think* we know about ancient Greek and Roman religion we know because some monk, priest, or imam decided to *let* later generations know it. They decided which scrolls and manuscripts would be reproduced and exactly how each of the tales would be told.

2. Such as *King, Warrior, Magician, Lover : Rediscovering the Archetypes of the Mature Masculine* by Robert Moore and Douglas Gillette; *Gods in Our Midst* by Christine Downing; and *Gods in Everyman* by Jean Shinoda Bolen.

3. See the writings of Georges Dumézil and his followers for details on these three functions. They are vital for understanding the *real* Old Religions of Europe.

4. See Margot Adler's *Drawing Down the Moon*.

5. It had previously been used negatively by the Roman Catholic Church to describe Renaissance artists who were painting and carving Pagan deities, and then by them to describe the Nazi's racist pseudo-Paganism.

6. This quasi theology finally left the dualism behind in the early twenty-first century novels based on the movies, when the next generation of heroes realized that the Force was neutral and that it was one's intent that made it good or evil.

Founding Fathers

1. These tend to have a bad habit of taking their living subjects' word for various controversial claims without bothering to fact-check them, so take what they have to say with a small Siberian salt mine.

2. A new (and supposedly much better) translation was published in 1998 by Phoenix Publishing.

3. St. Martin's Press published a lovely reprint in 1990 of the 1915 edition.

4. Both of these are sublaws of the magical law of association (things associated with each other interact magically). See my *Real Magic* for a detailed discussion of these and the other laws of magic.

5. You may consult my *Bonewits's Essential Guide to Witchcraft and Wicca* for all the proofs that the religion was new, as well as the details about the matters mentioned in this paragraph.

6. Borrowing it from the writings of Dion Fortune, a well-known occultist of the time.

7. Although I have pointed out before that religions placing a heavy emphasis on magical or psychic activities usually wind up being run by women.

8. Which should be on the bookshelf of every male Wiccan.

9. The first federally recognized (501-c-3, 1972) Wiccan church in America.

10. See Long's *The Secret Science Behind Miracles* and other works for details on his theories about Hawaiian Paleopaganism, most of which were ludicrous by anthropological standards even in his day.

11. The ninth degree, that is. The tenth (national head) and twelfth (world head) degrees are mostly administrative, and the eleventh is outside of the normal structure of the OTO.

12. See his posthumous *Book of Druidry*, edited by John Matthews and Philip Carr-Gomm, and *In the Grove of the Druids* by Carr-Gomm.

13. See my *Bonewits's Essential Guide to Druidism* for more about the OBOD.

14. His recordings of the *Elder Edda* are available from the English record company D.U.R.T.R.O. (United Dairies) as "Cur-

rent 93 [a Thelemic reference] Presents Sveinbjörn Beinteinsson: The Eddas."

15. See their Web site at www.runestone.org.

16. Published by Xlibris and available at amazon.com.

Pagan Men as Priests and Wizards

1. His Web site is www.mcbridemagic.com, and his performances are not to be missed!

2. Many more details will be found in the works of Georges Dumézil, already mentioned.

3. See *Archaic Roman Religion* by Dumezil.

4. At least until the French Revolution made it heroic to be an intellectual.

5. "Priesthood Is a State of Being," posted at www.witchvox.com. Reprinted by permission.

6. Those familiar with the sad story of Saint Pierre Teilhard de Chardin, the Jesuit paleontologist who was silenced and banished to the Gobi Desert by the Roman Catholic Church for daring to support the theory of evolution, and then trying to reconcile it with Catholic doctrine, will understand.

7. See *The Way of Four* and *Elements of Ritual*, both of which I highly recommend. Naturally, she has a Web site at www.deborahlipp.com.

8. See my *Real Magic* and *Rites of Worship* for technical details on this.

9. See *Bonewits's Essential Guide to Druidism* for details on how to perform such rites, or visit the Web sites of ADF at www.adf.org or Keltria at www.keltria.org.

10. Although I've been told by some Santeria priests that they began speaking English occasionally back in the 1990s.

11. And in those tales where he is a true wizard, he accepts the wise woman as his equal and colleague. See *Equal Rites* by Terry Pratchet for details.

12. Oberon himself has tended to look more and more like a classic Renaissance wizard over the last decade or so and has even been known to dress like his predecessor, Leonardo da Vinci.

13. And it's a thousand times better than the misogynistic dreck to be found in Douglas Monroe's *21 Lessons of Hogwash* (more formally known as *21 Lessons of Merlyn*).

14. At www.greyschool.com.

15. My own work, *Real Magic,* may be of some use as well.

Pagan Men as Artists and Musicians

1. Find them at www.mythicimages.com.

2. He has a Web site at www.amuletsbymerlin.com, where you can see many of his pieces.

3. He has a Web site at www.waterhawkcreations.com, where you can see more pictures.

4. His art will be online by late 2005 at www.nybormystical art.org.

5. Posted at www.witchvox.com/xpaganmusic.html, used by permission.

6. The organization's Web site is www.sca.org.

7. Yes, they named the house after Tolkien's "last friendly house" of the elves, then named their next house that, too!

8. The words and music for most of the songs in these two albums were published in *Wheel of the Year,* which I had a hand in typesetting and laying out.

9. Their music catalog is at www.rosencomet.com/catalog/ tapes.

10. From *People of the Earth* by Ellen Evert Hopman and Lawrence Bond.

11. Also available from ACE.

12. Along with his wife, Sue Parker, he is the poet laureate of ADF, as well as one of its chief liturgists.

13. His Web site is www.paganmusic.co.uk and his albums can be purchased at www.bardicarts.com/Shop.htm.

14. Their Web site is wiccabilly.com.

15. From the satirical Church of the Subgenius; info at www.subgenius.com. Expect to be very confused.

16. A "heyoka" is a follower of a Lakota medicine path that involves doing things backward or opposite from the normal way to teach spiritual lessons.

17. He both played on and recorded my first album, *Be Pagan Once Again*, for me.

18. Their Web site is at www.rosencomet.com.

19. This book is filled with the magic and mystery of drumming and contains much good advice, not only on how to choose and consecrate a drum, then learn to play it, but also on how to participate in drum circles as fire tenders, dancers, drummers, or members of a supportive community.

20. Go to www.rosencomet.com/catalog/tapes/drumming-tapes. html for a selection of excellent ritual drum music from the Starwood Festivals.

Pagan Men as Warriors and Hunters

1. He is also the author of the forthcoming *Witch Hunts: Out of the Broom Closet* (about the corruption, fraud, and deceit of famous anti-occult crusaders).

2. From www.gladsheim.org, the Web site of the Gladsheim Kindred, "an independent Asatru kindred." Used by permission.

3. By Chris Blackfox, reprinted by permission from www. knightsofherne.org. See more about them in chapter 9 on Pagan men's groups.

4. Their Web site is www.officersofavalon.com.

5. See *The Selfish Gene* by Richard Dawkins.

6. See www.milpagan.org for a lot more info about Pagans in the military than I could possible put here.

7. There is an American Pagan Veterans Headstone Campaign being waged over this very issue. There is also a discussion group at groups. yahoo.com/group/American-Pagan-Veterans-Headstone-Campaign.

8. U.S. military forces have gone into combat over 100 times since the end of World War II. Only some of those occasions were morally defensible ones by Neopagan (or basic human rights) values, while the United States avoided moral obligations to stop genocide on more than one occasion, all for the benefit of conservative politicians and the corporations who own and operate them.

9. Posted as an open letter on the Pagans in the Military Web site, February 13, 2003.

10. Yes, I'm familiar with all the arguments in favor of vegetarianism, but the archaeological record is clear that humans evolved eating small amounts of meat and that a lack of meat meant death by malnutrition until modern times.

11. See the last thirty years' of feminist and antifeminist writings for the arguments.

12. Yes, humans (in very good shape) can catch running deer (or antelope) if they just keep chasing them until the four-legged is exhausted.

Pagan Men as Fathers

1. Yes, I know that adds up to more than 100 percent of those raising kids, but the answers overlapped.

2. See *Pagan Parenting* and *Pagan Homeschooling* by Kristin Madden, *The Family Wicca Book* by Ashleen O'Gaea, and *The Pagan Family* by Ceisiwr Serith for excellent ideas and tools for Pagan parents to use in raising their kids in their faith(s).

3. I wrote this for Arthur shortly after he was born and used it on many occasions to sing him to sleep. It appears on the *Avalon Is Rising!* album as "Bran's Lullaby."

4. Both are available from www.rosencomet.com/catalog/tapes/drumming-tapes.html, noted previously.

5. This song can be found on his album *Canticles of Light*.

6. Deborah and I even wrote a Pagan-friendly seder script the family used for a few years.

Pagan Men as Brothers

1. See my *Real Magic* for a discussion of the magical Law of Names and the Law of Words of Power.

2. See www.tuathadekelti.com for details.

3. As mentioned before, they can be found online at www.knightsofherne.org.

4. Available online at www.paganparenting.net, a marvelous resource for Pagan parents of all genders.

5. This is a subgroup within the larger Unitarian Universalist Association. See www.cuups.org for details.

6. www.triadcuups.org is its Web site, not too surprisingly.

7. Ironically, it appears that one of the first local Masonic lodges that met together with three others to form the first grand lodge in England in 1717 usually met in the same tavern, the Apple Tree, in which the founders of the Mesopagan Druid movement met—in that same year! Perhaps this is an early example of the modern saying that "Pagans do it in small circles!"

8. George Washington, Thomas Jefferson, Benjamin Franklin, and many of the other founding fathers of the American Revolution were Freemasons, as were those of the French Revolution. For a huge list of famous men who were Masons, visit www.masonic info.com/famous.htm.

9. In at least some French lodges there is no such requirement and some have female members.

10. One California lodge even let a Thelemite use a copy of Crowley's *Book of the Law* for his initiation!

11. And if you would prefer your Masonry to be co-ed, you might want to investigate Co-Masonry, which initiates both men and women. See www.comasonic.org for details.

Pagan Men as "Queers"

1. Much of this is related to mammalian power and status displays. The "top dog" is such because he has the power to mate, forcibly if he wishes, with all the other dogs, male and female.

2. Freyja's name is variously spelled Frigg, Frigga, and Fricka (all verbs for intercourse), as well as Frija. Not surprisingly, she is often confused with Freya (Lady), who is the sister and lover of Frey (Lord), especially since the two(?) goddesses share much symbolism as love, fertility, marriage, and childbirth deities.

3. See the full essay at www.seidh.org/articles/sex-status-seidh.html.

4. These were women trained to entertain men intellectually, similar in some ways to Japanese geishas.

5. This ritual has similarities to the ancient Irish one for inaugurating a high king, involving him mating with a live mare, who was then sacrificed and eaten by the king.

6. For more examples, see *Cassell's Encyclopedia of Queer Myth, Symbol, and Spirit: Gay, Lesbian, Bisexual, and Trangender Lore* by Randy P. Conner, David Hatfield Sparks, and Mariya Sparks.

7. Penczak is also the author of *Sons of the Goddess* (my original title for this book!), *City Magick, Spirit Allies,* and others.

8. See my *Real Magic* and *Rites of Worship* for details.

9. Their Web site is www.adf.org/members/sigs/purple-feather/, but you have to join ADF to read it.

10. One of the best known is the Thiasos Olympikos, which can be found at home.pon.net/rhinoceroslodge/thiasos.htm.

Pagan Men, Pagan Women, and Sex

1. See chapter 13 for several other answers to those questions.

2. You can meet them at www.mysticwicks.com.

3. In an essay by her titled "A Bouquet of Lovers," originally published in *Green Egg* magazine. It is available online at www. caw.org/articles/bouquet.html and in print as part of *Polyamory: The New Love without Limits* by Deborah Anapol.

4. *Loving More: The Polyfidelity Primer* by Ryam Nearing will make the distinctions between the two clear.

5. A good introduction to the joys and woes of polyamory is *The Ethical Slut: A Guide to Infinite Sexual Possibilities* by Dossie Easton and Catherine A. Lisz.

6. Actually, they've been there all along, all the way back to Gerald Gardner, they just were a lot more private about it, for fear of harassment from their fellow Pagans.

Pagan Men and Ritual

1. The proportion is usually expressed as 1:φ (that's the Greek letter phi) or roughly 1:1.618. Cutting a square equal to the short side out of the rectangle will leave another smaller rectangle with the same proportions as the larger one. The followers of the philosopher-mystic Pythagoras believed that this proportion had great mystical and aesthetic power.

2. Although this is a Greco-Roman style of ritual, it would be easily adaptable to the worship of any culture that used temples, which includes most Indo-European and Asian ones, as well as some Native American ones.

3. This is one of the many reasons that terrorism is viewed with both contempt and fear, because it doesn't give its victims a chance to psyche themselves up for possibly dying or retaliating if they are warriors.

4. Janet and Stewart Farrar's *The Witches' God* and Aleister

Crowley's 777 will provide plenty of other deities who might be appropriate. The latter will also help with color and incense choices, as will the works of Scott Cunningham.

5. From *Puck of Pook's Hill*, published 1906. If you would like to sing it, look for an album called *Cold Iron* by Leslie Fish.

To Be a Pagan Man

1. An excellent book on ogham, the ancient Irish alphabet used for both writing and divination.

2. www.summerlands.com is where you'll find them.

3. This is really a great book on the topic and I highly recommend it.

4. Daven of www.davensjournal.com. All rights reserved.

5. The Jungian idea that all men have an internal female spirit (all women have an internal male one, the animus).

Bibliography

The following books may be of special interest to Pagan men. Some of them were mentioned in this book, others are classics of male literature, some are just amusing. I'm leaving out some Wiccan titles mentioned in the text, unless they are of particular interest to males as males, as they can be found in the bibliographies of hundreds of Wiccan books.

Adler, Margot. *Drawing Down the Moon.* Beacon Press, 1986.

Anapol, Deborah. *Polyamory: The New Love without Limits.* Intinet Resource Center, 1997.

Bishop, Beata, and Pat McNeill. *Eggshell Ego.* Enslow, 1979. (Published in England in 1977 as *Below the Belt*)

Bly, Robert. *Iron John.* Addison-Wesley, 1990.

Bolen, Jean Shinoda. *Gods in Everyman.* Quill, 1990.

Bonewits, Isaac. *Authentic Thaumaturgy.* Steve Jackson Games, 1998.

_____. *Bonewits's Essential Guide to Druidism.* Citadel Press, 2006.

———. *Bonewits's Essential Guide to Witchcraft and Wicca.* Citadel Press, 2006.

———. *Real Magic.* Weiser, 1989.

———. *Rites of Worship*. Earth Religions Press, 2004.

Carr-Gomm, Philip. *Druid Mysteries*. Rider, 2002.

———. *In the Grove of the Druids*. Watkins, 2002.

———. *The Rebirth of Druidry*. Thorsons, 2003.

Connor, Randy P., David Hatfield Sparks, and Mariya Sparks. *Cassell's Encyclopedia of Queer Myth, Symbol, and Spirit: Gay, Lesbian, Bisexual, and Transgender Lore*. Cassell, 1997.

Crowley, Aleister. *The Book of the Law* (100th anniversary edition). Red Wheel–Weiser, 2004.

Cuhulain, Kerr. *Full Contact Magic*. Llewellyn Publications, 2002.

———. *Law Enforcement Guide to Wicca*. Horned Owl Publishing, 1997.

———. *The Wiccan Warrior*. Llewellyn Publications, 2000.

———. *Witch Hunts: Out of the Broom Closet*. Spiral Publishing, 2005.

Dawkins, Richard. *The Selfish Gene*. Oxford University Press, 1990.

Dorsey, Lillith. *Voodoo and Afro-Caribbean Paganism*. Citadel Press, 2005.

Downing, Christine. *Gods in Our Midst*. Crossroad, 1993.

Drew, A. J. *Wicca for Men*. Citadel Press, 1998.

———. *Wicca Spellcraft for Men*. New Page Books, 2001.

Dumezil, Georges. *Archaic Roman Religion*. Johns Hopkins University Press, 1996.

———. *The Destiny of a King*. University of Chicago Press, 1988.

———. *Loki*. Flammarion, 1997.

———. *The Plight of a Sorcerer*. University of California Press, 1986.

———. *The Stakes of the Warrior*. University of California Press, 1983.

Easton, Dossie, and Catherine A. Lisz. *The Ethical Slut: A Guide to Infinite Sexual Possibilities*. Greenery Press, 1998.

Ellison, Skip. *The Solitary Druid.* Citadel Press, 2005.

Evans, Arthur. *Witchcraft and the Gay Counterculture.* Fag Rag Books, 1981.

Farrar, Stewart, and Janet Farrar. *The Witches' God.* Phoenix Publishing, 1989.

Firethorn, Ramfis S. *Blindfold on a Tightrope.* Xlibris, 2001.

Frazer, Sir James. *The Golden Bough.* St. Martin's Press, 1990.

Hopman, Ellen Evert, and Lawrence Bond. *People of the Earth.* Destiny Books, 1996.

Hutton, Ronald. *The Triumph of the Moon.* Oxford University Press, 2001.

———. *Witches, Druids, and King Arthur.* Hambledon and London, 2003.

Klein, Kenny. *The Flowering Rod.* Delphi Press, 1993.

Kraig, Donald Michael. *Modern Magick.* Llewellyn Publications, 1992.

Lamond, Frederick. *Fifty Years of Wicca.* Green Magic, 2004.

Lawlor, Robert. *Earth Honoring.* Inner Traditions, 1991.

Lipp, Deborah. *Elements of Ritual.* Llewellyn Publications, 2003.

———. *The Way of Four.* Llewellyn Publications, 2002.

Littleton, G. Scott. *The New Comparative Mythology.* University of California Press, 1982.

Long, Max Freedom. *The Secret Science behind Miracles.* 2nd ed. Huna Research Publications, 1954.

Madden, Kristin. *Pagan Homeschooling.* Spilled Candy Books, 2002.

———. *Pagan Parenting.* Spilled Candy Books, 2004.

Moore, Robert, and Douglas Gillette. *King, Warrior, Magician, Lover: Rediscovering the Archetypes of the Mature Masculine.* HarperSanFrancisco, 1991.

Moss, Harold. *Politics, Religion, and Sex.* Pasigram, 1996.

Nearing, Ryam. *Loving More: The Polyfidelity Primer.* Pep Publishing, 1992.

Nichols, Ross. *The Book of Druidry.* Thorsons Publishers, 1992.

Paxson, Diana. *Asatru and Northern Paganism.* Citadel Press, 2005.

Pearson, Carol S. *Awakening the Heroes Within.* HarperSan-Francisco, 1991.

Penczak, Christopher. *Gay Witchcraft.* Red Wheel–Weiser, 2003.

——. *Sons of the Goddess.* Llewellyn Publications, 2005.

Penderwyn, Gwydion. *Wheel of the Year.* Nemeton, 1979.

Pratchet, Terry. *Equal Rites.* Harper Torch, 2000.

Richardson, Alan. *Earth God Rising.* Llewellyn Publications, 1991.

Saemundar, Edda. *The Poetic Edda* (Oxford World Classics). Oxford University Press, 1999.

Serith, Ceisiwr. *The Pagan Family.* Llewellyn Publications, 1994.

Starhawk. *The Spiral Dance* (20th anniversary edition). Harper-SanFrancisco, 1999.

Sturlson, Snorri. *The Prose Edda.* Everyman's Library, 1995.

Telesco, Patricia, and Don Two Eagles Waterhawk. *Sacred Beat.* Red Wheel–Weiser, 2003.

Zell-Ravenheart, Oberon. *Grimoire for the Apprentice Wizard.* New Page Books, 2004.

Online Resources

Here are all of the Web sites mentioned in the Notes, all in one place for you. Be aware that there are tens of thousands of Pagan Web sites out there, hundreds of which are worth investigating. Visiting just the following, however, and reading all their materials should keep you busy for quite some time!

Note, all of these Web site addresses were good as of August 2005, and almost all of them should still be working for another few years.

GENERAL PAGAN INTEREST
www.witchvox.com ~ The Witches' Voice
www.gc.cuny.edu/faculty/research_briefs/aris/key_findings.htm ~ City University of New York's American Religious Identification Study
www.mysticwicks.com ~ Mystic Wicks

AFRICAN DIASPORIC PAGANISM
www.church-of-the-lukumi.org ~ Church of the Lukumi Babalu Aye (Santeria)
www.voodoospiritualtemple.org ~ Voodoo Spiritual Temple
www.orishanet.org ~ Orisha Net
www.ifafoundation.org ~ Ifa Foundation of North America

NORSE/GERMANIC PAGANISM/HEATHENISM

www.thetroth.org ~ The Troth
www.seidh.org ~ Seeing for the People (Seidh Site)
www.gladsheim.org ~ Gladsheim Kindred
www.runestone.org ~ Asatru Folk Assembly
www.geocities.com/theodish_belief ~ Gering Theod (Theodish Belief)

EGYPTIAN PAGANISM

www.oto-usa.org ~ Ordo Templi Orientis and Gnostic Catholic Church
www.egyptianmuseum.org ~ AMORC Egyptian Museum
www.cesidaho.org ~ Church of the Eternal Source
www.kemet.org ~ Kemetic Orthodox Faith
www.inkemetic.org ~ International Network of Kemetics
www.kemetonline.com ~ Kemet OnLine
www.netjer.org ~ House of Netjer

DRUIDISM, DRUIDRY, AND DRUIDECHT

www.adf.org ~ Ár nDraíocht Féin: A Druid Fellowship
www.adf.org/members/sigs/purple-feather ~ "Queer" ADFers (must get there via closed membership pages)
www.keltria.org ~ Henge of Keltria
www.druidry.org ~ Order of Bards Ovates and Druids
www.imbas.org ~ Imbas
www.summerlands.com ~ Summerlands

HELLENIC/GREEK AND ROMAN PAGANISM

homepage.mac.com/dodecatheon ~ Dodecatheon
istillworshipzeus.com ~ I Still Worship Zeus
www.hellenion.org ~ Hellenion
home.pon.net/rhinoceroslodge/thiasos.htm ~ Thiasos Olympikos
www.novaroma.org ~ Nova Roma

BALTIC AND SLAVIC PAGANISM
www.romuva.lt ~ Lietuvos Romuva (Lithuanian)
krugperuna.narod.ru ~ Krug Peruna (Russian)
www.geocities.com/gnievko ~ Rodzimy Kosciól Polski (Polish)

OTHER MISCELLANEOUS PAGANISMS
www.caw.org ~ Church of All Worlds
www.subgenius.com ~ Church of the Subgenius
www.cuups.org ~ Covenant of Unitarian Universalist Pagans

ARTISTS AND PERFORMERS
www.mythicimages.com ~ Mythic Images
www.amuletsbymerlin.com ~ Amulets by Merlin
www.waterhawkcreations.com ~ Waterhawk Creations
www.nybormysticalart.org ~ Nybor Mystical Art
www.mcbridemagic.com ~ McBride Magic
www.rosencomet.com/catalog/tapes ~ The Association for Consciousness Exploration's bardic and drum tapes catalog
www.paganmusic.co.uk ~ Damh the Bard
www.bardicarts.com/Shop.htm ~ Bardic Arts Shop
wiccabilly.com ~ Loke E. Coyote's Wiccabilly Circus

MEN'S GROUPS
www.knightsofherne.org ~ Knights of Herne
www.tuathadekelti.com ~ Tuatha de Kelti
www.masonicinfo.com/famous.htm ~ Famous Masons
www.comasonic.org ~ Order of International Co-Freemasonry (co-ed)

MILITARY AND POLICE
www.officersofavalon.com ~ Officers of Avalon
www.milpagan.org ~ Military Pagan Network
groups.yahoo.com/group/American-Pagan-Veterans-Headstone-Campaign ~ American Pagan Veterans Headstone Campaign

OTHER MISCELLANEOUS GROUP SITES MENTIONED

www.rosencomet.com ~ Association for Consciousness Exploration

www.greyschool.com ~ Grey School of Wizardry

www.sca.org ~ Society for Creative Anachronism

PAGAN PARENTING RESOURCES

www.spiralscouts.org ~ Spiral Scouts

www.paganparenting.net ~ Pagan Parenting

groups.yahoo.com/groups/Pagan_Parent ~ a Pagan parenting e-list (there are other, local, ones at Yahoo Groups too).

INDIVIDUALS' WEB SITES

www.davensjournal.com ~ Daven

www.deborahlipp.com ~ Deborah Lipp

www.neopagan.net ~ Isaac Bonewits

Index

Abbott, Stephen, 61–62
Adams, Frederick, 30
Adler, Margot, 133
Aed, 77
African Diasporic Paganism (Pagans), 14–18
  homosexuality in, 161
  manhood ideals of, 45–46
  priests in, 81
  Web sites, 239–40
Afterlife, 11
AIDS, 175–76
Akhenaten, 24
Alan, Todd, 107
Altars, 184–85
  ancestor, 191–94
Analog, 97
Ancestor invocation, 191–94
Ancient Druid Order (ADO), 62
Ancient Mystic Order Rosae Crucis, 25
Anderson, Victor, 60, 101
Animal sacrifices, 17
Aphrodite, 199–201
Apollo, 39, 157
Aradia, or the Gospel of the Witches (Leland), 51
Archetypes
  of manhood, 39–49
  of warriors, 114–16
Ár nDraíocht Féin: A Druid Fellowship (ADF), 28–29, 74, 160, 208
Artemis, 157
Arthurian myths, 41–42
"Arthur's Lullaby" (song), 130
Arts (artists), 87–98. *See also* Bards; *and specific artists*

Asatru, xii, 21, 63–64
  Nine Virtues of, 116–17
Asatru Folk Assembly, 64
Asatru Free Assembly (AFA), 64
Association for Consciousness Exploration (ACE), 104–5, 107
Astarte, 153
Athena, 104
Aubrey, John, 27
Avalon Is Rising!, 104
Avoidance of harm, 175–76
Aztecs, 19, 155

Baal, 157
Baltic and Slavic Paganism, 32–33
  Web sites, 241
Barbarians, 116–19
Bardic Circles, 100–101
Bards, 98–107
Beinteinsson, Sveinbjörn, 63–64
Beliefs of Pagans, 8–12, 170
Be Pagan Once Again!, 104
Bible, 148, 153–54
Bibliography, 235–38
Bisexuality, 153–54, 155–56
Blackfox, Chris, 137–38, 145–46, 147–48
Blackstone, Tracy, 100
Blindfold on a Tightrope (Firethorn), 210
Blue Knight, 107
Bondage and discipline (B&D), 176–77
Bone, Gavin, 56–57
Bonewits, Phaedra Heyman, 109, 111
Book of Shadows (Gardner), 34, 55
Book of Shadows (Lady Sheba), 59
Botkin, Gleb, 30

Brotherhood. *See* Men's groups
Buckland, Raymond, 57
*Buckland's Complete Book of
    Witchcraft,* 57
Buddheo-Pagans, 5–6
Buddhism, 3, 5–6, 154
Building the Temple of the Gods,
    184–91
"Burning Times" (song), 104

Campbell, Joseph, 48
Candles, for spells, 197
Candomble, 15–16
Carnivores, 123–25
Carr-Gomm, Philip, 29, 63
Celtic Tribe (Tuatha de Kelti), 143–45
Celts, 25–30, 41, 69–70. *See also*
    Druidism/Druidry/Druidecht
    use of term, 25–26
Centaurs, 157
Cernunnos, 88–89, 197
    spell for improving hunting and fish-
        ing, 203–4
Chango, xi–xii
Charity, 118, 119
Chief Seattle, 19
Child raising. *See* Fatherhood
Chin, 155
Chivalry, 42, 117–19, 145, 146
Christianity, 3, 4, 15, 16, 21, 26–27,
    41–42, 70–72, 148, 153–54, 221*n*
Christie, Lance, 47
Church of All Worlds (CAW), 4, 47,
    65, 160
Church of Aphrodite, 30
Church of the Eternal Source, 25,
    64–65
Classifications of Pagans, 3–8
Code of Chivalry, 118–19, 146
Coitophonic, 107
Committee for the Hellenic Religion of
    Dodecatheon, 30–31
Contraception, 175–76
Conversation, in men's groups, 142–43
Cops (police officers), 115, 119–20
    Web sites, 242
Corrigan, Ian, 105
Council of American Witches, 59
Courage, 116
    spell for, 201–3

Covenant of Unitarian Universalist
    Pagans (CUUPS), 147
Covens, 75–77
Coyote, 93
Crafting the Art of Magic (Kelly), 61
Crowley, Aleister, 24, 34, 52–54, 61–62
Cuhulain, Kerr, 114–15, 221*n*
Cunningham, Scott, 60
Cunning men, 81
CUNY's (City University of New
    York) American Religious
    Identification Study, 7
Cybele, 153

Dagda, 92, 197
    Shield of the, 194–96
Dalai Lama, 154
Damh the Bard, 105–6
Dancing (dancers), 107–11
Daven, 213
DeCles, Jon, 100
Defense, 118
Definitions of Paganism (Pagans), 1–2
Demeter, 150
Devil, 9, 16
Diet, 123–25
Dionysus, 39
Discipline, 117
Discordianism, 4
Divination, 10–11, 79–80, 208–9
Divinity, 8–9, 170
Domination and submission (D&S),
    176–77
Draconis, Zalon, 114
Dragon's blood, 197
Drawing down the moon, 76–78
Drawing Down the Moon (Adler), 133
Druidism/Druidry/Druidecht (Druids),
    4–5, 26–30, 209–10
    bards, 98–102
    founding fathers of, 62–63
    manhood ideals of, 41
    priesthood in, 69–70, 71, 73–74,
        79–80
    Web sites, 240
Druids' Alphabet, The (Ellison), 208
Drumming (drummers), 107–11
Dualism, 3–4, 9, 12–13, 35–36,
    148–49, 154, 224*n*
Dumézil, Georges, 224*n*

Earth Drum Council, 109
Earth Mother, 9–10, 65
Eddas, 21, 64
Egyptian Paganism (Pagans), 23–25
    founding fathers of, 25, 53, 64–65
    priesthood in, 80
    Web sites, 240
El-Dabh, Halim, 107–9
Eleusinian Mysteries, 66
Ellegua, 16
Ellison, Skip, 208–9
Enkidu, 153
Eosinophilia-Myalgia Syndrome,
    xv–xvi
Epic of Gilgamesh, 153
Eros, 199–201
Ethical Slut, The (Easton and Lisz),
    232*n*
Ethics and morality, 10, 170–71
Europa, 157
Evans, Arthur, 158–59
Evil, 9, 12
Exu (Eshu), 16

Fairy Shaman, The (Penderwen), 101
Fairy Wicca, 36, 60, 101
Farrar, Janet, 56–57
Farrar, Stewart, 56–57
Fatherhood (fathers), 127–36
    author's experience of, 129–36
Feminists, Pagan men as, 163–66,
    214–15
Feminist Wiccans (Wicca), 33–37, 159,
    165–66
Feraferia, 30
Fidelity, 117
Figure candles, 197
Fire dancing (jumping), 111, 166–69
Firefighters, 119–20, 242
Firethorn, Ramfis S., 31–32, 210–11
First Law of Sex, 170
Fishing, 123–25
    spell to improve, 203–4
Founding fathers, 50–66
Four Pillars of Knighthood, 146
Fraternal organizations, 150–51. *See
    also* Masons
Frazer, James, 51–52
Freedom, 11, 217
Freemasonry, 4, 24, 148–50, 230–31*n*

Friends, spell to make new Pagan,
    198–99
Frost, Gavin, 58
Frost, Yvonne, 58

Gagne, James, 107
Gaia
    Millennial (statue), 89–91, *90*
    spell to make new Pagan friends,
        198–99
Gaia thesis, 9–10, 65, 89–90
Gandalf, 44
Ganesh, 155
Ganymede, 157
Gardner, Gerald Brousseau, 34, 53,
    54–55, 61, 71–72, 75
Gay Paganism. *See* Queer Paganism
Gay Witchcraft (Penczak), 158
Gender equality, 8–9, 12, 163–66,
    214–15
Gender roles, xiii–xiv, 8–9, 36–37,
    163–69. *See also* Manhood; Sex
    and sexuality
    energy manipulation and, 183
Germanic Paganism. *See*
    Norse/Germanic Paganism
Germer, Karl, 61–62
Ghost Dance, 19
Gilchrist, James, 107
Gillette, Douglas, 82–83, 115
Gnostica, 59, 61
Gnostic Catholic Church, 24
Gods and goddesses, 8–9. *See also
    specific deities*
Golden Bough, The (Frazer), 51–52
Golden Dawn, 24, 53, 61
Golden Rectangle, 184, 232*n*
Grange, the (Patrons of Husbandry),
    150–51
Graves, Robert, 34, 54
Greek and Roman Paganism (Pagans),
    30–32, 150–51
    homosexuality in, 156–57, 161
    manhood ideals of, 39–40
    priesthood in, 69–70
    Web sites, 241
Greek Orthodox Church, 30–31
Green Egg, 65, 89, 97, 145
Green Tara, 6

Grey Council, 84–85
Grey School of Wizardry, 84
Grimoire for the Apprentice Wizard (Zell-Ravenheart), 84–85
Guenevere, 41–42
Gypsies, 24

Habondia, 88–89
Hades, 76
Hardin, Tim, 103
Harm avoidance, 175–76
Harrison, Donald, 25
Harry Potter books, 82, 84
Hasidic Druids of North America (HDNA), 28
Hawaiian Paleopaganism, 225n
Heathenism, 20–23, 222n
  Web sites, 240
Heidrick, William, 62
Heinlein, Robert, 47
Hellenic Paganism. *See* Greek and Roman Paganism
Hellenion, 31
Henge of Keltria, 28–29
Hera, 157
Heracles, 40
Hermes, 39
  spell for return of powers tools, 204–5
Hermes Council, xii, 138–43
Hermetic Order of the Golden Dawn (HOGD), 24, 53
Herne's Apprentice, 106
High priests/priestesses, 75–78
Hijras caste, 154, 155
Hills They Are Hollow, The, 106
Hinayana Buddhism, 5
Hinduism, 3–4, 154, 155, 157
Hitler, Adolf, 21–22
Hobbit, The (Tolkien), 43–44
Holy Grail, 41
Homophobia, 159, 161
Homosexuality. *See* Queer Paganism
Honor, 48–49, 116, 119, 210–11
Horned God, 76–77, 146
Hospitality, 117
Humility, 118, 119
Hunting (hunters), 123–25
  spell to improve, 203–4
Hyacinth, 157
"Hymn to the Dagda" (song), 103–4

Ian Corrigan Live at Starwood, 105
Iceland, 21, 63–64
Ifa, 16–17
Imbas, 29
Impotence, spell to prevent or cure, 205–7
Independent Order of Odd Fellows, 150
Industriousness, 117
Informed consent, 173–74
Initiations, 57, 149–50
International Network of Kemetics, 25
Iraq War, 122
Ishtar, 153
Ishvara, 155
Islam, 3, 4, 7, 16, 23, 148, 153–54
I Still Worship Zeus (movie), 31

Jackson, Peter, 44–45
Jason, 40
Jefferson, Thomas, 148
Jesus Christ, 154
Judaism, 153–54
Julius Caesar, 69
Jung, Carl, 192
Justice, 118–19

Karma, 10
Kelly, Aidan, 61
Kemetic (Egyptian) Orthodox Faith, 25
King, Warrior, Magician, Lover (Moore and Gillette), 82–83, 115
Kipling, Rudyard, 34, 202–3
Knighthood (knights), 116–19
  Code of Chivalry, 118–19, 146
Knights of Columbus, 145
Knights of Herne, xi, 118–19, 145–48
Knights of Pythias, 150
Knights Templar, 145
Knob candles, 197
Krishna, 155
Krug Peruna, 32

Lady Sheba, 59
Lamond, Fred, 209
Lancelot, 41–42
Larson, Robert, 73–74
Law enforcement, 115, 119–20
  Web sites, 242

Law Enforcement Guide to Wicca
    (Cuhulain), 115
Law of Names, xiii
Leather activities, 176–77
Leda, 157
Leland, Charles Godfrey, 34, 51
Leviticus, 153–54
"Light is Returning" (song), 132
Lipp, Deborah, 74, 129–32, 170n.
Lipp-Bonewits, Arthur, 124n., 129–36,
    140–41, 173–74
Living Wicca (Cunningham), 60
Llewellyn Publications, 59
Loke E. Coyote's Wiccabilly Circus,
    106
Lord, Garman, 23
Lord of the Rings, The (movie), 44–45
Lord of the Rings, The (Tolkien),
    43–44
Lovelock, James, 65
Lovers, spell to attract new Pagan,
    199–201
Loyalty, 118
Lucumi, 16, 81
Lunar cycles, 11
Lupercalia, xi
Luther, Martin, 5, 71–72

McLaren, Kirk, 91–95, 137, 142,
    143–45, 208, 217
McMurtry, Grady, 61–62
McNallen, Steve, 64
Macumba, 15–16, 161
Magic, 10–11. *See also* Rituals; Spells
    definition of, 182
    sex, 179–81
Magical/psychic protection, 194–96
Mahayana Buddhism, 5, 6
Mana, 183
Manhood (masculinity), 39–49,
    214–16, 218
    African and Native American influ-
        ences on, 45–46
    European influences on, 39–45
    fantasy and science-fiction influences
        on, 43–45, 46–48
Martial arts, 115–16
Maslow, Abraham, 47
Masons, 4, 24, 148–50, 230–31n.
Mayans, 155

Meat eaters, 123–25
Men's groups, 137–51
    Hermes Council, 138–43
    Knights of Herne, 118–19, 145–48
    Masons, 24, 148–50
    Tuatha de Kelti, 143–45
    Web sites, 241–42
Merlin, 41–42, 44
Mesopaganism (Mesopagans), 3–5,
    7–8
    beliefs, 8–12
    manhood ideals of, 39–49
    varieties of, 14–38
Military, 115, 120–22, 229n
    Web sites, 242
Military Pagan Network, 120–21, 122
Millennial Gaia (statue), 89–91, *90*
Minotaur, 157
Mithras, 201–3
Monotheism, 3–4
Moore, Robert, 82–83, 115
Morning Glory Ferns Zell-Ravenheart,
    65–66, 88–89, 172, 177
Moss, Harold, 25, 64–65
Mother Nature, 9–10, 65
Muhammad, 154
Murphy, Charlie, 104, 132
Murray, Margaret, 102–3
Music (musicians), 98–107
Mythic Images, 89
Myths (mythology) of manhood,
    39–49

Name changes, xiii
Native American religions, 18–20,
    45–46, 155
Neopaganism (Neopagans), 4–5, 7–8
    beliefs, 8–12
    manhood ideals of, 39–49
    varieties of, 14–38
New Reformed Druids of North
    America (NRDNA), 28
New Reformed Orthodox Order of the
    Golden Dawn, 61
Nichols, Ross, 29, 62–63
Nine Virtues of Asatru, 116–17
Nondiscrimination policies, 161
Norse/Germanic Paganism (Pagans),
    20–23
    founding fathers of, 63–64

Norse/Germanic Paganism (*cont.*)
  homosexuality in, 155–56, 161
  manhood ideals of, 40, 116–17
  priesthood in, 70–72, 80
  Web sites, 240
Nova Roma, 32
Nybor (James R. Odbert), 97–98
Nybor Tarot, 97

Odin, 155
Odinson, Aidan, 72, 74
O'Dubhain, Searles, 30, 209–10
Odysseus, 40
Officers of Avalon, 119
Once Around the Wheel, 105
Order of Bards Ovates and Druids
  (OBOD), 29, 62–63
Ordo Templi Orientis (OTO), 24,
  61–62
Orgies, 179–80
Original sin, 8, 130
Orthodox Druids of North America
  (ODNA), 28
Osirus, 153

Pagan Headstone Campaign, 229*n*
Paganism (Pagans)
  beliefs, 8–12
  definitions of, 1–2
  founding fathers, 50–66
  historical categories of, 3–8
  manhood ideals of, 39–49
  varieties of modern, 14–38
Pagan Religion and Spiritual Directory,
  32–33
Paleopaganism (Paleopagans), 3–6
  manhood ideals of, 39–45
Palo Mayombe, 15–16
Pan, 157
"Papa's Gonna Conjure" (song), 131
Paramedics, 119–20, 242
Parenting issues, 127–36
Parthenon (Athens), 184
Patrons of Husbandry (the Grange),
  150–51
Paxson, Diana L., 21–22, 100, 155–56
Penczak, Christopher, 158
Penderwen, Gwydion, 101–2
People of the Purple Feather, 160
Persephone, 76

Perseverance, 117
Police (police officers), 115, 119–20
  Web sites, 242
Politics, Religion, and Sex (Moss), 65
Polyamory, 66, 171, 177–79, 232*n*
Polyfidelity, 177–79
Polymorphous perversity, 155–58
Polytheism, 3–4, 6
Postmodernism, 13
Power tools, spell for return of, 204–5
Powwows, 19, 147
Prayers, versus spells, 196
Priapus, 205–7
Priesthood (priests), 67–81
  ancient history of, 68–72
  Pagan attitudes about, 74–81
  personal story, 72–74
Prose Edda, 21, 64
Protection
  Shield of the Dagda, 194–96
  spell for, before battles, 201–3
Prowess, 118
Pythagoras, 149, 150, 232*n*

Queer Paganism (Pagans), 152–62
  polymorphous perversity, 155–58
  sexual minorities, in mainstream
    religions, 153–54
  use of term, 152–53
  in Wicca, 158–60

Rabelais, François, 24
Ragnarok, 21
Rand, Ayn, 47
Ravenhawk, 124–25
Recon-Pagans, 4–5, 29, 30–31
Reeder, Sara, 145
Reformed Druids of North America
  (RDNA), 28–29, 73–74
Reincarnation, 11
Religious tolerance, 11
Religious upbringing, 127–29
Respect, 173–74, 211–12
Revivalist Paganism, 5
Rímur, 64
Rites of Worship (Bonewits), 183, 184
Rituals, 182–96
  ancestor invocation, 191–94
  Building the Temple of the Gods,
    184–91

overview of, 182–83
Shield of the Dagda, 194–96
Robin Hood and his Merry Men,
    42–43
Rodzimy Kosciol Polski, 32
Rogers, Kenny, 103
Role models, 127–28, 137–38
Roman Paganism. *See* Greek and
    Roman Paganism
Romuva, 32
Rosicrucianism, 4, 24–25
Rowling, J. K., 82, 84
Royal Order of the Knights of Herne,
    xi, 118–19, 145–48

Sacred Beat (Waterhawk and Telesco),
    109–10
Sadism and masochism (S&M),
    176–77
Salmi, Alan, 150–51
Sanders, Alex, 56
Santeria, xi–xii, 16, 81, 161
Satyrs, 157
Scandinavian Paganism. *See*
    Norse/Germanic Paganism
Schismatic Druids of North America
    (SDNA), 28
Science-fiction influences, on
    manhood, 43–45, 46–48
Seax Wicca, 57
Seidh, 22, 70, 155–56
Self-identification, as Pagans, 6–7
Self-protection meditation, 194–96
Self-reliance, 117
Seligman, Bill, 139
Set, 153
Sex and sexuality, 170–81
    avoidance of harm, 175–76
    basic principles of, 170–71
    leather activities, 176–77
    polyamory, 177–79
    simple rule for, 173–74
Sex magic, 179–81
Sexual ecstasy, 10, 170
Sexually transmitted diseases (STDs),
    175–76
Sexual minorities, in mainstream reli-
    gions, 153–54
Shamanism, 20, 222*n*
She Said!, 105

Shield of the Dagda, 194–96
Shinto, 3
Shrines, ancestor, 191–94
Sikhism, 3–4
Siuda, Tamara L., 25
Skalds, 70
Slavery (slave trade), 14–15, 18, 45
Slavic Paganism, 32–33
    Web sites, 241
Smith, Brian, 107
Snorri Sturluson, 21
Society for Creative Anachronism
    (SCA), 100–101
Solitary Druid, The (Ellison), 208
Solitary Wicca, 60
Songs for the Old Religion
    (Penderwen), 101
"Song to Mithras, A" (Kipling), 202–3
Spells, 196–207
    to attract new Pagan lovers,
        199–201
    for courage and protection before
        battle, 201–3
    to improve hunting and fishing,
        203–4
    to make new Pagan friends, 198–99
    to prevent or cure impotence, 205–7
    for return of power tools, 204–5
Spiral Castle, 106
Spiral Dance (Starhawk), 34–35
Spiritualism, 15, 222*n*
Starhawk, 34–35, 122
Star Wars (movies), 47–48
Starwood Festival, 107, 109, 133
Stonehenge, 27
Stranger in a Strange Land (Heinlein),
    47
Sturluson, Snorri, 21
Summerlands, 209–10
Sun Bear, 19
Supreme Council of Ethnikoi Hellenes,
    32

Talking sticks, 140, *141*
Tantra, *55*, 58
Taoism (Tao), 3, 47–48
Tarot Casters, 91–92
Teilhard de Chardin, Pierre, 226*n*
Telesco, Patricia, 109–10
Thelema, 24, 53

Theosophy, 4
Theravada Buddhism, 5
Thiasos Olympikos, 31–32, 210
Third sex, 154
Thor, xii
Thundercloud, 116
Tolkien, J. R. R., 43–45, 82
Tree, The: Complete Book of Saxon Witchcraft (Buckland), 57
Trickster (Loke E. Coyote), 106–7
Truth, 116, 118
Tuatha de Kelti, 143–45

Unitarian Universalist (UU), xi, 147
    Religious Education program, 128
United Ancient Order of Druids (UAOD), 28

Valhalla. See Norse/Germanic Paganism
Valiente, Doreen, 34
Valor, 118
Vegetarianism, 123–24, 229n
Viking Brotherhood, 64
Violence, and warriors, 114
Visualization, Shield of the Dagda, 194–96
Volvas, 70
Voodoo, 4, 16, 17

Wannabe Indians, 18–20
Warriors, 113–22
    definitions and archetypes of, 114–16
    military, 115, 120–22
    myths and manhood ideals, 41–43, 116–19
    police, 115, 119–20
    priesthood and, 69–71
    virtues and ideals of, 41–43, 116–19
Washington, George, 148
Waterhawk, Don Two Eagles, 95, 96, 109–10
Webbers Falls Native American Reservation, 147

Web sites, 239–42
Weschke, Carl, 59
Western African Paganism. See African Diasporic Paganism
What Witches Do (Farrar), 56
White Goddess, The (Graves), 54
White Tara, 6
Wicca (witchcraft), 6–7, 33–37, 223–24n
    definitions of, 1–2
    founding fathers of, 54–55, 57, 58, 60, 61
    homosexuality in, 158–60
    priesthood in, 71–72, 75–78
    Web sites, 239, 241
Wicca: A Guide for the Solitary Practitioner (Cunningham), 60
Wiccan Warrior, The (Cuhulain), 114–15
Witchcraft and the Gay Counterculture (Evans), 158–59
Witches' Voice, 32, 99
Witch Hunts (Cuhulain), 221n
Witch's Bible, The (Frost), 58
WitchVox, 99–101
"Wizard" (song), 103
Wizardry (wizards), 81–85
Worship, 182–83
Wu Tien Bao, 155

Xochipili, 155

Zell-Ravenheart, Morning Glory Ferns, 65–66, 88–89, 172, 177
Zell-Ravenheart, Oberon, 65–66, 172, 211–12
    art of, 88–91, 88, 90
    Church of All Worlds and, 47, 65, 160
    Grimoire for the Apprentice Wizard, 84–85
    Nybor and, 97
Zeus, 39, 157
Zimmer, Paul Edwin, 100
Zoosexuality, 157

About the Author

Isaac Bonewits made history at the age of twenty by becoming the first student to graduate with a bachelor's degree in magic from an accredited university (the University of California at Berkeley, 1970). He then published his first book, *Real Magic,* in 1971, which became a classic of occult literature (and is still in print). He became the editor of *Gnostica* (then the premiere occult journal in the English-speaking world) from 1973 to 1975. Over the course of his life, he has been present at some of the most important historical events in the American Neopagan community. His books, articles, speeches, and interviews have strongly influenced that community for thirty-five years.

He is probably the best-known representative of the modern Druid revival in North America and is an ordained Druid priest of both the Reformed Druids of North America and Ár nDraíocht Féin: A Druid Fellowship (ADF). The latter is the largest American-based Neopagan Druid organization and the first to insist on rigorous standards of scholarship and magical/spiritual/liturgical knowledge on the part of Druid clergy. He was the founder of the ADF and is now its first archdruid emeritus. He is also a third-degree member of the United Ancient Order of Druids, the world's largest Mesopagan Druid organization, as well as an honorary member of other Druidic groups.

Besides his Druidic credentials, Bonewits is an initiated high priest in both the Gardnerian (British Orthodox) and the NROOGD (California Heterodox) traditions of Wicca, was involved in the revival of Aleister Crowley's ceremonial magical order, the Ordo Templi Orientis, and has been initiated into Santeria.

His other books include: *The Druid Chronicles (Evolved)*— now part of *A Reformed Druid Anthology*; *Authentic Thaumaturgy*; *Witchcraft: A Concise Guide*; *Rites of Worship: A Neopagan Approach*; and the forthcoming *Bonewits's Essential Guide to Witchcraft and Wicca* and *Bonewits's Essential Guide to Druidism*. He is also working on new books of Neopagan anthropology and polytheology.

He lives in Rockland County, New York, with his wife, Phaedra, his son, Arthur, and two cats who are active in the war against literacy.